I AM A MAN!

I AM

Race, Manhood, and the Civil Rights Movement

A MAN!

Steve Estes

The University of North Carolina Press
Chapel Hill and London

Designed by April Leidig-Higgins
Set in Ehrhardt by Copperline Book Services, Inc.

The paper in this book meets the guidelines for permanence and
durability of the Committee on Production Guidelines for Book
Longevity of the Council on Library Resources.

Part of this book has been reprinted with permission in revised
form from "'I Am a Man!': Race, Masculinity, and the 1968
Memphis Sanitation Strike," *Labor History* 41, no. 2 (May 2000):
153–70; ⟨http://www.tandf.co.uk/journals⟩.

Library of Congress Cataloging-in-Publication Data
Estes, Steve.   I am a man!: race, manhood, and the civil rights
movement / Steve Estes.
p. cm.   Includes bibliographical references and index.
ISBN-13: 978-0-8078-2929-5 (cloth: alk. paper)
ISBN-10: 0-8078-2929-3 (cloth: alk. paper)
ISBN-13: 978-0-8078-5593-5 (pbk.: alk. paper)
ISBN-10: 0-8078-5593-6 (pbk.: alk. paper)
1. African Americans—Civil rights—History—20th century.
2. Civil rights movements—United States—History—20th
century.   3. African American civil rights workers—
Attitudes—History—20th century.   4. African American
men—Attitudes—History—20th century.   5. Rhetoric—
Political aspects—United States—History—20th century.
6. Masculinity—Political aspects—United States—
History—20th century.   7. Sex role—Political aspects—United
States—History—20th century.   8. Sexism—United States—
History—20th century.   9. Racism—United States—
History—20th century.   10. United States—Race relations.
I. Title.
E185.61.E76 2005   323.1196'073—dc22   2004019092

cloth   10 09 08 07 06   6 5 4 3 2
paper   10 09 08 07 06   6 5 4 3 2

Contents

Illustrations

Acknowledgments

I couldn't have finished this book without the help of my students, colleagues, mentors, and of course, friends and family. Though it's a cliché, it is also true that every book is a journey. This one began in Athens, Georgia, and ended in San Francisco, California. Along the way, I incurred more debts than any written thanks could ever repay, but I hope that all of the people who helped me take these acknowledgments as a first installment toward full repayment.

Like most intellectual projects, this one really began with the guidance of incredible teachers. At the University of Georgia, Bob Pratt and Bryant Simon fostered my early interest in the civil rights movement. In North Carolina, Peter Filene, Gerald Horne, Bill Chafe, Beth Millwood, Leon Fink, and most of all, Jacquelyn Hall taught me how to "listen for a change" and how to learn history from the people who made it. In Washington, D.C., Donna Walker James, Betsy Brand, Glenda Partee, and Sam Halperin helped me climb down from the Ivory Tower, so that I could try to make a difference in the real world. Once I returned to academia and began presenting this work at conferences, I acquired the help of a new cadre of teachers. Glenda Gilmore, Ernestine Jenkins, Ted Owenby, Nancy McLean, Glenn Eskew, Clyde Woods, Linda Norton, and Robert Allen all read and commented on portions of the manuscript. In the publication process, Michael Honey and Tim Tyson were amazingly patient and insightful readers, while Chuck Grench, Amanda McMillan, and Eric Combest were untiring editors. Perhaps the most important teachers that guided this project were the civil rights activists who graciously shared their time and stories with me in interviews.

Half of the way through this project, I started writing for students as well as teachers. Students at Towson University, the College of Charleston, and Sonoma State University never failed to remind me that people like them would most probably be reading this book some day. Working with the Sunflower County Freedom Project in the Mississippi Delta taught me more about civil rights than all of the sources and citations in this book put together. For that opportunity, I owe a great deal to my friend Chris Myers and all of the amazing folks that I met in Mississippi.

The research for this book took me across the country from New York to California, and I wouldn't have been able to visit these far-flung places without funding from a variety of sources. The National Endowment for the Humanities, the Center for the Study of the American South, the Lyndon B. Johnson Presidential Library, the American Youth Policy Forum, the Southern Oral History Program of the University of North Carolina, and Sonoma State University generously supported me as I researched and wrote the book.

Friends and family were untiring in their support as well, lending me everything from cash to couches, burritos to books, and most of all, love and support. I couldn't have made it out of Athens without Aristide Sechandice, Rick Fogarty, Michael Blickenstaff, and Vicki Grieve. In North Carolina, Alan McPherson, Rene Hayden, Kris Ray, Angela Hornsby, David Sartorius, Chris Endy, Will Jones, Holloway Sparks, Brian Griffin, Sherry Honeycutt, Natalie Fousekis, Leah Potter, and Melynn Glusman read portions of this manuscript, bought me a beer, or jammed with me. In their own ways, all were crucial to this project.

Carol Spector dragged me away from Chapel Hill at the best possible moment, and then let me drag her to California. Even though I promised her that I wouldn't talk to her about this book, she let me do that, too. But she also reminded me that the present is just as important as the past, and that love is more important than just about everything else.

I have to reserve the last thanks for the person who taught me how to be not just a man, but a good one. This book is dedicated to Dr. Gene Elizabeth Burges, MD-PhD (aka Mama).

I AM A MAN!

I am an invisible man. No, I am not a spook like those who haunted Edgar Allan Poe; nor am I one of your Hollywood-movie ectoplasms. I am a man of substance, of flesh and bone, fiber and liquids — and I might even be said to possess a mind. I am invisible, understand, simply because people refuse to see me. — Ralph Ellison, *Invisible Man* (1952)

Introduction

Am I Not a Man and a Brother?

He had no name. At least, we never knew it. Yet we knew, or thought we knew, intimate details about his life. Raised and educated in the South, he attended one of the most prestigious institutions of higher learning open to African Americans early in the twentieth century. A bright, bookish young man, he had not learned a lesson that other black south-erners seemed to internalize from early in their youth—that African Americans, especially African American men, had to hide their true selves behind masks of deference to whites. Expelled from school for offending one of his university's white benefactors, this man traveled to the North where he became active in the struggle for racial equality. As he rose through the ranks of an integrated civil rights organization, he honed his skills as a public speaker and activist, fighting for the rights of the dispossessed in Harlem. Then, almost without warning, the white leaders of his organization withdrew their support for him after a relatively minor dispute over movement strategy. Shorn of his position and persona as an activist, the man came to understand that it did not matter what identity he chose; others could not see him, and in some sense, he had never really been able to see himself.

Published in 1952, Ralph Ellison's novel *Invisible Man* chronicled the life of this unnamed protagonist, exploring the racial blind spot in the mind's eye of white America. In the first half of the twentieth century, racism forced African

Americans to hide their true thoughts and identities, and it blinded whites to black humanity. For black men, such social subterfuge was all the more essential, because the ever-present threat of lynching for supposed sexual improprieties meant that their survival could depend on their ability to mask their masculinity. It thus behooved black men to become invisible, lest they become highly visible examples of the racial rules that governed American society. This posed a serious dilemma for black men who, like the protagonist of Ellison's novel, wanted to become activists or leaders in the crusade for racial equality. It also meant that white allies in this struggle worked with blinders that obscured some of the very problems they were trying to solve. These dilemmas had confounded the movement for racial equality from its inception.[1]

In the 1780s, the British Society for the Abolition of Slavery adopted as its official seal a woodcut of a kneeling slave above a banner that read: "Am I not a man and a brother?" By the middle of the 1800s, this illustration had graced the covers of countless abolitionist handbills in America. This image of an African man imploring an unseen master for his freedom came to symbolize the struggle for abolition of the "peculiar institution" in the nineteenth century. As the woodcut reveals, many white Americans, even abolitionists, expected African Americans to adopt a submissive posture of supplication when seeking emancipation. African American abolitionists such as Frederick Douglass and Sojourner Truth did not beg for their freedom, however; they demanded it. And they left a heritage of untiring struggle that would inspire the modern civil rights movement. As eloquent as these African American abolitionists were in their advocacy of equal rights, they were not powerful enough to sway the paternalistic vision of emancipation held by many white abolitionists and lawmakers. These white leaders and their former opponents in the South would define and limit the rights of African American citizens after the Civil War. A century after emancipation, African Americans were still not truly free and equal citizens of the United States. Civil rights activists in the second half of the twentieth century sought to remedy this injustice. No longer willing to wait for an answer to the question, "Am I not a man and a brother?" they demanded freedom with the slogan, "I AM a Man!"[2]

The civil rights movement was first and foremost a struggle for racial equality, but questions of gender lay deeply embedded within this overtly racial conflict. From the outset, the African American quest for emancipation and equality in the United States was a struggle for recognition of black humanity and citizenship. In this sense, demands for recognition of black manhood were calls for an acknowledgment of the human rights of both black men *and* women. Yet men

Abolitionists argued that the brotherhood of man included African and African American slaves. From John Greenleaf Whittier, "Our Countrymen in Chains" (New York: Anti-Slavery Office, 1837). Rare Book and Special Collections Division, Library of Congress.

dominated the social and political arenas in which the struggle for rights took place, and this was reflected in the language used to discuss civil rights. The political philosophy of republican citizenship, which Americans originally borrowed from European Enlightenment thinkers, equated the "rights of man" with the rights of all citizens. Since men were the only voters in most nineteenth century political contests, voting rights and citizenship were directly linked to manhood. This connection between citizenship and manhood shaped the language, strategies and objectives of political and social reform. Like the political leaders of their respective times, abolitionists and civil rights activists also used a gendered language to call for white Americans to live up to the country's egalitarian ideals by recognizing the equal rights of all men regardless of the color of their skin. The gender component of their rhetoric was not simply a matter of semantics, however. In fact, the struggle for black equality since the era of slavery has also had specific implications for gender relations and gender identity in America. The "I *AM* a Man!" slogan represents a demand for recognition and respect of black manhood as well as black humanity. This demand, and the racial oppression that inspired it, reflect the ways that race and racism have contributed to our understanding of both black and white manhood in America.

In the eighteenth and nineteenth centuries, definitions of white manhood—and especially, southern white manhood—rested on mastery over plantations, farms, and households that contained numerous dependents. The legal status of dependence (the subordination of women, children, and slaves) defined white manhood and independence. The Virginians who led the revolt against "enslavement" to a despotic British monarch did so, in part, because they understood only too well what slavery and dependence meant. In 1776 these same men pledged "our lives, our fortunes, and our sacred honor" to the cause of independence from England. With few exceptions, citizenship, honor, and manhood in the young American nation would remain the exclusive purview of these white men and their white male progeny.[3]

Along with black women and white abolitionists, African American men struggled for independence on the fields of plantations and the fields of battle in a herculean effort to win emancipation. This struggle was often tied to their identity as men. Since slavery rested on the violent suppression of black bondsmen, black men in the antebellum period often spoke of physical confrontation with whites as a rite of passage into manhood. In his autobiography, Frederick Douglass wrote about such a confrontation when describing his first fight for freedom. After winning a bloody, two-hour brawl with a white overseer, Douglass realized his own power and will to be free. "This battle with Mr. Covey," Douglass wrote, "was the turning point in my career as a slave. It rekindled the few expiring embers of freedom, and revived within me a sense of my own manhood. It recalled the departed self-confidence and inspired me again with a determination to be free." Slave revolts and escapes represented only two of the many forms of rebellion against bondage that imbued black men with a "resistant masculinity." The Civil War offered black men a chance to fight for their own freedom, for the liberation of all slaves, and for their manhood. The struggle for emancipation during the Civil War imparted a new sense of pride in black soldiers. When a white man asked one black Union soldier from South Carolina, "What are you, anyhow?" the soldier responded proudly, "When God made me I wasn't much, but I's a man now."[4]

In the tumultuous years that followed the Civil War, black men won citizenship, the vote, and political office only to see these things stripped from them in the waning years of the nineteenth century. Conferring equal citizenship and the vote, the Fourteenth and Fifteenth Amendments provided the legal and political foundations for black equality. Reconstruction established biracial political leadership in the South after the Civil War, but it did not insure that African Americans had the economic wherewithal to maintain independence from white landowners. Sharecropping allowed black families a certain amount of autonomy and distance from former masters and overseers, enabling black men to exercise authority in their households comparable to the limited patriarchy of white yeomen. Yet a cycle of debt to landlords and merchants produced grinding poverty and an equality of oppression for black and white people who worked the land. When the Populists and a small number of other progressive politicians attempted to organize these black and white farmers along class lines in the 1880s and 1890s, elite white southerners trumped this interracial alliance with white male supremacy. Adopting the rhetoric of civilization and manliness that pervaded American culture at the turn of the twentieth century, white southern men banded together across class lines, ostensibly to protect white women from "uncivilized" and "beastly" black men. White night riders, Klansmen, and state legislators hid behind the masks of chivalry and protection of white womanhood as they stole the vote from black men. Lynching, disfranchisement, and segregation solidified a social order in the American South based on white male supremacy. Race men and women such as W. E. B. Du Bois and Ida B. Wells would fight against this tide of virulent racism that swept across the South and the nation in the first half of the twentieth century.[5]

Racial separation became the rule in southern society when the Supreme Court upheld segregation in its *Plessy v. Ferguson* decision in 1896. Segregation defined the region's labor market, educational system, worship patterns, recreational activities, and sexual mores. Wealthy white men manipulated the sense of racial loyalty inherent in segregation to undercut class solidarity between black and white workers, and all white men could use segregation to protect and control "their" women. Segregation offered no such protection for black women, however, for under the cover of darkness and even in the light of day, white men reserved the "right" to rape black women with impunity. Certainly, not all white men took advantage of this "right," but segregation buttressed the social structure that made such atrocities possible. In short, segregation supported a system that gave elite white men complete control over southern society, guaranteeing the allegiance of white women and working-class white men by offering them a sense of psychological superiority over their black neighbors and coworkers.[6]

Segregation's high walls also confined black men. For them, any transgression in the white world might lead to lynching or castration for supposed sexual improprieties. "You couldn't even smile at a white woman," a black man from rural Mississippi remembered. "If you did, you'd be hung from a limb." This terrifying period when the segregated social order became entrenched is often called the Jim Crow era, named after the character—really, a racist caricature of African American men—in blackface minstrel shows of the nineteenth century. Historians often refer to this time as the "nadir of race relations," because of the ghastly lynching campaign that reinforced white supremacy. From 1889 to 1922, the National Association for the Advancement of Colored People (NAACP) calculated that 3,436 Americans were lynched, the majority of them African Americans and all but 83 of them men. Though accusations of rape were made in less than a third of the cases for which the "cause" of the vigilante justice was known, sexual assault by black men remained the popular justification for such lynchings. When around whites, especially white women, black men had to cloak their sexuality and mask their manhood for fear of trespassing on the race and gender prerogatives of white men. Benjamin Mays, a black South Carolina native who would become Martin Luther King Jr.'s mentor at Morehouse College, looked back on his upbringing during the Jim Crow era and concluded, "To exercise manhood, as white men displayed it, was to invite disaster."[7]

When black men and women confronted segregation and disfranchisement in the 1950s and 1960s, they contested white supremacy in the South and questioned long-held assumptions about race and gender in American society. During the Montgomery bus boycott of 1955–56, one of the first major campaigns of the modern movement for racial equality, activists addressed the gender implications of civil rights protest. Rosa Parks, a local black activist who refused to abide by segregation on a Montgomery bus, initiated the boycott, but she and other organizers at first found it difficult to enlist the support of the city's black male ministers. One local leader who had supported the boycott from the beginning was E. D. Nixon. A union man and president of the Montgomery chapter of the NAACP, Nixon met with Montgomery's black ministers and chastised them for not publicly supporting the boycott begun by courageous women from their community. "We are acting like little boys," Nixon told the ministers, "and if we're afraid, we might as well just fold up right now. We must also be men enough to discuss [this] in the open. . . . We'd better decide if we're going to be fearless men or scared boys." Martin Luther King Jr. responded to Nixon's call to action, becoming the leader of the Montgomery Improvement Association and one of the most eloquent spokesmen of the civil rights movement. Another of the ministers who heeded Nixon's call that night, Reverend Ralph Abernathy, later noted that the struggle in Montgomery raised questions not only about black manhood but white manhood as well. When white city officials refused to desegregate the city's buses without a court order, Abernathy explained, "They could not appear to be giving in to black pressure. It was a matter of racial pride, their manhood."[8]

As the modern civil rights movement began, both white and black Americans shared basic definitions of manhood. Manhood entailed an economic, social, and political status ideally achievable by all men. A man was the head of his household: he made enough money to support his family as the primary if not the only breadwinner. He also had a political voice in deciding how his community, his state, and his country were run. Racism kept many men, especially working-class black men, from achieving these attributes of manhood. This was partly by design in that white men used racism to reduce competition for jobs, for political offices, and even for women. When overt racial discrimination in the South came under attack in the 1950s, southern white men used masculinist rhetoric to defend the privileges that whiteness and manhood had afforded them in the economic, political, and sexual spheres. It should come as no surprise, then, that some civil rights activists and their allies responded to this defense of white male supremacy by using masculinist strategies of racial uplift with the express goals of gaining economic autonomy, political power, and social status for black men.[9]

In contrast to feminism, which attempts to overturn social inequalities that result from gender discrimination, "masculinism" embraces the notion that men are more powerful than women, that they should have control over their own lives and authority over others. Masculinist rhetoric uses the traditional power wielded by men to woo supporters and attack opponents. It rallies supporters to a cause by urging them to be manly or to support traditional ideas of manhood. It challenges opponents by feminizing them, and therefore linking them to "weakness." When political leaders harness the power of masculinism to forward their agendas, they often simplify complex issues into binary oppositions, placing themselves and their allies in the dominant position. During the civil rights movement, masculinist rhetoric used by both sides served to obscure the questions of racial and economic equality that lay at the heart of the original struggle, complicating and sometimes conflating these issues with the related question of what it meant to be a man.[10]

Early accounts of the movement focused primarily on men without consciously acknowledging the role of women or gender in shaping the course of the struggle. Journalists who chronicled the movement in the 1950s and 1960s highlighted the actions of male leaders in civil rights organizations in part because chauvinism in the wider American culture led them to assume that men were the "natural" leaders of any movement or organization. For many years, civil rights historians replicated this bias, favoring male movement leaders in their narratives, despite the fact that women did much of the tough local organizing. Recently, civil rights scholars have reversed this trend, lauding the admirable achievements of movement women such as Rosa Parks, Ella Baker, and Fannie Lou Hamer. The analysis of gender in these accounts of the movement along with demonstrations by black men in events like the Million Man March raised important questions about the interplay between race and masculinity in struggles for black equality. How did participation in the American military affect black men's conceptions of themselves as men and as citizens? What role did these veterans play in the emerging movement for civil rights? What role did masculinity play in the strategic choices activists made—for instance, the choice between nonviolent protest and armed self-defense? How did notions of manhood shape the responses of southern leaders, federal policymakers, and Americans of all races to the movement? Finally, how did movement activists influence racial and gender identities in American society, and what can we learn from their experiences, both the triumphs and tribulations?[11]

This book seeks to answer these questions and explore some of the dilemmas that arose during the civil rights movement and still bedevil race and gender relations today. When both segregationists and civil rights workers framed their actions in terms of claiming or defending manhood, they found a powerful organizing tactic that rested on traditional assumptions about race, gender, and sexuality. This tactic bound men together in struggle and revealed both the possibilities and limitations of campaigns based on a quest for manhood. This is a book about men emerging from the shadows of prejudice and discrimination to challenge stereotypes about who they were and the types of men they could be. But it is also, at its heart, the story of men *and* women working together to fight for their rights. It is my hope that an understanding of connections between race and manhood in the civil rights movement will inform new histories of this struggle and guide campaigns for social justice today and in the future.

I spent four years in the army to free a bunch of Frenchmen and Dutchmen, and I'm hanged if I'm going to let the Alabama version of the Germans kick me around when I get back home. No sirreee-bob! I went into the army a nigger; I'm comin' out a *man*.
—Black corporal, U.S. Army (1945)

Chapter One

Man the Guns

S hells from a Japanese cruiser streaked across the bow of the USS *Gregory* as Ray Carter rushed to his battle station. The *Gregory* was supporting the American invasion of Guadalcanal in the midst of a bloody island hopping campaign to retake the Pacific from the Japanese during World War II. Ray Carter was the "hot shell man" for a four-inch deck-gun on the *Gregory*. He wore asbestos gloves in order to catch the white-hot shell casings ejected from the gun. Suddenly, one of the Japanese cruiser's shots landed a devastating hit on the *Gregory*, killing the American captain instantly and crippling the vessel. A surviving officer ordered all hands to abandon ship. "I donned a life jacket," Carter later remembered, "and took a running jump, landing as far out as possible from the ship." Like his fellow sailors, Carter scrambled onto one of the life rafts. The men looked back and watched as the *Gregory* sank beneath the waves. Feeling lucky to be alive, Carter talked about the bond that formed between the men. "Talk about togetherness; we were straight out of *The Three Musketeers*, all for one and one for all." Such combat-forged camaraderie is a common theme in stories from the "Good War." Yet it does not tell the whole story of Raymond Carter's wartime experiences or the experiences of other black men and women who served during World War II.[1]

Ray Carter enlisted in the Navy early in the 1940s as a fresh-faced nineteen-year-old from Detroit, Michigan. Perhaps he had seen a poster urging young recruits to "Man the Guns" or one featuring a pin-up girl that read, "Gee, I wish I were a Man!! I'd join the Navy." More likely, posters and newspaper stories featuring the black World War II hero, Dorie Miller, inspired Carter to sign up. Miller was a messman on the USS *West Virginia* stationed in Pearl Harbor on December 7, 1941. During the Japanese surprise attack that morning, Miller risked his own life to drag his dying captain from harm's way, before manning a deck-mounted machine gun. Though he had not been allowed to train on the weapon because of his race and rank, Miller took aim at Japanese planes until a fire on the deck drove him from his position. Likely hoping to follow Miller's example and to man the guns himself, Ray Carter joined the Navy.[2]

Because of his tan complexion, the Navy recruiter asked Carter about his nationality and was clearly surprised when Carter responded that he was "colored." The white officer quickly crossed out Carter's original duty assignment and wrote "steward" on the recruiting forms. It was official policy of the Navy in the early 1940s that "colored men are enlisted only in the messman branch" as cooks and personal attendants for white officers. It was a "waste of time and effort," the Navy reasoned, to recruit and train black sailors for other positions that were assumed beyond their capacity. Carter wondered why the Navy issued white coats in addition to normal uniforms for himself and the other black recruits. "Oh man, was I a real dum-dum!" he later exclaimed with a mixture of humor and sadness. "I had enlisted to fight for my country and my great contribution to the war effort was to wait on whites."[3]

More than one million African Americans served in the U.S. Armed Forces during World War II, and hundreds of thousands more contributed to the war effort in war-related industries. Though many black soldiers were relegated to labor battalions in the early years of the war, manpower needs and political pressure eventually brought thousands of them into combat. Similarly, many war industries had initially hired white men only. As white American men went off to war, however, positions began to open up for white women and African Americans. Scholars of the war argue that these changes in domestic race and gender relations were "central to the whole campaign for civil rights" in the 1950s and 1960s. Previous studies of the war have explored how Rosie riveted a new identity for women and how the Tuskegee Airmen earned the movement its wings. This chapter investigates the ways that World War II altered conceptions of African American manhood and how these changes set the stage for the civil rights movement.[4]

Although it is certainly not the only defining experience for boys becoming men, military service—especially during a time of war—has traditionally been viewed as a rite of passage into manhood. In the context of wartime service, "man" becomes not just a noun but a verb, not just an identity but an action, as soldiers and sailors are ordered to "man the guns." Military action, then, shapes a masculine identity. The tests of physical prowess, courage, and mettle in the military are supposed to harden young boys into men, to prove that they can fulfill their traditional roles as husbands and fathers, protecting their families and communities from harm. On a political level, wartime military service has also been seen as an obligation of citizenship in modern republics and democracies. Citizen-soldiers must protect and defend the state in return for the right to have a say in how the state is run. Well into the twentieth century, the segregation of the armed forces and the relegation of women and minority men to noncombat roles excluded them from this band of brothers, for this was where manhood and citizenship were defined. Still, there was a sense among African American men that participation and valorous service in war could uplift their race and gain them respect and recognition as men. Such had been the case during the Civil War, when nearly 200,000 black soldiers fought in combat and 300,000 African Americans labored behind the lines for the Union Army. Black military service helped to inspire passage of the Thirteenth, Fourteenth and Fifteenth Amendments to the Constitution, ending slavery and laying the groundwork for Reconstruction. Yet these rights had been rolled back in succeeding decades, despite evidence of African American patriotism during the Spanish-American War and calls by black leaders like W. E. B. Du Bois for Americans to "close ranks" and share the burden of battle in World War I. It seemed that the political and social legacies of black heroism and martial manhood had a limited half-life when the military crisis of the moment had passed. Understanding that their civil rights had been curtailed rather than expanded after these conflicts, black men and women exhibited deep ambivalence at the outset of World War II. Navy steward Ray Carter continued to feel this ambivalence when he spoke to an interviewer more than two decades after the war in the midst of the civil rights movement. He wondered how "I or my people benefited from the time I spent in the service and the insults and humiliation I endured as a man." But one legacy of his service was clear. When asked what he thought about young militants in the civil rights movement, he said that he was proud of them. "After all," he explained, "they were sired by the men of World War II."[5]

Even before the attack on Pearl Harbor brought the United States formally into the war, the battle lines were drawn at home. Industries in the United States began gearing up for war production in 1939, and in 1940 President Franklin D.

McClelland Barclay's recruiting poster for the Navy entitled "Man the Guns" (1942) emphasizes the manly duty to serve with its arresting image of a muscular white seaman ramming home a shell in the midst of battle. David Stone Martin's "Above and Beyond the Call of Duty" (n.d.) foregrounds the loyalty of black seaman Dorie Miller against the

abstract backdrop of Pearl Harbor without explicitly showing Miller's heroic action or his assigned role as a messman. Miller received the Navy Cross only after much pressure from the NAACP and the black press. Still Picture Branch (NWDNS-44-PA-24 and NWDNS-208-PMP-68), National Archives and Records Administration.

Roosevelt began shipping arms to aid the British in the fight against Germany. After the record unemployment of the Great Depression, employers in these burgeoning war industries could pick and choose their workers. In the second half of 1940, white unemployment declined from nearly 18 percent to 13 percent, but black unemployment in this same period remained at an astonishing 22 percent. In the immediate wake of the Pearl Harbor attacks, less than three percent of the workers in American defense industries were African Americans, and many of these black war workers were relegated to low-paying, unskilled positions. "While we are in complete sympathy with the Negro," one executive at the North American Aviation Company explained, "it is against company policy to employ them as aircraft workers or mechanics. . . . There will be some jobs as janitors for Negroes."[6]

Black labor and civil rights leaders pressured the government to deal with rampant workplace discrimination. Black trade unionist A. Philip Randolph came up with the idea for a March on Washington in 1941. Backed by Walter White of the NAACP, and other black leaders, the march would protest racial discrimination among defense contractors, federal agencies, and the armed forces. "If American democracy will not insure equality of opportunity, freedom and justice to its citizens, black and white," Randolph argued, "it is a hollow mockery and belies the principles for which it is supposed to stand." The blues singer Josh White put it even more simply in "Defense Factory Blues": "Well, it sho' don' make no sense, when a Negro can't work in the National Defense." Initially planned for 10,000 people, Randolph predicted a few weeks before the scheduled date of the march that more than 100,000 African American protesters might come to the nation's capital. This was no empty threat. Randolph could count on the support of the militant followers in his powerful union, the Brotherhood of Sleeping Car Porters, as well as thousands more demonstrators organized by local March on Washington committees in cities across the country. President Franklin D. Roosevelt met with black leaders in the summer of 1941 to try to persuade them to drop their demands. He was unsuccessful. A few days after the meeting, the president issued Executive Order 8802, which forbid racial discrimination by employers and labor unions working with defense contracts and also set up a Fair Employment Practices Committee (FEPC) to investigate racism in war industries. Randolph called off his march, but he would go on to lead an even greater pilgrimage for jobs and freedom two decades later.[7]

During the early 1940s, despite a small staff and an unenthusiastic southern chairman, the FEPC held hearings around the country, examining the hiring practices of various defense contractors. Earl Dickerson, an outspoken black insurance man and politician from Chicago, served on the FEPC and remembered heading to Los Angeles for hearings early in the war. The aviation contractor Lockheed had around 20,000 employees in southern California, only nine of whom were African Americans. When Dickerson asked where the black employees worked and how long they had been with the company, the Lockheed spokesman sheepishly admitted that they were all janitors, who had been hired just before the hearing. Without the political clout to enforce the president's nondiscrimination order, the FEPC could do little more than slap companies on the wrist with warnings. Integration would come to the defense industries, but only after millions of white men were shipped overseas to fight in the war.[8]

The American military faced an even more delicate task of recruiting minorities while still trying to maintain racial segregation. Despite the heroism of black soldiers in World War I, there still were doubts among top military officials about the combat capabilities of African Americans. A 1925 study conducted by what is now the Army War College based its conclusions on the tenets of social Darwinism: "In the process of evolution the American Negro has not progressed as far as the other subspecies of the human family. . . . His mental inferiority and inherent weakness of his character are factors that must be considered . . . [in] any plans for his employment in war." Such assumptions were still widely held by military brass at the outset of World War II, but political pressures led to gradual policy adjustments that opened the door for more black military participation. Fearing a challenge from Republicans for black votes in the 1940 elections, FDR and some liberal Democrats crafted a Selective Service Act, calling for "any person, regardless of race or color" to be included in the draft and be given the opportunity to enlist voluntarily. So as not to ruffle the feathers of white southern Democrats and military leaders, however, the White House and War Department quickly assured the public that such legislation would not jeopardize the military's policy of racial segregation, which had "proven satisfactory over a long period of years."[9]

To African Americans, Washington's Jim Crow pronouncements whispered the same white supremacist dogma shouted by Adolph Hitler and the fascist Nazi Party in Germany. In *Mein Kampf*, Hitler had outlined conspiracy theories based on anti-Semitism and racism to explain the depressed state of the German economy after World War I. "It was and it is the Jews who bring Negroes into the Rhineland, always with the same secret thought and clear aim of ruining the hated white race," Hitler warned. In his eyes, the men of these "bastard" races presented a clear danger to German womanhood and the German nation. Yet denigration of other races was only half of the Nazi propaganda strategy. Idealization of Aryan manhood and athleticism were just as central to the Third

Reich. Hitler and his followers viewed the 1936 Olympics in Berlin as a perfect opportunity to showcase German superiority. When black track star Jesse Owens raced to victory and four gold medals in the Berlin games, the Nazis' white supremacist theories took a beating. Two years later, African American boxer Joe Louis knocked out the German champ Max Schmeling, deemed the embodiment of Aryan manhood, in the first round of a heavyweight title bout. Yet when conflict came with the United States, Hitler continued to harp on Jewish and black inferiority, reportedly telling his senior staff that Germany would surely defeat the "half Judaized, and the other half Negrified" American people.[10]

The declaration of war in the United States brought a rush of enlistments, a draft, and calls to arms based on the obligations of citizenship and manhood. For young white men, service in the armed forces during World War II was a chance to prove themselves. Bob Rasmus, a white Chicagoan who volunteered as an infantry rifleman, explained in an interview years later: "I was a skinny, gaunt kind of mama's boy. I was going to gain my manhood then. I would forever be liberated from the sense that I wasn't rugged. I would prove that I had the guts and the manhood to stand up to these things." Black servicemen discussed some of the same traditional themes, but with different political implications. Draftee Jack Crittendon explained to the graduating class at his high school why he was proud to serve, recalling Dorie Miller's heroism. "He proved himself capable. And when more black men are given the opportunity to serve their country they will prove themselves worthy of the trust placed in them. Give them a chance, [because] . . . a man is still a man!" Such sentiments gave parents, black and white, cause for concern. When Nelson Peery told his mother that he was enlisting, she steeled herself for the waiting and worrying to come. "I knew you'd go," she told her son. "I can't stop you. I guess men have to fight to prove something to themselves. It's just that I hate to think that I raised seven sons to become cannon fodder."[11]

Not all young black men wanted to fight, kill, and perhaps die in a segregated army, despite the seemingly laudable aims of defeating Hitler and defending democracy. Bayard Rustin, an organizer for the Fellowship of Reconciliation, refused to serve because of his Quaker upbringing and his commitment to the philosophy of nonviolence advocated by Mohandas Gandhi. In addition to political opposition to service in a segregated army, Rustin and other pacifists sought an alternative path to manhood that did not rest on military service or physical aggression. Elijah Muhammad, the leader of the group that would later become the Nation of Islam, opposed the draft not because he disagreed with traditional ideas about martial manhood, but because he felt that the black man's struggle lay closer to home and that his natural allies were the Japanese and other people of color. "The Asiatic race is made up of all dark-skinned people, including the Japanese and the Asiatic black man," Muhammad explained to his followers, urging them to ignore the draft. "The Japanese will win the war, because the white man cannot successfully oppose Asiatics." Rustin and Muhammad both served jail time for their philosophical and ideological opposition to the U.S. war effort. Other black men wanted to avoid the war for more pragmatic reasons. Howard McGhee was an up-and-coming jazz trumpeter during World War II. When he was called down to the induction center for a psychiatric evaluation, he asked the army psychiatrist, "Man, why should I fight? I ain't mad at nobody out there. . . . I wouldn't know the difference. . . . If he's white, I'm going to shoot him. Whether he's a Frenchman, a German, or whatever, how the fuck would I know the difference?" As he had intended, that answer got McGhee classified as 4-F, psychologically unfit for service. During the war, he got a chance to join Count Basie's band, replacing a horn player who had been drafted. Afterwards, McGhee explained, "I wasn't ready to dodge no bullets for nobody. And I like America. But I didn't like it *that* much. I mean it's all right to be a second class citizen . . . but shit, to be shot at, that's another damn story."[12]

Rustin, Muhammad, and McGhee were certainly not alone in denouncing the war, but the majority of young black men who were called to serve did so. Still, the armed forces relegated them almost exclusively to labor and service battalions for the first two years of the war. Trained under white southern officers who supposedly "knew the Negro" better than their northern counterparts, 80 percent of black recruits and draftees were stationed at bases in the South, surrounded by communities that were hostile to black men in uniform. John Griffin, a black Marine Corps recruit from Chicago, learned this lesson first hand. The Marines had, in fact, rejected black volunteers for nearly a century and a half after the Revolutionary War, from 1798 to 1941. The Corps only reluctantly began accepting African Americans early in World War II. Even before he arrived for training at the segregated base attached to Camp Lejeune in North Carolina, Griffin faced the humiliation of having to move to the back of a segregated train as it traveled into the South. For much of the war, the commanding officer of the black training facilities at Camp Lejeune was Colonel Samuel A. Woods Jr., a native of South Carolina and an alumnus of that state's all-white military college, The Citadel. According to an official history of black Marines in World War II, Colonel Woods "cultivated a paternalistic relationship with his men," who dubbed him the "Great White Father." One imagines that this was said with different inflection around the colonel and in the barracks. But Woods appeared enlightened compared to another camp commander who joked that overseas he had seen "women Marines" and "dog Marines," but he knew that the war was serious when he saw black men "wearing our uniform."[13]

Life and labor on southern bases was brutal by design. The explicit intention of military training is to harden a civilian into a soldier, one who will take orders to kill or be killed with no questions asked. Black draftees and recruits understood this. "I wasn't looking for an easy spot or a bed of roses to lay in," one explained. But the majority of black soldiers endured the normal rigors of military life, only to face continued discrimination and segregation once they had completed basic training. Black GIs vented their frustrations in letters to black editors, members of the Roosevelt administration, and the NAACP, decrying segregation and discrimination in the armed forces. "A U.S. Army uniform to a colored man makes him feel about as free as a man on a Georgia chain gang and you know that's hell," explained one letter to the *Baltimore Afro-American* signed by 300 black soldiers in Alabama. On base, black soldiers were forced to go to segregated Post Exchanges, theaters, and other recreational facilities. The most galling aspect of this Jim Crow policy was that German prisoners were often allowed to use these white facilities, while loyal African American soldiers were shunted off to substandard "colored" ones. A black lieutenant stationed in Texas remembered watching German POWs and white American troops eating together, and he thought, "I was a citizen soldier in the uniform of my country and I had to go through an alley to the back door while some of Hitler's storm troopers lapped up the hospitality of my country. I think the army, the government, or white people . . . purposely humiliated blacks in uniform to attempt to make them feel they were less than men."[14]

Institutional racism within the military was less visible but just as insidious as segregation. An officially sanctioned racial hierarchy in assignments and advancement infuriated black troops. After Samuel A. Conner's battalion was trained for artillery and radio operations, they were reassigned to a job the military felt better suited them. "To our dismay," he wrote to the *Afro-American*, "we found that some brass hat in Washington had given orders to form a Construction Battalion. . . . To be frank, we must toss away the months, in some cases, years of training." Promotion and advancement proved difficult as well. By the end of the war, less than two percent of the officers in the U.S. military were black, and these officers frequently were denied access to Officers' Clubs or positions other than chaplain.[15]

Black enlisted men and officers faced brutality if they trespassed across the color line in or around military bases. In 1941 Private Felix Hall was lynched in his uniform at Fort Benning, Georgia. Local authorities refused to rule out the possibility of suicide, even though his hands and feet had been bound. Black troops who protested against segregated buses and other public facilities in towns near military bases were beaten, arrested, and even shot by local white authorities. The military did nothing. Fed up with brutality, injustice, and segregation, the tone of soldiers' letters became more strident. A letter to Walter White from an anonymous soldier in Alabama explained, "Negro soldiers are treated like slaves on this post." The soldier continued, "Unless something is done at once to change these conditions, I am afraid something serious will happen at this camp." It was only a matter of time before frustration exploded into confrontation. Although problems were worse in the South where segregation was the order of the day, the War Department acknowledged that "smoldering unrest, which is likely to erupt at any time," existed at posts across the country. In 1943 a department memo reported "riots of a racial character" at Camp Van Dorn, Mississippi; Camp Stewart, Georgia; March Field and San Luis Obispo, California; Fort Bliss, Texas; and Camp Breckenridge, Kentucky. Nelson Peery, a black infantryman trained in Louisiana and Mississippi, recalled the sense of rage and frustration among black troops in the wake of these uprisings. "The final realization of the black man's impotence weighed on my chest," he wrote. At the time, he remembered feeling as if the "black man will never be anything but a boy in this country. Even if you kill one of these white bastards, you're not a brave man; you're a dangerous crazy nigger."[16]

When black soldiers and sailors finally went overseas, discrimination and continued assignments to labor battalions were constant sources of tension. Staff Sergeant Bill Stevens from the famed black 24th Infantry Regiment later joked about the situation. Assigned to dock work during the Guadalcanal campaign "under the guise of keeping physically fit," Stevens explained, "If totin' that barge and liftin' that bale was a physical fitness program, then [we] should have been in superb physical condition compared to similar white units." In fact, Stevens's regiment was assigned to manual labor so often that he thought they should have been renamed the "24th Stevedores." Infantry training had nothing to do with their assignments. Not all black troops were anxious to "prove themselves" at the front, however. As one soldier from a labor battalion remembered, "We were glad that we were not being sent up into the hand-to-hand combat area. We wanted to survive . . . [and] we felt we were performing an important job." Service assignments were not only important jobs; they also could be dangerous ones. As the Allies advanced in Europe, construction battalions were asked to rebuild bridges while battles continued to rage around them. Leon Bass remembered the "glorious day" that his battalion of combat engineers completed a bridge in spite of inclement weather, strafing, and shelling from German howitzers. But he also recalled thinking that his battalion had "paid a heck of a price for that glory" as he stood in the snow "and looked at the grave registration trucks on which the bodies of so many friends were placed."[17]

With black soldiers working and dying for their country, the black press and black officials demanded an end to the hypocrisy of a segregated army fighting to save freedom and democracy throughout the world. Early in 1942, the *Pittsburgh Courier* launched the "Double V" campaign for victory over fascism abroad and discrimination at home. The Double V caught on with fashion, songs, and numerous editorials in the black press. Yet the NAACP's magazine, *The Crisis*, had been demanding similar action since 1940. In an editorial entitled "For Manhood in National Defense," the NAACP explained, "This is no fight merely to wear a uniform. This is a struggle for status, a struggle to take democracy off of a parchment and give it life." It was, in short, a "continuing battle for manhood citizenship rights." White policymakers and pundits understood the relationship between military service, citizenship, and manhood as well, but they argued — disingenuously — that war was not the time for rabble rousing and protest. To conservative whites like J. Edgar Hoover, the director of the FBI, black editors' criticism of government policies during wartime bordered on treason and sedition. Hoover and some members of the mainstream white press argued that black editors should be muzzled. The white Scripps-Howard columnist Westbrook Pegler accused the *Pittsburgh Courier* and the *Chicago Defender* of "exploiting the war emergency as an opportunity to push the aspirations of the Negro." Even Pegler acknowledged, however, "If I were a Negro, I would live in constant fury. . . . I would not be a sub-American, sub-human being, and in docile patience forever yield my rightful aspiration to be a man." Black editors felt the same way, and they continued to fight for the Double V.[18]

The strongest critic of Jim Crow military policies within the Roosevelt administration was William Hastie, the dean of the Howard University Law School and former federal district judge in the U.S. Virgin Islands. Hastie had been appointed as Civilian Aide on Negro Affairs in the War Department in October 1940. Letters from irate black soldiers and his own investigations of discrimination in the armed forces led Hastie to conclude that segregation had a disastrous effect on military morale and effectiveness. In a 1941 memo to his superiors, he challenged the assumption that southern white officers were the best choice to train and lead black troops, and he also chastised the War Department for "insufficient effort" to "persuade southern communities to accept and treat the

Negro man in uniform as a man and a soldier." The heart of Hastie's critique related to the psychological effects of segregation and discrimination on black soldiers: "In the army, the Negro is taught to be a man, a fighting man; in brief, a soldier. It is impossible to create a dual personality which will be on the one hand a fighting man toward a foreign enemy, and on the other hand a craven who will accept treatment as less than a man at home." Understanding that wartime military service reinforced traditional notions of manhood that rested on physical strength, courage, duty, and honor, Hastie saw that such cultural expectations placed black recruits in a Catch-22. Black soldiers were trained to exhibit these traditional attributes of manhood to help win the war, but these same qualities that helped them survive military service were perceived as dangerous to an American social order that rested on white male supremacy. These paradoxical expectations created a psychic dissonance for black veterans, many of whom would channel their frustrations into a movement for equal rights after the war. Hastie's insightful critique of the military predicted just such a scenario, but his words fell on deaf ears in the War Department. Responding to Hastie's salvo, department officials argued that the "level of intelligence and occupational skill of the Negro population is considerably below that of the white" and warned of the dangers of "social experimentation" in the military during wartime as a justification for continued segregation. Hastie resigned his post in protest against these policies.[19]

As the military reinforced traditional ideas about manhood and stubbornly clung to Jim Crow policies, manpower needs on the home front inspired a massive migration of workers and shifts in the labor force that undermined white male supremacy. With the bulk of young white men serving overseas, there were new job opportunities for women and minorities in the economy, especially in the burgeoning war industries. Even if some of these opportunities proved fleeting, they had an important impact on manhood and race in America. As historian George Lipsitz argues, the mobilization for war "not only realigned the economy, it brought dramatic changes as well in gender roles" and allowed African Americans to take "control of their own destinies." These changes began with what amounted to a second Great Migration of farmwomen and black sharecroppers from fields to factories. Just as in World War I, millions of rural Americans, especially in the South, headed to southern urban centers and cities in the industrial Northeast and Midwest. But the new promised land of the 1940s was the West Coast, especially California. Many of the 338,000 black migrants who headed to California ended up in Los Angeles and the San Francisco Bay Area. They were part of a flood of more than 3.5 million new workers that came to the state in a wave of migration that journalists and scholars have dubbed the "Second Gold Rush."[20]

Eddie Eaton was one of these migrants. His grandfather had been born a slave, and Eaton himself had been born in a log cabin. Maybe migration was in Eaton's blood; Eaton's parents had joined one of the earlier migrations from the rural South to the city of Houston, Texas to find work. In 1943, when he heard about high paying jobs in the California shipyards, Eaton took the train with his sweetheart, Myrtle, and headed west. The train was undoubtedly packed with other migrants—black and white, many of them from Texas, Louisiana, Oklahoma, and Arkansas—hoping to find a job and the good life. "From what I heard," Eaton said, "it was a better place to live than Texas. You were a little more freer in California than you were in Texas." Another Texas migrant had similar expectations after an uncle waxed poetic about his work on the Golden Gate Bridge in letters home. Images of her uncle standing high atop one of the bridge towers and gazing out into the expanse of the Pacific Ocean inspired this young black woman to move west. "It just sounded like a fantasy," she remembered.[21]

Like thousands of other migrants to the Bay Area, Eddie and Myrtle got jobs at the Kaiser shipyards in the town of Richmond, just northeast of San Francisco. Finding a job wasn't the problem; housing was. The population of Richmond exploded during the war. In 1940 there were 23,000 residents in the bayside town. Four years later the population had more than quadrupled. Schools, apartments, and other city facilities creaked under the weight of all the newcomers. Housing was especially tight for the 18,000 new African American workers at the Kaiser shipyards, who were often excluded from certain homes and neighborhoods. Eddie and Myrtle Eaton moved in with a friend for a time, before they married and finally found their own place. "They tried to keep the blacks in an area and the whites in an area," Eaton remembered, "but finally, they kind of gelled and went to moving in and around each other and it worked out fine." The influx of both black and white migrants from the South was both exciting and unsettling for longtime residents of the Bay Area. One middle-class black resident of Richmond admitted in an interview years later that she was suspicious of both black and white newcomers, who seemed less educated and more racially prejudiced than her family. "They brought a lot of that with them from the South. I'm not talking about just whites, I'm talking about blacks too, because they would go around, a lot of them, with chips on their shoulders."[22]

It is no wonder that many of the migrants had chips on their shoulders, because they often faced discrimination in the shifting terrain of the wartime workplace. Most unsettling to older residents and workers were the women who took "men's jobs" in the shipyards, women like Myrtle Eaton. Challenging traditional gender ideas, these women had simply answered the federal government's call to join the workforce like Rosie the Riveter. To minimize the social impact of women entering the shipyards, leadermen and managers tried to stop women from wearing nail polish, lipstick, makeup, or sweaters in the yards. Historian Kevin Starr notes that such rules did not apply to women who did more traditional clerical work at the shipyards, but when women "came into competition with men as welders or electricians, they were forced to suppress all signs of femininity." This was too much for some men, who didn't want their wives to get jobs at the shipyards, and some women, who looked askance at such jobs. Marguerite Williams was tempted by the high pay but decided against applying for a shipyard job because the women "looked so mannish" and they "had to work like men." Myrtle Eaton didn't seem to mind. Beaming from the Eaton family album is a beautiful picture of a young Myrtle smiling, her face framed by a raised welder's visor during a sunny afternoon break at the shipyard. Evidently, Myrtle Eaton was happy to have a high paying job even if she couldn't wear lipstick while she welded.[23]

Migrant men also struggled to find their place in the new war industries. Older California residents derided the white southern migrants as ignorant "peckerwoods" and Okies. They hung signs over ship bulkheads that read, "Okie, This Is a Door" and drew labels on urinals that said, "Drinking Fountain." But the white southern migrant could take solace in the fact that he was not the "low man" on the job site at Kaiser. Unions made this clear when they barred black workers from joining or shunted them into segregated auxiliary locals that had little say in negotiations. Racism infected the workplace in other ways. As an internal Kaiser company memo noted, "The men from the South complain more about the fact that the shipyards employ, and they must mingle with, all races, creeds, and colors." Much of this tension came from the simple fact that black and white migrants were competing for jobs and raises. But the presence of women in a racially integrated workplace—and the implicit possibility of interracial relationships—further complicated the economic competition in the shipyards. No one captured the drama of these conflicts better than the novelist Chester Himes.[24]

Himes was himself a migrant. Born and raised predominantly in the Midwest, he had spent a short time in the South where his father taught in black colleges. He was too old for the initial draft in World War II and later was deemed medically unfit because of a horrible accident, a fall down an elevator shaft, in his youth. In the early 1940s he traveled with thousands of other migrants in search of work in California, a place that he found was no "land of the free." Himes had twenty-three jobs in the first three years of the war. Only two of them were skilled positions: a ship-fitter for Kaiser in Richmond and a shipwright's helper in a Los Angeles shipyard. Himes later wrote in his autobiography that "the mental corrosion of race prejudice in Los Angeles" left him "bitter and saturated with hate." He channeled that anger into several essays and short stories for the NAACP magazine, *The Crisis*, and also into what he called a "bitter novel of protest," *If He Hollers Let Him Go*.[25]

Bob Jones, the main character of *If He Hollers Let Him Go*, is a black shipyard worker in Los Angeles who must deal with the racism that faced Himes and other black workers in wartime industries. Jones is also a leaderman, a man in a position of authority over a crew of other black workers. His light-skinned, middle-class girlfriend and her family constantly remind him of his potential, if only he would apply himself and get an education. But higher education and attaining a respectable middle-class life are not necessarily priorities for Jones, especially if he has to hold his tongue about the racism that he faces in Los Angeles and the shipyards to get them. The sky of the narrative darkens when Jones must supervise a white woman from Texas. "I ain't gonna work with no nigger!" Madge Perkins tells Jones when he first gives her an assignment. To which Bob replies, "Screw you, you cracker bitch!" From this first altercation springs a work relationship fraught with sexual tension. At one point, Bob finds himself drawn to the hotel where Madge is staying. They argue and tussle until they find themselves locked in an embrace. In a psychological power play, Madge hisses her lustful desire, "All right, rape me then, nigger!" Alarm bells peal through Bob's consciousness and he breaks off the encounter immediately. But he hasn't escaped yet. The next day at work, he stumbles upon Madge sleeping in a compartment of the ship where they are working. Before Bob can figure out what to do, Madge begins to scream for help, claiming that she's being raped. Beaten to a bloody pulp by his white coworkers at the shipyards, Bob is then taken before a judge. "Suppose I give you a break, boy," the judge says, acknowledging the weakness of the case against Bob. "If I let you join the armed forces—any branch you want—will you give me your word that you'll stay away from white women and keep out of trouble?" Feeling like "half a man," Bob Jones joins the army.[26]

The conflicts and anxieties that drove *If He Hollers Let Him Go* were rife in the factories and cities that had been transformed by war industries and migration. In 1943 these tensions exploded into race riots in Los Angeles, Harlem, and Beaumont, Texas, but the worst racial violence took place in Detroit. It had begun more than a year earlier as the federal government attempted to deal with the housing shortage caused by massive migration. In 1942 the government had planned to build the Sojourner Truth Homes for black war workers in a predominantly white neighborhood. A rash of white protests made the government redesignate the homes for whites only despite the fact that they were named in honor of the prominent African American abolitionist. A second reversal followed the outcry from liberal and civil rights leaders, but when the first black family attempted to move in, it was greeted by an angry white mob. Though violence quickly dissipated, residual racial tensions simmered in Detroit until they boiled over again in June 1943. One rumor that a black woman and her child had been assaulted and another about the supposed rape of a white woman sparked the conflict that raged for three days. When the smoke cleared, thirty-four people were dead—twenty-five were black and nine were white. Seventeen of the black casualties had been killed by the city's predominantly white police force. After an investigation of the riot, the NAACP's Walter White argued that competition for housing and jobs along with the stresses and strains that accompanied black and white migration from the South were primarily to blame. Finding that nearly 70 percent of the rioters were young white and black men, White further speculated, "A compensatory bravado seems to have been created in some of these young men who by the physical violence of mobbing sought to convince themselves and others that they were as physically able as those who had gone into the army." As White suggested, it was difficult to untangle the social and psychological causes of the 1943 race riots in Detroit and other cities. Black men on the home front were frustrated with limitations placed on new wartime job opportunities, and white men who remained at home saw the social hierarchy that they dominated before the war begin to shift beneath them. Avoiding the traditional rite of passage offered by the military for whatever reason, these men on the home front may have felt even more adrift in the sea of social changes brought on by the war.[27]

The military was not without its own social problems, and the case of the Port Chicago mutiny made it impossible for folks on the home front to ignore these problems any longer. Not far from Kaiser's Richmond shipyards in the northeast corner of the San Francisco Bay stood Port Chicago and the Mare Island Naval Station. Liberty ships would sail in and dock at Port Chicago to be loaded with ammunition that would resupply Allied forces overseas. All of the enlisted men loading the munitions were black, while the vast majority of their superior officers were white. Though the detonators had not been placed in most of the bombs that the men loaded onto the ships, they were still filled with tons of explosive and incendiary materials. Boxcars were loaded within two feet of the ceiling, and the men would climb onto the pile of bombs and roll them down a ramp into a net on the dock. Winch operators would then use cranes to lift the nets of shells into the cargo holds that were 30–40 feet deep. Joe Small, a winch operator, remembered, "If a bomb fell out or the net came loose and dumped the load into the hold, it would mean disaster. There is absolutely no place to run or hide in the hold of a Liberty ship being loaded with ammunition." Despite the danger, officers would make small wagers on which units could load the most munitions in an eight-hour shift. Such informal speed-ups were even more dangerous, because the Navy had not offered the black sailors any special training in loading munitions.[28]

On July 17, 1944, the Port Chicago men's worst nightmare became a reality. An explosion on or near the loading dock set off a chain reaction that decimated the Port Chicago facilities and two ships, killing 320 sailors. An Army Air Force plane flying nearby reported seeing a fireball three miles wide, and Bay Area residents as far as forty miles away felt the blast. Joe Small, who was not working at the time, rolled out of his bunk and used his mattress to protect himself from shards flying out of the explosion. Everyone who survived at the base was shaken by the devastating experience. Given that more than 200 of the sailors killed were African Americans, the tragedy was especially difficult for the black survivors.[29]

Less than a month after the explosion, the black sailors who had survived the disaster were asked to return to work loading munitions again. When 258 of them refused, they were imprisoned in a barge to await questioning. Frustrated, scared, and angry, some of the men passed around a petition stating that they would agree to any assignment other than loading munitions, while others began to fashion weapons out of metal tools and implements on the barge. Joe Small, an unofficial leader of the men, gathered them together to try to calm them down and keep them united. "We've got the officers by the balls," he said. "They can do nothing to us if we don't do anything to them. If we stick together, they can't do anything to us." But Small was wrong. The Navy announced that fifty of the "ringleaders" would be charged for mutiny, and mutiny during a time of war carried a possible death sentence.[30]

The Port Chicago mutiny became a cause célèbre, a case in which black manhood and courage were literally on trial. A *Chicago Defender* headline trumpeted the cause of the "Fifty New Martyrs." The NAACP sent its top litigant, Thurgood Marshall, to advise the defense team, and a young Lieutenant Commander James Coakley, who would later prosecute members of the Black Panther Party as the District Attorney of Oakland, served as the Navy's judge advocate. The fifty men pled not guilty, arguing that many of them had not been directly ordered to load ammunition and that those who had were not technically guilty of mutiny, because they had not attempted to "usurp, subvert, or override" the authority of their officers. Most of all, the defense rested its argument on the fact that the men had agreed to accept any other assignment, just not loading munitions, because of the paralyzing fear that crippled them after the explosion. In response, the prosecution sought to prove that the meeting on the barge was clear evidence of conspiracy and that fear was no excuse for disobeying an order during a war that saw American soldiers and sailors dying by the thousands overseas. The officers called to testify by the Navy included a chaplain at Mare Island who spoke with the men after they were imprisoned. All of the officers testified that they had tried to persuade the men to do the right thing. The chaplain had "appealed to their race pride and mentioned the fact that they were letting down the loyal men of their race and their friends." A white officer who commanded one of the accused units testified that he "explained the seriousness of the charge and went on to explain that there were women doing more hazardous work with explosives than they were called to perform." After building a case for a sensitive officer corps commanding cowardly enlisted units, the prosecution used Small's comment that the enlisted men "had the officers by the balls" to prove he had led a conspiracy to "usurp and subvert" the white officers' authority.[31]

It took the court eighty minutes, including a lunch break, to decide that the fifty men were guilty. They were sentenced to fifteen years in prison and dishonorable discharges. In an appellate brief completed after the sentence was handed down, Thurgood Marshall and other NAACP attorneys cited a lack of training for the black sailors and also poor leadership by white officers as leading to both the explosion and the alleged mutiny. For these reasons, and also because this was the largest court martial trial ever held, Marshall asked the navy to reconsider the verdict. "This is not an isolated case," he wrote. "This is a case which will break down completely all consideration of a Negro as a seaman." Marshall understood that the prosecution's arguments and the original verdict in this case reinforced negative stereotypes about black manhood, morale, and military service without critically examining the racism within the armed forces that was at the root of these problems. The poor morale of the Port Chicago men was the logical result of racist assignments to the most dangerous and unrewarding tasks in the navy duty rosters. Far from an exhibition of cowardice, the "mutiny" was an example of courage, of men fighting for the right to fight. The Port Chicago verdict tarred the reputation of fifty seamen, few of whom had ever even gotten a chance to go to sea. Ironically, Joe Small and many of his comrades from Port Chicago finally got assigned aboard ships after the war ended. In 1946 the Port Chicago mutineers were released and stationed on several integrated ships to complete their terms of service. It was on one of these ships that Small had one last confrontation with racism in the navy—this time, with a white sailor from Alabama who refused to eat in an integrated ship's mess with him. Small launched his five-and-a-half foot, 170-pound frame into the six-foot plus, 250-pound southerner. After the fight, the two eventually became friends, and the Alabamian admitted, "I found something out. A man is a man." To Small, this was something of a vindication of his struggle. It was long overdue.[32]

While Small and the other black men from Port Chicago literally fought for their lives in the mutiny trial, subtle changes were finally taking place in the branches of the military as a result of political, intellectual, and social pressures in the wider society. President Roosevelt acknowledged the racism in the armed forces in a 1944 press conference before the Negro Newspaper Publishers Association. "It is perfectly true," FDR said, "there is definite discrimination in the actual treatment of the colored engineer troops and others." While FDR's election-year mea culpa seemed a political ploy, Eleanor Roosevelt's stance was a more principled and proactive one. "I think we will have to do a little educating among our Southern white men and officers," she wrote to Secretary of War Henry Stimson, urging him to take action against discrimination. Slowly, the military began to respond to these criticisms. In 1944 the army produced a training manual called "Leadership and the Negro Soldier" that cited "competent scholars . . . [who] are almost unanimous in the opinion that race 'superiority' and 'inferiority' have not been demonstrated." The manual praised the patriotism of black troops and urged officers (most of them white) to remember that black soldiers were "citizens in a country which prides itself on its democracy and individual liberty." The army's new line echoed the thesis of the groundbreaking work that the Swedish sociologist Gunnar Myrdal completed on American race relations in 1944 entitled *An American Dilemma*. Myrdal's exhaustive study concluded that racism pervaded all sections of American society, but also emphasized that if Americans could address this "dilemma," they had an opportunity to lead the postwar world by living up to the national ideals of liberty and justice for all. The obvious first step down this path was equal treatment in the armed services and, as the black press had argued all along, that meant African American troops deserved the right to *fight* for their country.[33]

The fight for the right to fight began early in the war as African Americans struggled to gain entry into the heralded Army Air Corps. Air Corps pilots were the surgeons of the skies, and when they came back down to earth, they had a confident swagger that has become legend. The very embodiment of martial manhood and technological mastery, positions for fighter pilots were reserved for whites only. So when Charles W. Dryden went down to enlist in the Army Air Corps in New York City, the recruiter shook his head and said, "The United States Army is not training any colored pilots." As one of the first black graduates of the New Deal's civilian pilot training program, Dryden was as qualified as any young man in America to sign up in 1940, but he would have to wait. Finally, in the summer of 1941, the Bronx native was accepted into a segregated fighter squadron that would train at an airfield attached to the black university in Tuskegee, Alabama. When Dryden and his fellow cadets completed their training courses and earned their wings, it was front-page news in the black press. Yet at home in New York on leave, Dryden was mistaken for a porter at Penn Station. "Here, boy, carry my bag," an elderly white socialite demanded of him. "Madame, I am an officer of the United States Army Air Forces," Dryden replied with as much patience as he could muster in the face of such disrespect.[34]

Two years after Dryden arrived at Tuskegee, he and the other members of the 99th fighter squadron were finally sent into combat in North Africa and the European theater. Saddling up for what he later called "an aerial *danse macabre*," Dryden took part in the Tuskegee Airmen's first dogfights with the German Air Force, or Luftwaffe. He nicknamed his planes "A-Train," after the popular tune played by Duke Ellington's band about a subway train in New York, and the planes served him well. On a clear day over the coast of Sicily, Dryden and other Tuskegee-trained pilots joined a fighter escort for bombers who had targeted Axis airstrips on the island. When two "bandits" appeared in the sky ahead, Dryden's wingman didn't see them. Tracer bullets came frighteningly close to Dryden's plane as he joined the fray to protect his buddy. Surviving the first barrage of enemy fire, it was his turn to attack. With A-Train's .50 caliber guns, Dryden sought to tattoo lines of bullet holes on the German fighters. Although none of the German planes went down, the dogfight was over in minutes. The enemy had fled. "Race base, this is race ace," the black pilots would radio to their control tower after a mission. "Give me the word, and I'll make like a bird."[35]

When reports of the Tuskegee Airmen's early exploits reached the States, they were lauded in the black press but viewed with skepticism by military brass and the white media. *Time* magazine grudgingly admitted that the 99th fighter squadron had "done fairly well." But the story went on to cite unnamed military sources, concluding, "The top air command was not altogether successful with the performance." The mainstream media and military officials echoed old stereotypes about black soldiers, implying that the 99th fighter squadron suffered from a "lack of aggressive spirit." Historical accounts do not bear this out. If anything, the Tuskegee Airmen were plagued not by cowardice but by the cocksureness that is legend among fighter pilots. "The fact is, we were vainglorious," one pilot later remembered. "I'm old enough now to know this is quite human for a bunch of young men." This must have been especially true for young men who fought with the heavy responsibility of representing their race. "Let's face it, it was an honor in that our people were so proud of us for having picked up the challenge when it was offered," this same airman concluded.[36]

As the men of the 99th fighter squadron saw their first combat in Europe, U.S. transports with African American reinforcements were zigzagging across the Atlantic to avoid German subs. Arriving in Britain was a welcome relief to all, but it was especially so for black troops, who stepped off the ships and into a society with a reputation for more tolerant race relations. The first African American soldiers arrived in Britain in May 1942. Having never seen African Americans before, many British people were receptive to the newcomers and critical of American racism. Some pubs mocked American segregation, advertising: "For British people and coloured Americans only." The liberal *Daily Mirror* in London printed a cartoon of an African American and an Indian soldier passing a sign in a shop window that read: "No colored people admitted," with the black soldier commenting, "We didn't see *that* notice in the trenches." When Europeans did not evince the proper deference to American racial customs, some white soldiers took umbrage. An Italian American soldier went so far as to print up leaflets ordering Italian women not to consort with black GIs, warning, "The machine gun will cut down the prostitute who sells the honor of her race, and the people will seek revenge upon her and her black son." In Britain, white troops spread rumors that their black comrades in arms were endowed with tails. Since few British women had seen a black man before the war, they were naturally curious. "They would come up and pat you on your butt to see if you got a tail," remembered one black veteran. "And some of the smarter brothers told them, 'Yes, I may have a tail . . . [but] my tail doesn't come out until late at night.'" This kind of interracial flirtation was the worst nightmare of many southern white troops. As one white corporal explained, he didn't mind the advancement of black troops, but he did object "to Negro men sexing with white women. We're not fighting for that kind of 'democracy'."[37]

British attitudes toward race relations subtly shifted as more American troops, black and white, poured into the country in anticipation of the D-Day invasion. The historian Graham Smith argues that the British were not uniformly opposed to segregation or theories of white supremacy and such racist sentiments actually grew in some circles during the war. Sympathy for segregation was clear in British military memos and civilian pronouncements, but it crystallized around the case of a black American GI named Leroy Henry, who was accused of raping a British farmer's wife in 1944. The rape accusation led to Henry's swift conviction in a U.S. military tribunal, and he was sentenced "to be hanged by the neck until dead." The case was widely publicized in the British press, as liberal Brits attempted to distance themselves from the racial atrocities they had long criticized in the United States. Many believed Henry's claim that he had paid his British partner for sex in the past but that on the night in question she had demanded twice her normal fee. When he refused to pay, she played to white Americans' basest racial fears. A thorough investigation by members of General Eisenhower's staff supported Henry's story, and the black GI was freed to return to duty. Other African American soldiers were not so lucky. African Americans made up less than 10 percent of American military personnel in the European theater, but they represented 21 percent of the soldiers convicted of criminal activity and 42 percent of those convicted of sexual assault. This wasn't the sort of justice they were fighting for, and it revealed the lengths to which military officials would go to export Jim Crow.[38]

Timuel Black saw this injustice first hand when one of the members of his Quartermaster Battalion was hung for supposedly raping a British woman during their stay on the island before the D-Day invasion. This must have weighed heavily on Black's mind as he joined the invasion of Normandy two days after D-Day. On the trip across the English Channel to Utah Beach, Black remembered "young men cryin' for their mothers, wetting and defecating themselves. Others tellin' jokes. Most of us were just solemn." After the landing, African American supply companies served as the arteries of the Allied forces, pumping the lifeblood of supplies and munitions to the front lines. The 23,000 black drivers and support staff collectively known as the Red Ball Express brought more than 412,000 tons of food, fuel, weapons, and ammunition from the beachhead to the advancing Allied armies within one three-month period in 1944.[39]

While the companies in the Red Ball Express distinguished themselves in the types of support positions where blacks had traditionally served, new opportunities were finally opening up for black troops on the battlefield in the European theater. The most acclaimed of these was the 761st Tank Battalion, nicknamed the Black Panthers. When the Black Panther battalion joined the advancing Third Army, General Patton explained to the soldiers what he expected of them. "Men, you are the first Negro tankers ever to fight in the American army," the gruff commander barked. "I don't care what color you are as long as you go up and kill those Kraut sons-of-bitches." Captain John Long, the commander of B Company in the 761st Battalion, was actually nicknamed the "black Patton" by his men. Although the army and the American public rarely recognized them, Long and other black combat officers exhibited an attribute of martial manhood that would prove valuable in the struggles that followed the war: leadership. "Johnnie was every inch a soldier," one of the men from B Company recalled. "He asked nothing of his men that he would not do himself. He was courageous, shrewd, able and an evil s.o.b. There were times when we hated his guts, but we had to respect him." One can still sense awe and fear in the testimony of men from B Company who told of Captain Long getting out of his tank personally to check for booby traps and mines underneath a bridge that they had to cross, leaving himself open to enemy sniper fire.[40]

Though they served in a segregated battalion, the Black Panther tankers found themselves involuntarily integrated with white units by the chaos of modern warfare. When a German round slammed into Sergeant Johnnie Stevens's tank, he climbed out with three surviving comrades but found himself too injured and shocked to crawl out of range of the mortars that continued to rain down on his position. A white soldier from the 26th Division saw him. "Hey Sarge, you hit?" he asked. "I'm hit hard as hell," Stevens called back. The white soldier hopped over a protective embankment, scooped Stevens up in his arms, and carried him to safety. Just before the white soldier ducked down behind the embankment himself, a German sniper killed him. Stevens never learned the name of the man who saved his life. But he did come to understand what another black soldier believed was one of the central ironies of war: "You don't have time for prejudice in a foxhole."[41]

One of the few black combat units on the front lines at the conclusion of the war, the Black Panther battalion was also one of the first American units to witness the devastation of the Holocaust. Seeing the atrocities of the concentration camps seared horrifying images into the minds and memories of these men. When asked about his impressions of the camps, Captain John Long could only initially respond with a question for his interviewer: "Have you ever seen a stack of bones with skin stretched over it?" The exact role of the Black Panthers in liberating the camps is a matter of dispute, but Captain Long remembers, "When we busted in the gate, the inmates just staggered out with no purpose or direction until they saw a dead horse recently struck by a shell." To Long's shock and horror, the prisoners began tearing at the animal's carcass, "eating the raw flesh." As black soldiers came to grips with the meaning of the atrocities that they saw at the end of World War II, they began to reflect on their own conditions in the United

States. "If this [Holocaust] could happen here, . . . it could happen to black folk in America. I guess more than any single event, it was this sight that crystallized my determination to do as much as I could to bring about some sanity to a very insane world."[42]

In fact, many of the American troops, black and white, who survived the war came to similar conclusions about the need for activism when they returned to the United States. One black chaplain stationed in the Pacific gave a final sermon to his men at the conclusion of hostilities that summed up this new militancy among black troops. "We have won the military battle for democracy," he said, "but the fight is not over. Don't be satisfied with the way things were. . . . Don't let anyone ever again tell you you are inferior because you are black. . . . Be a man! We owe it to ourselves." Black troops were not the only ones who saw racial injustice in a new light after the war. The scales had fallen from the eyes of a few white veterans as well. Captain Hyman Samuelson may have gone into the war more predisposed to understanding racial prejudice because of his Jewish heritage, but he also carried racist assumptions of his Louisiana upbringing. Samuelson came to respect and admire the black men he commanded in an engineering battalion stationed in the South Pacific. He tired of constantly defending them in front of other white officers and resolved to do something about this when he returned home. "Before I die," he wrote in his diary in 1943, "I must help stamp out this crazy idea that the white man has about his superiority over the colored man. . . . It's wrong—damn wrong!" This was a powerful epiphany, yet after Samuelson returned from the war, he did little to support the emerging struggle for racial equality.[43]

One of the reasons that the war may have altered race relations, if only temporarily, was the formation of strong friendships—a type of male bonding that some veterans argue cannot be fully understood by civilians. "The buddy becomes father, brother, drinking companion, banker, untiring confidant to all the hopes and hurts and fears," wrote Nelson Peery, a black infantryman who served in the Pacific theater. "Buddy becomes . . . more of a man by confidently giving that dignified special kind of love that exists between men of combat." Black troops who fought together in segregated units gained strength in this bond and a new consciousness of shared racism that they all faced, regardless of where they came from in the United States. Northern blacks realized the trials and tribulations that segregation inflicted on their southern brethren, and southern blacks saw that they were not alone in fighting such discrimination. Despite the segregation and discrimination in the armed forces, camaraderie did bridge racial and class divides during the war. But black soldiers looked on such newfound friendships with a mixture of hope and skepticism, fearing that once the war ended, so would the relationships it wrought. "Oh, we accepted the friendship offered," a black soldier remembered, "but we never forgot that one day we would be going home and not to take this bit for real." Another later said, "My best friend while I was in the Pacific was white. We went through hell together, gambled together, chased girls together, and came back together until we passed under the Golden Gate Bridge, and my buddy disappeared. . . . The bridge said it, we were back home again, back to reality."[44]

The reality may not have changed, but black soldiers had. A new sense of confidence and camaraderie forged during the war became a powerful weapon for civil rights groups afterwards. NAACP membership and activism grew by leaps and bounds as veterans swelled the ranks of the organization. The number of local chapters nearly tripled and national membership soared from 50,556 in 1940 to almost 450,000 by 1946. In Mississippi, for instance, black veterans like Amzie Moore, Aaron Henry, and Medgar Evers spearheaded successful local organizing drives for the NAACP in the 1940s and 1950s. Southern white leaders fought back, attempting to defend the racial hierarchy that existed before the war. Mississippi Senator Theodore "The Man" Bilbo admonished his constituents to quell the rising militancy of black veterans and their efforts to regain the vote after the war. "The white people of Mississippi are sleeping on a volcano," he warned, "and it is left up to you red-blooded men to do something about it." Such calls to arms did not go unheeded. In 1946 Isaac Woodard, a black veteran, was returning to his South Carolina home after completing three years of service in the army when he asked the white bus driver if it would be possible to stop so that he could use the bathroom. "Hell, no!" the driver said. Still wearing the uniform that symbolized his service to his country, Woodard seethed: "Dammit, you've got to talk to me like a man." The bus driver then radioed ahead to the police, who pulled Woodard off the bus at the next stop and beat him until he was blind. In the face of such local resistance, the NAACP harnessed the organizing energy of returning veterans into a national campaign to overthrow Jim Crow. "After World War II, as a result of black servicemen, really, the whole attitude in the country about the race relations problem changed," according to NAACP attorney Constance Baker Motley. Motley, Thurgood Marshall, and their colleagues in the NAACP Legal Defense Fund focused on a challenge to segregation that was ultimately successful in the Supreme Court's 1954 *Brown v. Board of Education* decision.[45]

The social and cultural revolutions that took place in the 1950s and 1960s were clearly rooted in changes that began during the war. In framing the war as a fight for democracy and self-determination, the United States had inspired a desire for freedom at home and abroad. The combination of this idealistic rhetoric and the decimation of European economies during the war led to the rise of anticolonial movements in Africa and Asia that would, in turn, inspire the civil rights movement in the United States. The migration of African Americans from the South to the North and West altered the domestic political landscape. Politicians with national ambitions had to appeal to this black voting block. Franklin Roosevelt's successor, Harry Truman, recognized this new political reality. Motivated both by political expediency and moral repulsion at the beating of Isaac Woodard, Truman signed an executive order to desegregate the armed forces and pushed for a civil rights agenda in Congress in the months before the 1948 elections. Though this would lose him white southern votes as the Dixiecrats bolted from the Democratic Party, it gained him votes in the urban North and West. The national consciousness was finally awakening to social justice, but the change had begun in the hearts and minds of the men who served in World War II.

The dissonance between the idealistic rhetoric of World War II and the racist reality of 1940s America created the new militance among black veterans that spurred the early civil rights movement. While calls to arms reinvigorated traditional notions of manhood during the war, they further illuminated the gulf between what was expected of black men as soldiers and as civilians. Here were black men fighting to protect democracy in Europe despite the fact that they could not vote in Alabama or Mississippi. Here were citizen-soldiers who did not enjoy basic rights of citizenship such as equal protection of the law. Here were black youth joining up to "man the guns" in a segregated military that rarely treated them as men and armed them with mops and shovels instead of weapons. Despite these paradoxes and prejudices, World War II military service gave many black soldiers the opportunity to prove themselves as men in a very traditional sense. Having survived the traditional rite of passage into manhood in military service, black veterans felt differently about themselves even if many white Americans still did not. The discrimination against black veterans, and massive resistance to early civil rights victories like the *Brown* decision, revealed the limits of the positive legacies of black military service. The confidence and strength that black veterans gained as soldiers was simply a foundation for future struggle. Whites might reluctantly acknowledge black sacrifice, service, and even manhood during a time of military crisis, but when the crisis passed, African Americans' civil rights were still not fully recognized. That fight was just beginning, and it would be a struggle for a more enduring equality. When Nelson

Peery returned from service in the Pacific, he understood on a personal level that "the most important phase of my becoming a man and a revolutionary was drawing to a close." He knew that black veterans had "stood together and gained a new pride and unity . . . [and] that when the moment came . . . these men were going to be the cutting edge of a movement that would change America."[46]

Preservation of our institutions has become for [southern congressmen] a fight to the death — and the fact that the battle has not been lost is due largely to the steadfast efforts of that strong and stubborn group of "Southern Gentlemen" . . . who have taken an impregnable position behind a fortress of truth, honor, and integrity, and who refuse to surrender to enemies from without and within who would destroy us. — *Councilor Newsletter* (1957)

Chapter Two

A Question of Honor

Howard University professor Roosevelt Williams gripped the podium with both hands as he addressed the Mississippi NAACP audience in December 1954. Williams began by paying his respects to the black Mississippians who helped to pave the way for the Supreme Court's *Brown v. Board of Education* decision, which overturned racial segregation. "It is to your everlasting honor," Williams said, "that you have not given up in the difficult struggle . . . for equality." Referring to the efforts of African American soldiers in World War II and Korea, he proclaimed, "Our people have fearlessly fought and died in the front lines while the white soldiers crouched in the back areas," proving once again that "the negro is the white man's superior." As he moved on to the heart of his speech, a discussion of relations between white women and black men, Williams leaned toward the audience as if he were divulging a secret. He explained that southern white women supported black equality, because they "have been subjected to the same persecution that we have," but he believed that there was a deeper reason why "millions of southern white women" fought for integration. Black men, Williams claimed, "have long known that the white woman is violently dissatisfied with the white man and we know of the millions of clandestine meetings sought by the white woman. They, along with us, demand the right to win and love the negro man of their choice and shout to the world, 'This is my man and he is a man in every respect.'"[1]

Roosevelt Williams never gave this speech to the NAACP in Mississippi. In fact, Roosevelt Williams existed only in the minds of southern white men, the Citizens' Council leaders who drafted, recorded, and distributed this speech to state legislatures and opponents of integration all over the South.[2] National NAACP president Roy Wilkins dubbed the speech "an obvious fake," pointing out that Howard University did not employ a Roosevelt Williams and that no such person belonged to the NAACP. Robert "Tut" Patterson, executive secretary of the Citizens' Council, could only respond by saying that the council had "never claimed [the speech] to be authentic."[3] As a figment of the council's imagination, the fraudulent speech provides stark evidence of the fears about race, sex, and gender that animated the campaign of massive resistance throughout the Deep South.

In the 1950s southern white men faced a stiff challenge for control of a social order they had long dominated. The "race mixers" in the NAACP and Supreme Court seemed hellbent on overturning a gender and racial hierarchy that rested on the solid foundations of black disfranchisement and segregation.[4] The Williams speech called into question white women's loyalty and white men's performances on the battlefield and in the bedroom. Rather than revealing the secret desires of black men and white women, this speech illustrates the anxieties about manhood that spurred "massive resistance" to integration. It also shows the lengths to which segregationists would go to band white men together in defense of their race and region, their women and children, and their status as white men.

The debate between the Citizens' Councils and their opponents reveals intersections between the segregationists' rhetoric of manhood and themes of southern honor, social control, and racial violence.[5] Massive resistance was not a "crisis of masculinity," but it was a struggle for power often expressed in gendered terms. Segregation gave elite white men control of black workers in white homes, shops, fields, and factories, and it kept wages low for working-class blacks *and* whites. To retain their economic and social authority, white southern leaders in the Citizens' Councils demonized black men's sexuality and galvanized southern white men with ideals of whiteness, honor, and manhood. This gendered rhetoric was not simply a mask that hid race and class conflict, however. It was both a reflection of male insecurities in the larger society of 1950s America, and a response to "assaults" on southern society by the civil rights movement and an increasingly interventionist federal government. While the reliance on honor and masculinist rhetoric did help the Citizens' Councils mobilize white men and women for massive resistance campaigns, these strategies had unforeseen consequences. By demonizing black manhood and resurrecting nineteenth-century conceptions of honor, the councils created hysteria in the South that encouraged vigilante violence in defense of segregation. The violent extremism inspired by this masculinist rhetoric eventually gave civil rights officials and the federal government the moral authority to dismantle legal segregation.

For nights after he learned of the impending *Brown v. Board of Education* decision at a school board meeting in Indianola, Mississippi, Robert Patterson, the future executive secretary of the Citizens' Councils of America, lay awake in his home, worrying about sending his daughter to first grade in an integrated school. Finally, he rose from bed and wrote a letter of protest, calling for other men to join him in defense of segregation. "I, for one," he vowed, "would gladly lay down my life to prevent mongrelization. . . . There is no greater cause." While some southern whites resigned themselves to accepting the Court's decision, Patterson, a World War II paratrooper, Mississippi State football hero, and manager of a 1,585 acre plantation in LeFlore County, was not the sort of man to give up the fight that easily. In July 1954 he met with thirteen like-minded businessmen and politicians from Indianola and formed the first Citizens' Council to battle the integrationists. Looking back on that first meeting two years later, Patterson recalled that the men present had "no idea that such a small beginning would, in a few months time, expand miraculously into a virile and potent organization." The majority of new recruits to this "virile and potent organization" were middle-class white men. By the summer of 1956 the councils claimed to have over 80,000 members in Mississippi alone. Though there were chapters in sixty-five out of the state's eighty-two counties, membership was highest in Delta counties where the majority of the state's black population lived and worked for a white minority.[6]

The Citizens' Councils quickly spread from Mississippi to other Deep South states. In December 1954, six months after the first council meeting in Mississippi, segregationists from the Magnolia State were invited to lead a revival-style meeting in western Alabama. As dusk settled on the sleepy town of 1,300, pick-up trucks and large sedans cruised up to the county courthouse. "When they parked," one observer recalled, "only men — white men — emerged and all walked silently" to the meeting. A local state senator warmed up the crowd, preaching, "This is a white man's county. It always was and always will be if the white men will unite to keep it so." Speakers hammered on one theme over and over again. School integration, they argued, would inevitably lead to sexual relations between black men and white women. In the words of one councilor, "The door to the school room is the door to the bedroom." To slam those doors shut, southern white men felt that they must band together to squash the movement for integration. Although the potential for violent reprisals against civil rights activism was discussed, economic pressure was the preferred method of "persuasion" for the council leaders. They urged bankers, for instance, to refuse credit to black and white "trouble makers," and employers clearly understood their responsibility if hired help so much as hinted at support for integration. At the conclusion of the meeting, most of the four hundred men present anted up the three-dollar annual dues to join the Citizens' Council.[7]

Though they used much the same recruiting approach, council organizers in the upper South were not as successful as those in Alabama and Mississippi. In the border states of the old Confederacy, politicians who held fast to massive resistance vied with business leaders who sought to project a "progressive" image of race relations in order to attract outside investment in the boom years of the 1950s.[8] Virginia, North Carolina, and other border states may not have witnessed the level of grassroots organizing that Mississippi and Alabama did, but segregationists in the upper South were just as worried about "miscegenation" and "race mixing" as their Deep South counterparts. Dr. Wesley Critz George, a professor of anatomy at the University of North Carolina at Chapel Hill, responded to the *Brown* decision by lending his scientific credentials to the defense of segregation. George theorized that integration allowed for "the illicit and illegitimate crossing of blood" between the two races that would inevitably lead to a "lowering of the quality of our race and [destruction] of our civilization." He helped found the Patriots of North Carolina, a group with approximately 20,000 members affiliated with the Citizens' Councils of America.[9]

Hundreds of white men and women from all over North Carolina wrote to George to praise him for his courageous defiance of integration. A few even hailed him as a paragon of southern white manhood. Eugene Hood, a working-class segregationist from Greensboro, commended the segregationist intellectual for leading the "common folk." "It's difficult to see how a man can retain his own 'self-respect' unless he also maintains his pride in his race," Hood wrote in a letter to a Greensboro newspaper. "It is to men of the type of Dr. W. C. George, of the faculty of the University of North Carolina, to whom we are indebted . . . for some of us being able to maintain our 'own self-respect' and possibly our racial integrity." The psychological wages of "self-respect" and "pride in race" may have made up for the fact that working-class white men were not paid much more than their black coworkers in a segregated southern labor market that depressed all paychecks. As important as self-respect was, it did not put food on the table in workingmen's homes. Despite its costs, segregation served another function for working-class households in the eyes of some white women. White North Carolina women thanked George for protecting their children from integration. "I sure do wish we had some more men just like you," wrote Mrs. J. P. Thornton. "This is the saddest thing that has ever faced the mothers of the South."[10]

Black North Carolinians were less enamored with Wesley George than their white neighbors. Dr. F. W. Avant was one of the few black North Carolinians to write to George, and he targeted the segregationist's assumptions about "race mixing" in his response. "The disgusting thing that has been such a problem to thinking Negroes all of the time," Avant observed, "has been how to keep the white man out of our back yards, debauching our Negro women, and crossing the races in this diabolical, dishonorable, disgusting manner." Avant then went on to argue that rather than leading to a destruction of American civilization, "the crossings of the human beings here in America have produced a very . . . sturdy specimen of manhood and womanhood." An anonymous African American woman testified to the true origins of "miscegenation" in her rebuttal to George. "I have passed by hundreds of white men in my life and they winked their eyes," she wrote. "But to keep from being disgraced I kept my mouth shut, because Negroes have no protection."[11]

In a strange twist of fate, segregationists in North Carolina turned to black men for support (at least rhetorically) when their organization began to falter in the late 1950s. The North Carolina Patriots folded in 1958, in large part because local governments had coopted their agenda. By then, education policymakers had formulated plans to forestall real integration by accepting a few black students into white schools. Unwilling to let even one black child attend school with their sons and daughters, diehard Tar Heel segregationists resorted to desperate measures, even attempting to muster a *biracial* coalition of men to combat integration. The charter for the North Carolina Defenders of State's Rights, which succeeded the Patriots, called for all men "who have pride in their race, whether they be white or Negro . . . to show it. Let honorable men take their stand for their inalienable rights, their race, and their country." Evidently, no black men answered the call.[12]

The clearest statement of the Citizens' Councils' ideology during their early years was a call to arms written by Judge Tom P. Brady in Brookhaven, Mississippi, on July 23, 1954. Brady's *Black Monday* provided a history of "racial amalgamation," a censure of the Supreme Court decision, and a call for grassroots political organizations to defend segregation through nonviolent, legal means. Brady began by "proving scientifically" that the "species" Homo Africanus was vastly inferior to Homo Caucasius, using the pseudo-scientific theories of southern academics like Wesley George and George McIlhenny. McIlhenny's research on cellular biology and his rabid support for segregation led him to suggest that "every male Negro of puberty should be considered a potential rapist, until clinical tests prove beyond any reasonable doubt that he does not possess the sickling gene."[13] The scientific link between the "sickling gene" and sexual assault was more than a bit tenuous. Regardless, Brady used such theories to explain what he saw as black male pathology, and he elaborated on his paternalistic vision of race and gender relations in the South, arguing that the Supreme Court should not meddle in the social affairs of the South until it "knew the Negro" as southern white men supposedly did. *Black Monday* did not confine itself to men, however. Brady reconstructed the Old South pedestal for "the loveliest and purest of God's creatures, . . . the well-bred, cultured Southern white woman or her blue-eyed, golden-haired little girl." Then, he gently latched the door of segregation's gilded cage, arguing that the "peaceful and harmonious relationship" between blacks and whites in the South rested on the "inviolability of Southern Womanhood." Brady's tract implicitly acknowledged that segregation restricted not only the social mobility of black women and men, but the sexuality of white women as well. Although he carefully emphasized that only a nonviolent organization could successfully defend segregation, Brady warned ominously that "trouble" would inevitably come to Mississippi if a "supercilious glib young negro who has sojourned in Chicago or New York" ever performed "an obscene act or [made] an obscene remark, or a vile overture or assault upon some white girl." Brady concluded his book with a strident appeal to white southern manhood: "No true, loyal, Southern man will ever agree to [integration] or permit it. It shall not be!"[14]

Brady's warning proved prophetic. A year after the publication of *Black Monday*, two white men named Roy Bryant and J. W. Milam lynched Emmett Till, a black youth from Chicago who supposedly whistled at a white woman in Money, Mississippi. Although Bryant and Milam were acquitted in the Till murder trial by an all-white jury, they later told a journalist their story for $4,000 in "portrayal rights." When they picked up Till, Bryant and Milam claimed that they had only intended to scare him. But after Till supposedly boasted of having a white girlfriend back in Chicago, the white men decided to make an example of him. "Well, when he told me about this white girl he had," Milam told the journalist, "my friend, that's what this war's about down here, now. That's what we got to fight to protect. And I just looked at him and I said, 'Boy, you ain't never going to see the sun come up again.'"[15] It is doubtful that Till boasted of a white girlfriend to his kidnappers, but in Milam's mind, even the hint of interracial relationships made the youth's murder a justifiable homicide. Citizens' Council spokesmen offered little comment on the Till case, except to say that it was "regrettable" and to deny responsibility. The NAACP saw things differently. They argued that the councils should have been held accountable for Till's death because the group had fomented intense racial animosity in Mississippi and all but demanded such vigilantism in Brady's *Black Monday*. As Milam's belated admission of guilt revealed, calls for the protection of white womanhood and defense of white manhood led directly to violence against black men.[16]

The national media spotlight focused on the Mississippi Delta during the Till murder trial, and white Mississippians were angered by what they viewed as the "biased" nature of the press reports. To combat this coverage of the struggle, the Citizens' Council began publishing its own monthly newspaper. The first issue rushed off the Jackson press in October 1955. William J. Simmons, the son of a prominent Jackson banker, edited and wrote most of the articles for the paper and eventually supplanted Patterson as the leading spokesperson for the organization. In the *Citizens' Council*, Simmons kept Mississippians, and ultimately over 40,000 subscribers across the South, apprised of the status of the organization and the results of integration in northern cities.[17]

Nearly every month in the first several years of publication, the *Citizens' Council* "documented" the inevitable sexual repercussions of racial integration in schools, calling on white men to do their paternal duty by protecting their children from this menace. Headlines shocked readers with stories of "Rape [and] Assault in New York Schools," "Sex Atrocities in Massachusetts: Blacks Rape White Girl Repeatedly" and "Brotherly Love Stained in Philadelphia." The specter of rape and miscegenation struck a chord with white readers. The segregationist paper published an open letter to President Dwight Eisenhower from a former Air Force officer explaining why he, as a father, had to fight against integration: "Do you think any American father with any red blood in his veins is going to allow his dear, little girl to be insulted, possibly sexually molested and exposed to disease" through integration? Such sentiment actually found a sympathetic ear in the White House. "These [segregationists] are not bad people," President Eisenhower confided to Supreme Court Chief Justice Earl Warren. "All they are concerned about is to see that their sweet little girls are not required to sit in school alongside some big overgrown Negroes." Positioning themselves as loyal husbands and fathers, council leaders won at least tacit support from the president and other white men by arguing that they were simply protecting the flower of southern womanhood from black men who supposedly could not control their "animalistic" passions.[18]

Southern editors and politicians described integration and the Supreme

Court's "attack" on the region in similar sensationalist tones. The *Richmond News Leader* denounced the *Brown* decision as a "rape of the Constitution" in its call for "a valiant effort to halt the evil."[19] Senator Strom Thurmond of South Carolina observed, "The court has flung a challenge of integration directly into the South's face. . . . This means as much as a demand for surrender."[20] The Richmond editor's equation of the Court decision with rape dipped into a deep well of racial animosity by linking the integration of schools to sexual violence and miscegenation. Strom Thurmond's mixture of the metaphor of the duel with allusions to the South's surrender in the Civil War tapped into yet another historical reservoir of ideals of southern white manhood.[21]

Southern whites had abandoned dueling years before and had lost and found the cause of the Civil War many times since 1865, but these calls still resonated in the hearts of many southern white men. Arguments based on historical southern obligations and protection of white womanhood represented self-conscious resurrection and reinterpretation of regional "traditions" that gave the fight for segregation and white male supremacy a powerful but false sense of timelessness. Although they borrowed from the language and symbols of earlier southern struggles, these arguments must be viewed in the specific context of the 1950s and 1960s, during a time when southern white men's status as leaders of their society was being challenged by black activists and the federal judiciary. Nowhere was the resurrection and reinterpretation of southern traditions more apparent than in the campaign to raise the Confederate battle flag over southern state houses in the late 1950s and early 1960s. While claiming that the flags simply commemorated the Civil War centennial, state and local politicians recognized the unifying value of such militaristic icons as symbols of manly independence and resistance to the federal government. At the same time that they hoisted the rebel flag, segregationist leaders unfurled a highly purposeful heritage of hatred and honor to bring white southerners together.[22]

Segregationists called upon ancestral obligations from the antebellum and Civil War eras to reinvigorate the concept of southern honor. They hoped that a combination of honor and shame would galvanize white community consensus against integration and discipline southern whites with questionable allegiance to segregation. In the first half of the nineteenth century, a challenge to a southern white man's honor was a challenge to his manhood, and such challenges often necessitated dueling. This rather brutal form of conflict resolution faded from southern society after the Civil War, but the concept of honor endured, retaining its association with militarism and a willingness to defend one's good name or community with force. Honor's salience in southern society, it seems, ebbed during relatively stable periods of race and gender relations and flowed during challenges to white male authority and identity. During the late 1950s, southern white opponents of integration consciously resurrected this code of judgment by community and regional consensus to forge a "Solid South" in which staunch segregationists would be held in high esteem, while "moderates" and racial liberals would be dishonored and ostracized.[23]

"The Citizens' Councils . . . deserve the sanction and participation of all who are willing to mutually pledge their lives, their fortunes and their honor to the preservation of an unsullied race," argued Representative Wilma Sledge from the floor of the Mississippi House of Representatives in 1954. The councils certainly appreciated Sledge's support, but as a woman, she would not have been welcomed into their ranks in 1954. In the first few years after the *Brown* decision, many prosegregation groups restricted their membership to men only.[24] The names of these groups suggested their gender exclusivity: White Men, Inc., White Brotherhood, and Southern Gentlemen.[25] Many councilmen did not originally believe that women's participation in the organization was necessary or appropriate. "Women will not be allowed to join," announced one Alabama organizer late in 1954, "because we feel that it is a job for men." One historian of massive resistance has observed, "As defenders of white 'racial purity' and guardians against the evils of 'miscegenation,' council members viewed themselves as fighting a battle to which women should not be exposed."[26] The skewed demographics of local Citizens' Councils reflected this mindset in the mid 1950s. As of 1956, the roster of one Citizens' Council chapter in Forrest, Mississippi, included only 15 women out of 190 total members. However, a note at the bottom of the membership list read, "Ladies invited to join also," indicating that some in the councils were not above recruiting the "gentler sex" if it meant more dues-paying members. While men would continue to dominate the councils' leadership and membership, they quickly realized that they could not ignore the vast pool of potential support and voting power represented by southern white women.[27]

By the end of 1956, the *Citizens' Council* had begun to acknowledge the need for women's activism in the segregationist crusade. "Special attention should be given to bringing ladies into active, working membership in your Council," William Simmons wrote. "Determined ladies will put backbone in some of your timid men." Women in the segregation struggle believed they could do more than stiffen the flagging fealty of their men, however. Council member Janice Neill wrote, "We women have an opportunity to do a job that is peculiarly ours: [teach] the children. . . . Men of the present generation can fight a delaying action, but if we women do our job we can play a part in attaining victory in the next generation."[28] Another self-styled "Southern Lady" asked women to use their vote to elect prosegregation candidates. In a telling (if implicit) admission that southern white women might be tempted to join the campaign against white male supremacy, she warned her white sisters to avoid integrationist organizations that were "part of the shrewd, premeditated campaign to enlist the sympathies of inexperienced women."[29]

Most women who joined the councils were relegated to low profile positions, but Sara McCorkle, director of the Councils' Youth Activities Division, appeared in the pages of the *Citizens' Council* several times. McCorkle, who argued that "women must fight along side of men in this war," coordinated a high school essay contest about the advantages of racial segregation and fought against sales of a toy that portrayed a family with a dark skinned father and a white mother.[30] The *Citizens' Council* supplemented McCorkle's efforts in the field of youth education by publishing a serial primer for white children that told the "true" story of American history and race relations. "Our country is very big," one installment of this "Manual for Southerners" began. "And white men built it all. . . . Did you know our country will grow weak if we mix our races? It will. . . . We do not want our country to grow weak. White men worked hard to build our country."[31] The councils' defense of segregated schooling and alternate lesson plans for southern youth would eventually fuel the private school movement in the South during the 1960s. In the 1950s, the obsession with protecting the racially divided pubic school system revealed fears that the younger generation would be easily swayed by integrationist propaganda and ideas. "For although to most persons today the idea of mixed mating is disagreeable or even repugnant," one council spokesman warned, "this would not be true of the new generation brought up in mixed schools."[32]

Nowhere was the issue of "mixed schools" more explosive than in Little Rock, Arkansas, where President Eisenhower grudgingly enforced racial integration with the presence of the National Guard in 1957.[33] "Remember Little Rock" became a rallying cry for Citizens' Councils, and council leaders blamed the defeat of segregation in Arkansas on southern white moderates who had exposed cracks in the "Solid South." Segregationists responded to moderate men's heretical positions with attacks that depicted them as women, for in the eyes of Citizens' Councilors, no true southern white man would ever question Jim Crow. After Harry Ashmore, editor of the *Arkansas Gazette*, won two Pulitzer Prizes for his critical assessments of Governor Orval Faubus's segregationist stance, one *Citizens' Council* cartoonist portrayed Ashmore as an old woman named "Pussyfoot," who won prizes for her articles in the "Carpetbag Chronicle." William Simmons

A Prize For Pussyfoot

CITIZENS' COUNCIL, JACKSON, MISS.

This cartoon, published in the *Citizens' Council* in 1958, portrays Arkansas newspaper editor Harry Ashmore as a woman named "Pussyfoot," because Ashmore was not man enough to stand up for segregation. Rare Book Collection, University of North Carolina, Chapel Hill.

later characterized moderate editors like Ashmore and Mississippi's own Hodding Carter as "recognition-starved printing-press prostitutes."[34]

Southern journalists like Ashmore and Carter did not view themselves as radicals or integrationists, because they upheld the concept of honor, remaining loyal southern men even as they rewrote what that identity meant. Describing a 1948 broadcast of the ABC radio and television program "Town Hall On the Air," Ashmore remembered that Walter White, then president of the NAACP, was demanding desegregation and "Hodding and I were defending the honor of the South." At the same time that these southern moderates were performing their duty as men in defending the honor of the South, they were performing race as well, literally assuming masks of whiteness for the television cameras. Ashmore remembered that when the show's crew was "putting [our] make-up on, they had to lighten up Hodding and darken down Walter." ABC could not very well have their representatives of the white South looking "blacker" than the president of the NAACP.[35] Even though Carter defended segregation in the *Greenville (Miss.) Delta Democrat-Times* throughout the 1950s, he had to withstand boycotts and threats of violence for his condemnation of council tactics. "Any white who didn't agree with the white majority was more than a dissenter," Carter remembered. "He was a traitor, and was to be treated as a traitor would be treated in war time."[36] Moderate southern editors like Hodding Carter and Atlanta's Ralph McGill abhorred the strategies of arch segregationist groups, but social mores and personal prejudices made them reluctant to advocate immediate integration. Straddling the fence on racial issues, these moderates garnered scathing criticism from both segregationists and civil rights activists. Martin Luther King Jr. articulated his disappointment with the slow pace of change proposed by racial moderates in his "Letter from the Birmingham Jail." "I have almost reached the regrettable conclusion," King wrote, "that the Negro's great stumbling block in his stride toward freedom is not the White Citizens' Councilor or the Ku Klux Klanner, but the white moderate who is more devoted to 'order' than to justice." The black comedian and activist Dick Gregory offered a more scathing satirical indictment. To Gregory, the southern moderate was "a cat who'll lynch you from a low tree." Moderate southern whites may have seemed no different from arch-segregationists in the eyes of movement activists, but their acceptance of gradual reform served as a harbinger of future change. Explaining the ambivalent regional allegiances of newsmen like Harry Ashmore, Ralph McGill, and her husband, Betty Carter said, "You see they never wanted to be anything but loyal sons of the South. But the South wasn't going to be what they wanted [it] to be. So they struggled to make the South be what they wanted."[37]

Southern moderates represented one threat to the councils' goal of regional hegemony, but violent supporters of segregation represented an even more dangerous problem because their actions ran the risk of provoking federal intervention. From the very beginning, most council spokesmen publicly distanced themselves from other white supremacist organizations like the Ku Klux Klan by denouncing their proclivity for violence. In one early council address, Judge Tom Brady surveyed his audience and surmised, "None of you men look like Ku Kluxers to me. I wouldn't join a Ku Klux [Klan] . . . because they hid their faces; because they did things you and I wouldn't approve of." However, realizing that it might be politically expedient to soften criticism of the Klan in Mississippi, Brady continued, "I'm not going to find fault with anyone who did [join the Klan]. Every man looks at the proposition not in the same way."[38] Although officially nonviolent, the councils issued mixed messages about the uses of violent tactics by supporters of segregation, just as their masculinist discourse and rhetoric of honor carried the implication that, if pushed, the only honorable course of action for white southern men might be to "defend" their communities by force. Violent acts committed by noncouncil members also allowed council leaders to claim that their defense of segregation offered a peaceful solution to the region's racial tensions, but council members who openly used violent tactics undercut these claims.

One council member who "looked at the proposition" of violence and Klan membership in a slightly different way was Asa "Ace" Carter, executive secretary of the North Alabama Citizens' Councils. Unlike most of the Mississippi Delta councils, which were dominated by leading businessmen and planters, the North Alabama Citizens' Council consisted mainly of laborers and union men. To Carter, this was the type of man that the Citizens' Councils should recruit because "through his veins flow the fire, the initiative, the stalwartness of the Anglo Saxon. Proof of his enviable reputation is the attack upon him. For such has been coined the words 'red neck' and wool hatter' . . . 'cracker,' and 'hillbilly.'" When he wasn't waxing poetic about the "calling card of cocksureness" adopted by southern "crackers," Carter ran into trouble with the state and national leadership of the councils. His working-class roots, propensity for violence, outspoken anti-Semitism, and membership in the "Original Ku Klux Klan of the Confederacy" proved too much for white-collar council leaders, who refused to recognize the North Alabama chapter. Despite this rejection from the official state organization, Carter continued to agitate openly for segregation until members of his klavern were arrested and convicted for castrating a black man in an initiation ceremony in 1957.[39] Castration of black men, a more common occurrence during the nadir of race relations around the turn of the century, continued through the 1960s, clearly underlining the salience of masculinity and sexual control in the struggle for civil rights.[40] The Birmingham castration incident damaged Carter's public position in the segregationist movement, but he continued to work behind the scenes and would later become a speechwriter for Alabama governor and perennial presidential candidate George Wallace. National Council leaders nonetheless distanced themselves from Carter in the late 1950s. "Ace Carter is an Alabama problem," William Simmons observed. "He has no standing with our group. . . . However, it might be added that the NAACP never feels it necessary to apologize for every Nigger rapist or for the Commies who help their cause."[41]

If southern moderates and vigilantes undercut council strategies of massive resistance from within, a new breed of northern bohemians in the 1950s represented an entirely different alternative to segregationist ideology. Norman Mailer sketched the complicated relationship between white and black youth in the generation of the beatniks and hipsters in an essay entitled "The White Negro." Like many men of his generation, Mailer worried that the crushing conformity of the post–World War II years threatened to wipe creativity, originality, and even "true" masculinity from the American scene. The only beacon of hope for Mailer and other white writers of the Beat generation was the "Negro hipster" or jazz musician. "Indeed, if one is to be a man [in the 1950s]," Mailer argued, "almost any kind of unconventional action often takes disproportionate courage. So it is no accident that the source of Hip is the Negro for he has been living on the margin between totalitarianism and democracy for two centuries." Mailer's homage to black manhood had paternalistic and racist undertones. He believed that black hipsters were "true" men, immune to the emasculating effects of conformist culture, not only because they were politically marginalized, but also because they were hypersexual "psychopaths." Yet despite the highly problematic nature of Mailer's argument, his essay did capture the Beat counterpoint to segregationist fears of "miscegenation." Positioning himself in direct opposition to the Citizens' Councils, Mailer argued that "it is the absolute human right of the Negro to mate with the White, and matings there undoubtedly will be, for there will be Negro high school boys brave enough to chance their lives."[42]

Mailer's fear that white American manhood was somehow on the decline in the 1950s tapped into an undercurrent of white male insecurity evident in the politics and popular culture of the era. This male angst reinforced the anxieties of white southern men who felt that they were losing control of their region. The masculinist rhetoric wielded by the Citizens' Councils against integration echoed the national debates concerning America's response to the Cold War. As historian K. A. Cuordileone has argued, politicians of this era attempted to position themselves not only as staunch anticommunists, but also as "hard," manly Cold Warriors who were imminently more capable of defending America than their "soft," sometimes "queer" or "effete" opponents. Senators Strom Thurmond, James Eastland, and Richard Russell were leading segregationists and national political figures who aligned themselves with the "hard" Cold Warriors, brooking no quarter for communist "subversives" or for liberals who appeared "soft" on communism and civil rights. Leander H. Perez, a powerful Louisiana politician and Citizens' Council leader, likened the national Democratic platform in 1960 to the Communist Manifesto because of its moderate support for civil rights. "How can we preserve *our* constitutional rights, *our* liberty and freedom under law, *our* status as first class citizens, *our* self-respect and manhood," Perez demanded, "IF we continue to run from the negroes" and bow to "the worldwide Communist conspiracy." As staunch anticommunists and segregationists, southern leaders saw little inconsistency with defending democracy abroad and denying it at home.[43]

Shifts in American society and popular culture reinforced and reflected the gender anxieties that were rife in the political arena. As men and women settled down to domestic bliss in the cookie-cutter suburban subdivisions that sprang up across the country in the 1950s, some husbands began to wonder if they controlled their domains and their destinies to the same extent that their fathers had. Films of the era such as *The Man in the Gray Flannel Suit* depict men grappling with insecurities that accompanied conformity and domesticity, but no picture was more emblematic of this male angst than *Rebel Without a Cause*. At the heart of the story is a dysfunctional relationship between a father and son. James Dean is the archetypal rebellious son who cannot understand why his father, played by Jim Backus, has exchanged his manhood for domestic servility. In one especially telling scene, the effete father, wearing a striking full-length, flower-print apron, futilely attempts to bond with the troubled teen. The son flees from the house and rushes to defend his "honor" in a game of chicken. With his smoldering intensity, Dean's character eventually teaches his father to be a strong man who stands up for himself and his son. One moral of the story is clearly that men must be careful not to become too domesticated or feminized in the rush to conjugal bliss. By the late 1950s and early 1960s, pop culture paeans to the patriarchal nuclear family such as *Leave it to Beaver* and *Father Knows Best* reassured American men that they were still masters of their domains. Yet the reassurances may have seemed hollow to southern white men who struggled to shield their families from integration.[44]

Rock 'n' roll music, television shows, and major motion pictures "invaded" homes and hamlets throughout the South in the late 1950s, challenging the basic tenets of segregation with interracial casts and integrationist themes. The Citizens' Councils railed against what they saw as the insidious tendency toward integration in American popular culture. When Asa Carter defended six members of the North Alabama council who assaulted Nat "King" Cole in 1956, he called Cole a "vicious agitator for integration." If Cole and other popular black crossover artists threatened segregation by attracting black and white fans to their concerts, Elvis Presley, Jerry Lee Lewis, and the white rockers of the 1950s seemed even more dangerous. They personally embodied integration. Unabashedly mingling black rhythm and blues with white country music, Elvis was the undisputed "king" of the white rockers who gained popularity by embracing black music, clothes, and dance styles. Elvis blurred gender lines as well. Dressed to the nines in meticulous outfits with bold pink accents or done up in the eye shadow that he liked to wear for shows, Elvis tapped into a tender masculinity that made girls swoon without letting go of the motorcycle machismo that inspired boys to rock. Like other rockers broadcast to even the most remote areas of the South by radio, Elvis presented a serious problem for segregationists bent on defending a traditional ideal of southern manhood and keeping white culture "pure" of black influences. The airwaves crackled with more than the insidious sounds of R & B and rock 'n' roll; they carried the images of television programs, which also seemed tainted by integration. Robert Patterson referred to the abominable influence of "Hellavision" on impressionable southern children, who might see "white men hugging Eartha Kitt or Pearl Bailey or some other form of interracial brainwash." And William Simmons frequently worried about the implications of television programs like Ed Sullivan's "mixed entertainment."[45]

Hollywood similarly shocked segregationist sensibilities in the 1950s, daring to depict interracial relationships on the silver screen. *Island in the Sun* (1957) revolved around an interracial relationship between a black man (Harry Belafonte) and a white woman (Joan Fontaine). Belafonte's character ultimately decides against interracial marriage, explaining that a white wife "would only mean snubs and misery. Besides, the girl would forget herself one day and call me a nigger." In a subplot, however, a white British officer does successfully woo an Afro-Caribbean woman. Despite the fact that the interracial couples are never seen kissing in the film, *Jet* dubbed *Island in the Sun* "the most frank portrayal of interracial love ever to hit the screen." Segregationists called for whites to picket theaters that screened the film. In fact, a posse of Citizens' Councilors cut the power and blocked the entrance to one rural Alabama drive-in that dared to show it. The angry councilors even assaulted a journalist sent from the state capital to photograph the protest and then boasted, "Niggers may run wild in Montgomery, but Elmore County is going to take care of itself."[46] To segregationists, *Island in the Sun* was only the beginning. Don Whelply, a council member from Atlanta, responded to Hollywood's purported slander against the southern white men and women in a *Citizens' Council* article entitled "What They Say About Dixie." He decried what he saw as celluloid caricatures of "the spineless Southern male [and] the sickly simpering belle," noting that "overnight, the southern gentleman vanished. In his place stood the beefy bigot, with blacksnake whip poised over the poor 'kneegrow.'" For Whelply, the last straw was the 1957 film *Band of Angels*, which cast Yvonne DeCarlo, a "luscious, very Anglo-Saxon young starlet as a Negress." Writers like Erskine Caldwell and Tennessee Williams, whose novels and plays became movies in the 1950s, also fell under Whelply's caustic critique for their gothic depictions "of the masses' strange doings in the land of cotton."[47]

If Citizens' Council members felt besieged by popular national culture and the press, they could take solace in the fact that distant echoes of their rhetoric returned in the words of at least a few vociferous northern segregationists. Carleton Putnam, an alumnus of Princeton with a law degree from Columbia, had grown up in New England, but his career as an executive in the airlines industry had taken him across the country, including a long stint in the South. In the late 1950s, he became a vocal opponent of racial integration, writing letters to the president and southern newspapers that eventually became the book, *Race and Reason: A Yankee View*. Putnam argued that Africans and African Americans were uncivilized, with generalizations such as "the earth has never known a bloodier race than the African Negro." It was clear to him that the "complete integration of these races, especially in the heavy black belts of the South, can result only in a parasitic deterioration of white culture." To an even greater extent than Putnam, Patricia and Lambert Schuyler believed that interracial sex would be the vehicle for such "cultural contamination," and they commended segregationists for their vigilance in a 1957 book entitled *Close That Bedroom Door*. Residents of Seattle, Washington, the Schuylers worried that "white men, it seems are no longer selfish of their women" and that "outside the South, where men are still conscious of their basic duty as defenders of their race, our men have abdicated" their role as protectors. The Schuylers' true fears are best summed up by their own fictitious integrated school bulletin. The fictional bulletin informed parents that a daughter "must not discriminate at school even in bestowal of her sexual favors," and it detailed the horrors of a white homecoming queen and a black homecoming king, noting, "Whatever they might do in a parked car after the ceremony is obviously to be expected and has the blessing of the entire faculty."[48]

In the late 1950s, the Schuylers were the exception rather than the rule outside the South. National sentiment and the federal government favored at least gradual desegregation in Dixie. By 1958 and 1959 politicians in the border states were beginning to view token integration as an acceptable alternative to federal intervention. When Governor J. Lindsay Almond of Virginia "surrendered" to the opponents of segregation by agreeing to token integration in Virginia schools, one Tennessee paper suggested that the Governor had "emerged with the honor that is due wisdom and courage and good citizenship." As a spokesman for the Citizens' Councils, William Simmons vehemently disagreed, noting, "The only 'honor' Almond emerged with is that accorded by others of like persuasion of whom, mercifully, there are but few in the deep South." Simmons termed Almond's action a "massive betrayal," and he felt certain that white Virginians had "enough pride and honor to make certain that [this] never happens again."[49] Moderate southern whites in border states had begun to redefine the "honorable" position in the integration crisis as massive resistance lost its already tenuous hold on the upper South.

Meanwhile, in the Deep South, Mississippi segregationists were about to elect one of their own to the highest office in the state. In his 1959 campaign for governor of Mississippi, Ross Barnett made it crystal clear that no other candidate could offer a stronger defense of segregation than he could. A longtime member of the Citizens' Councils, Barnett's election as governor represented the political high-water mark for the organization. At a council dinner to commemorate his election, Barnett hammered away at racial moderates with a masculinist rhetoric that had become the staple of segregationists. "Physical courage is a trait sadly lacking in altogether too many of the South's so-called leaders," Barnett said. "We must separate the men from the boys. We must identify the traitors in our midst. We must eliminate the cowards from the front lines." Barnett beseeched other southern leaders to harness "the FULL POWER of our State governments into this fight as OFFENSIVE weapons," and he wasted no time in diverting funds to the Citizens' Councils from the coffers of the Magnolia State.[50]

The primary vehicle through which Barnett channeled state money to the Citizens' Councils was the Mississippi State Sovereignty Commission, an investigative bureau and propaganda machine for the segregationist crusade that had been created in 1956. Under Barnett's predecessor, the Sovereignty Commission had languished in relative obscurity, but beginning in 1960, the Commission and the Citizens' Councils began a "real two-pronged offensive" against integration.

A QUESTION OF HONOR

Investigators for the Sovereignty Commission kept tabs on civil rights activists all over the state, showing up at mass meetings and conspicuously copying down the license plates of those in attendance. They seemed particularly interested in digging up dirt about the political activities, sexuality, and drinking habits of suspected civil rights sympathizers, making liberal use of hearsay to tar fellow Mississippians as communists, homosexuals, adulterers, and drunks. The Sovereignty Commission would then turn this information over to local police officers or Citizens' Council members so that "appropriate measures" could be taken to see that racial unrest was kept to a minimum. The Commission paid black editors to oppose integration and black informants to spy on movement activists in their communities. But the bulk of Commission "donations" went to the Mississippi Citizens' Councils, which received as much as $2,000 per month during the Barnett administration.[51]

Ross Barnett's outspoken opposition to integration set him on a collision course with the federal government, which by 1962 was no longer willing to delay the desegregation of the University of Mississippi. In that year, President John F. Kennedy and his brother, Attorney General Robert Kennedy, pressured Governor Barnett to accept court-ordered integration of Ole Miss. Publicly, Barnett had vowed never to permit integration. In early negotiations, he told Bobby Kennedy, "A lot of states haven't got the guts to take a stand. . . . They are weak-kneed." In contrast, Governor Barnett promised the public that he would "spend the rest of my life in a penitentiary" before letting a black man attend Ole Miss. The Governor also told Bobby Kennedy that James Meredith, a black applicant to Ole Miss, had been rejected primarily because of his criminal record (for civil rights protests) and that race was only one of many reasons he could not attend the university. "That's *one* of the reasons," the attorney general responded incredulously. "We're talking man to man. That's *the* reason—you don't want a Negro going to the University." After several more tense conversations, Barnett cut a secret deal with the Kennedy brothers that would allow him to save face even as he "surrendered" to the federal government by registering Meredith at Ole Miss. Final negotiations almost broke down when Barnett asked the attorney general to promise that Meredith would be led onto campus by a phalanx of federal marshals, who would all draw their guns as they forced the governor to step aside. Kennedy suggested that only the lead marshal draw his gun and "the rest of them [would] have their hands on their guns and their holsters." But this wasn't good enough. "I was under the impression that they were all going to pull their guns," Barnett complained. "We got a big crowd here and if one pulls his gun and we all turn, it would be very embarrassing. Isn't it possible to have them

A member of the Citizens' Councils and governor of Mississippi (1960–64), Ross Barnett
called on southern white men to do their honorable duty to defend the region from
integration. Here, he waves the Confederate battle flag and cheers on the Rebels of
Ole Miss. Photograph by Marion Trikosko, 1962. U.S. News & World Report
Magazine Collection, Prints and Photographs Division (LC-U9-8554,
frame 30), Library of Congress.

all pull their guns?" Clearly frustrated, Kennedy finally agreed, sealing the deal
to integrate Ole Miss with the staged confrontation. In Barnett's mind, this cho-
reographed showdown, reminiscent of a duel, would be the only way to convince
Mississippians that he had done his manly duty and acted honorably to defend
them against integration.[52]

Even the governor realized that this hollow performance of manliness would
not be enough to rationalize surrender in the eyes of Mississippians whipped into
a frenzy by his own rabid rhetoric. At the last minute, Barnett reneged on the
deal, withdrawing state troopers and highway patrolmen from the campus and
leaving the federal marshals, assigned to ensure order as Meredith integrated
Ole Miss, to face a mob of angry students and armed vigilantes. In the riot that
followed Meredith's entrance into the university, thirty-five marshals were shot
and two people were killed. Unaware of the violence erupting in Mississippi,
President Kennedy delivered a nationally televised speech concerning the integration of Ole Miss just as the marshals began to return the fire coming from the
mob. In his speech, Kennedy coopted white Mississippians' own conceptions of

manhood and honor as he asked Ole Miss students to accept Meredith, saying, "You have a great tradition to uphold, a tradition of honor and courage, won on the battlefield and the gridiron, as well as the university campus. . . . I am certain the great majority of the students will uphold that honor."[53]

Vigilante violence was a direct result of the masculinist demagoguery used by segregationists. The 1955 lynching of Emmett Till, the 1956 beating of Nat "King" Cole, the 1957 castration in Birmingham, the 1962 riots at Ole Miss, and countless lesser known acts of violence (primarily directed against black men) in the 1950s and 1960s had the unintended consequence of undermining the segregationist crusade. Segregation had constituted a solid foundation for white male supremacy in the South. Understanding this, the Citizens' Councils recruited thousands of southern white men into the fight against integration with ideals of manhood and honor. The council's manipulation of honor and a hateful heritage of militant white male supremacy led directly to violence against black citizens, civil rights activists, and federal officials. Once the struggle against integration became a question of honor, violence became the only recourse for militant white supremacists when political and legal actions failed.

Rather than cowing African Americans, these violent episodes spurred black activism for integration and voting rights. With the protection of the federal government, James Meredith finally enrolled at the University of Mississippi in September 1962. Twelve years later, Aaron Henry, a longtime civil rights activist and NAACP leader in Mississippi, told an interviewer that he had fought against segregation because "you don't learn from osmosis that other people are just like you. Except you have the opportunity of dealing with them man to man, or person to person. . . . White boys get the idea that they're better than black boys because they are separate from black boys." Though armed allies often protected them, African American civil rights activists could not hope to outgun white supremacists backed by the full authority of southern states. Nonviolent protests against segregation and disfranchisement brilliantly caricatured the macho posturing and racial violence on which southern white male supremacy rested. Through nonviolence, civil rights activists demanded respect for black manhood and carved out new possibilities for white manhood as well. Aaron Henry summed up this movement as an effort "to convince as many members of the total community as I could that there was a situation . . . where all men were men, where nobody was inferior to another." When Henry and activists in the Student Nonviolent Coordinating Committee brought the movement to Mississippi, they did just that.[54]

How many roads must a man walk down / Before you call him a man?
— Bob Dylan, "Blowin' in the Wind," *The Freewheelin' Bob Dylan* (1963)

Chapter Three

Freedom Summer and the Mississippi Movement

s Charles McLaurin walked down the street in Ruleville, Mississippi, during the summer of 1962, he chatted with anyone who would listen about the importance of registering to vote. A field secretary for the Student Nonviolent Coordinating Committee (SNCC), McLaurin had just begun a voter registration drive in the sleepy Delta town. The mayor of Ruleville and a local police officer confronted the stranger and the small group of black citizens that surrounded him. Mayor Charles Dorrough was a white man. He had been elected without the support of Ruleville's black residents, less than 2 percent of whom could vote in 1962. Dorrough ordered the people listening to McLaurin to get off the street and go home. When McLaurin told them to stay put, the Mayor had him arrested. McLaurin was released later that day, and he returned to the very same street to talk to the very same people about their right to vote.[1]

As a black Mississippian himself, McLaurin understood why most of the folks he spoke with were reluctant to join him on the trip to the county courthouse. He knew that when these folks got home from trying to register, they would be fired, evicted, or even jailed. But despite the threats of retaliation, or perhaps because they were no longer beholden to the white men who once paid them little more than subsistence wages, three older women from Ruleville agreed to ride with

McLaurin down to the courthouse in Indianola. There they would face a hostile white registrar in the birthplace of the Citizens' Councils of America.

Early on the morning of August 22, McLaurin took the three brave women to register. Their car rolled south from Ruleville, passing cotton plantations where "men, women, and children, moving to the rhythm [and] beat of the hoe," labored for the arch-segregationist Senator James O. Eastland and other wealthy planters. McLaurin followed the women up to the daunting white columns that stood like silent sentinels guarding the Indianola courthouse. He waited anxiously while they tried to register and drove them home after the registrar rejected them because they were black. McLaurin brought dozens of Ruleville residents down to the courthouse that summer. Among them was a sharecropper named Fannie Lou Hamer, who became one of the most powerful advocates for the rights of women, minorities, and the poor. Looking back, that first trip to the courthouse remained one of McLaurin most enduring memories. "I will always remember August 22, 1962," he said years later, "as the day I became a man."[2]

Charles McLaurin's reminiscences might seem strange at first. He himself did very little. He did not register to vote or face the white registrar; the women did. Yet McLaurin found his strength that day by helping the women find theirs. He claimed his manhood by helping the women reclaim a bit of their dignity. Coming of age in Mississippi, where respect for black men was all too rare, it is not surprising that McLaurin and other SNCC men look back on their activism as a rite of passage into manhood. Responding to segregationists who had demonized black masculinity, the young men in the movement created militant new models of black manhood. The rite of passage for SNCC activists and other young men in the southern movement avoided many of the traditional trappings of manhood that rested on power and domination. These men were leaders whose primary goal was to find local leaders to replace them. Though SNCC men occasionally used masculinist rhetoric, their advocacy of participatory democracy led them to an inclusive, humanistic organizing strategy that welcomed both men and women into the leadership of the movement.[3]

The Mississippi movement and especially the summer project of 1964 raised broad questions about the gender, racial, and sexual mores of the segregated South. During the summer project, hundreds of young white men and women lived and worked alongside black activists in an attempt to replace segregation with the "beloved community," a society based on equality, democracy, and love that knew no racial boundaries. For segregationists, it surely must have seemed that the "race mixing" apocalypse had arrived. This made local men's participation in the struggle especially difficult as their attempts to challenge white male supremacy alongside white women elicited particularly violent responses from the white community. Local blacks and civil rights organizers fought back against racial violence and oppression both with armed self-defense and nonviolent political protest. Armed self-defense safeguarded activists and the black community, fending off the attacks of white vigilantes. Local men and more than a few women took up arms in self-defense as a practical necessity. For the men in particular, this was also an important way to reclaim their manhood by protecting their families. However, because it was by nature defensive, this strategy could never produce lasting change in the southern social order. Nonviolent activism, perhaps seen as a more "passive" form of resistance, was actually the potent moral force and savvy political strategy that brought about real change in the southern society. Southern civil rights organizers showed that nonviolent activism could be courageous and even manly. Above all, they demonstrated that nonviolent protest was an effective way to undercut the violence upon which white male supremacy rested and also a way to gain political power for disfranchised African Americans in the South.

The Citizens' Councils and other segregationist groups succeeded in thwarting the Supreme Court's desegregation mandate during the second half of the 1950s because the federal government was unwilling to force southern states to comply with *Brown v. Board*, and because of the violent white backlash elicited by the decision. A temporary lull in the direct action phase of the movement after the Montgomery bus boycott and the Little Rock school crisis also contributed to the haltingly slow progress of desegregation. By the end of the 1950s, a new generation of African Americans had grown tired of waiting for older civil rights leaders and federal officials to act. On a blustery February day in 1960, four freshmen at North Carolina A & T, a historically black college in Greensboro, sat down and ordered food at the "whites only" Woolworth's lunch counter. When refused service because of their race, the four black men remained at the counter in protest against segregation. "I probably felt better than I've ever felt in my life," one of the students later said. "I felt as though I had gained my manhood." This simple act of protest sent shock waves throughout the South. By the end of the month, college and high-school students had begun sit-ins in thirty-one cities across the region.[4]

To harness the power of these various protests, student leaders met in mid-April in Raleigh, North Carolina, with support from Martin Luther King Jr.'s organization, the Southern Christian Leadership Conference (SCLC). There to guide the students were veteran activists Jim Lawson, a proponent of nonviolent protest and mentor to student demonstrators in Nashville, Tennessee, and Ella Baker, a movement veteran who had worked with both the NAACP and SCLC. Though employed by SCLC at the time of the conference, Baker advised the student leaders to remain independent of King's organization, which reflected the traditional male–dominated, hierarchical structure of the black church. The sit-in leaders listened to Baker and founded the Student Nonviolent Coordinating Committee (SNCC) as an autonomous band of young activists wedded to "group-centered leadership" and intent on using grassroots organizing and nonviolence to overturn white supremacy in the South.[5]

When Bob Moses, one of the first field secretaries for the young organization, accepted a call to lead a voter registration drive in southwest Mississippi in the summer of 1961, he faced the strongest bastion of white supremacy in the Deep South. Moses had grown up in a Harlem housing project. His sharp mind and intellectual curiosity spurred him to undertake graduate work at Harvard, and his admiration for the existentialist philosophy of Albert Camus fueled an early passion for social activism. Arriving in Mississippi on assignment for SNCC, Moses found that the Citizens' Councils had a stranglehold on most public institutions in the Magnolia State. Through the guidance of local activists such as veteran NAACP organizer Amzie Moore, Moses came to believe that the only way to wrest control of the state from the councils was to organize the voting power of black Mississippians.[6]

A strict social hierarchy of gender and race had long restricted citizenship and voting rights in Mississippi and the rest of the American South. Black men had won citizenship and the vote after the Civil War, but a concerted campaign to disfranchise African American male voters in the South at the end of the nineteenth century stripped them of these rights. Race riots throughout the region punctuated the disfranchisement campaign. One particularly heinous bloodbath in Wilmington, North Carolina, took place in 1898 after a black newspaper editor named Alexander Manly had the temerity to suggest that some white women might actually desire relationships with black men. Manly's offices were subsequently burned, and hundreds of black citizens fled the city after a massacre that accompanied local elections and the rise of a white supremacist government. White mobs wreaked similar havoc in New Orleans and Atlanta. The white southerners who shouldered shotguns during the riots and led disfranchisement campaigns argued that segregation alone would not afford white men the necessary power to protect white women from supposedly uncivilized black men. Thus elite southern white men sought not only control of the public space though segregation, but also sole jurisdiction over public office through disfranchisement. Having removed black men from electoral politics, many white southerners also fought against the Nineteenth Amendment to give women the right to vote, fearing that it would undermine traditional racial and gender norms. The political activism of the 1950s and 1960s directly confronted the interlocking system of racial and gender oppression. Marion Barry, a SNCC activist who accompanied Bob Moses into Mississippi, talked about this when he explained what the struggle meant to him. Barry fought against segregation and disfranchisement because he realized that if he "was not a free man, I was not a man at all. I was only part of a man, and I felt in order to be a whole man I must be an American citizen as anybody else."[7]

During the summer of 1961, SNCC voter registration workers confronted both legal and extralegal obstacles to black voting in Mississippi. After ascertaining that Bob Moses was the person "who's been trying to register our niggers," police officers threw the SNCC activist in jail for two days. Less than a week later, Moses took another group down to register, and this time a local white man attacked him. A staunch advocate of nonviolence, Moses refused to fight back. His assailant, who turned out to be the sheriff's cousin, was acquitted by an all-white jury. One month after Moses was beaten and jailed, E. H. Hurst, the state representative from Liberty, Mississippi, and also a member of the local Citizens' Council, shot and killed Herbert Lee, a black man who had been active in the voter registration drive that summer. Claiming self-defense, Hurst was never tried for Lee's murder. To the black residents of Liberty, the name of their hometown must have seemed, at best, ironic.[8]

In the face of vigilante reprisals and official police repression, Bob Moses and the others who helped organize the first voter registration drives in Mississippi remained true to the code of nonviolence. The idea of nonviolent protest, used so effectively in the Montgomery bus boycott and the student sit-ins, had come to the movement from many sources. American writer Henry David Thoreau had espoused nonviolent civil disobedience to protest against the Mexican War in the nineteenth century, and Mahatma Gandhi used similar passive resistance techniques to contest British colonialism in India during the twentieth century. As a man of color fighting both colonial oppression and an ethnic caste system in his native land, Gandhi won special admiration from African American leaders. Gandhi was, in the words of W. E. B. Du Bois, "not an impressive figure of a man but small and thin, weighing only about 100 pounds." Despite Gandhi's slight physical stature, Du Bois saw his nonviolent struggle as a model for how "to achieve freedom and manhood." Movement mentors James Lawson and Martin

Luther King Jr. merged Thoreau's and Gandhi's protest philosophies with the Judeo-Christian ethos of loving one's enemies. African Americans in the rural South may have been unfamiliar with Thoreau and Gandhi, but they did understand the moral strength of nonviolent protest as a modern version of Christian teachings to turn the other cheek.[9]

Though many rural black southerners accepted nonviolence as a tactic for demonstrations, most did not adopt it as a way of life. Local activists, especially black veterans, viewed armed self-defense as a practical necessity in the fight against white vigilantes. National civil rights leaders, on the other hand, understood that black activists could not outgun both vigilantes and southern authorities, and they feared that armed self-defense would undermine the movement's moral high ground. This debate came to a head in 1959. That year, the national leadership of the NAACP denounced the militant stance taken by Robert Williams. A veteran of the Marine Corps and director of the local NAACP chapter in Monroe, North Carolina, Williams had led black activists armed with shotguns and hunting rifles in fending off attacks by Klan nightriders. During an NAACP convention in 1959, Williams demanded that national officials reconsider their position against self-defense: "We as men should stand up as men and protect our women and children. I am a man and I will walk upright as a man should, I WILL NOT CRAWL." Williams conceded that nonviolence was a fine tactic when media cameras and the national conscience held white vigilantes in check, but on lonely nights in rural North Carolina, he understood that the only place for the moral high ground of nonviolence might be six feet under.[10]

As SNCC moved its voter registration drive into the Mississippi Delta in 1962 and 1963, student organizers had to make peace with local activists who, like Robert Williams, believed strongly in armed self-defense. Among the most visible advocates of self-defense were the men of Holmes County, Mississippi. Though it had been difficult for Charles McLaurin to persuade large numbers of Ruleville men to try to register, the men in Holmes County practically dragged SNCC organizers to the courthouse. Holmes County had been the site of a New Deal land grant experiment that helped black tenant farmers become landowners. Independent farmers could challenge white authority in ways that other men could not. Hartman Turnbow was one of the black landowners who accompanied fourteen other Holmes County residents on a trip to the courthouse. The sheriff met them at the door. Patting his side arm, he said, "Now, who will be first?" Turnbow stepped forward. Late one night, about a week after his unsuccessful registration attempt, gunshots poured into the windows of Turnbow's house and firebombs exploded outside. As his wife and daughter ran for cover,

Turnbow grabbed his rifle and trained it on his assailants. The attackers quickly fled. "They can't stand when a black man go to throwing fire," one black resident from Holmes County remembered. "When you stop and return fire, they moves." Though white officials arrested Turnbow the next morning for supposedly firebombing his own house, vigilantes in Holmes County probably thought twice about attacking his home in the future.[11]

Hartman Turnbow and Robert Williams believed that it was a man's duty to protect his wife and children against racial violence. The rationale that black men had a responsibility to protect their women and children was, in fact, very similar to the Citizens' Council argument that white fathers needed to fight against integration to protect their wives and daughters. For both black and white men, civil rights historian Tim Tyson notes, "the rhetoric of protecting women was fraught with the politics of controlling women." Though the gender politics may have been similar in these two instances, the parallel breaks down when one considers that black children, armed only with books and pencils, posed much less of a threat than white vigilantes with bombs and guns. As the attack on the Turnbow home illustrates, there were times when African American men had real reasons to defend their wives and children with arms, whereas white men's armed defense of segregation primarily protected their control of southern society, not the lives of white women and children. Black women did not remain silent in this debate about self-defense as protection for the "weaker sex." Women demanded that politically apathetic men stand up for them and take part in the movement, even as the women themselves occasionally took up arms to defend their families. In this way, according to Tyson, black women "both deployed and defied gender stereotypes," demanding protection to spur black men to activism, but protecting themselves when necessary.[12]

Tragically, it was not always possible to anticipate or defend against vigilante violence. Earlier in the same summer when Hartman Turnbow stood his ground against nightriders in the Delta, an assassin gunned down Medgar Evers, a field secretary for the NAACP, in front of his home in Jackson. The only prints found on the rifle belonged to Byron De La Beckwith, a member of a Delta Citizens' Council, who reportedly later said, "We're going to have to do a lot of shooting to protect our wives and our children from bad Negroes and sorry white folks and federal interference." Armed self-defense alone might slow this sort of violent suppression of the movement, but as a purely *defensive* strategy, it could not transform the political landscape of the state.[13]

Evers's assassination and the concerted attacks against voter registration drives in the summer of 1963 forced civil rights leaders to reevaluate their strategies.

"We were getting smashed by violence [and] terrorism," remembers Reverend Ed King, a white activist minister at predominantly black Tougaloo College in Jackson. "We either had to withdraw or move in a new direction." Mississippi activists refocused their energies on the gubernatorial campaign of state NAACP president Aaron Henry. As Henry's campaign manager, SNCC's Bob Moses asked Ed King to sign on as a candidate for lieutenant governor, creating the first biracial ticket in Mississippi since Reconstruction.[14]

King and Henry solicited "freedom votes" from black Mississippians, who were excluded from the official election by white registrars. The Henry campaign hoped to garner enough of these alternate ballots to prove to federal authorities that black Mississippians wanted to participate in the electoral process but were denied solely on the basis of race. According to the U.S. Commission on Civil Rights, just over 6 percent of the eligible nonwhite voters in Mississippi in the early 1960s were registered to vote. In twelve counties with a total population of nearly 35,000 eligible nonwhite voters, no black residents were registered at all. Far from apologetic about the scarcity of registered blacks, white Mississippians such as Citizens' Council leader William Simmons argued that racial disfranchisement was necessary to defend against "nigra political domination."[15]

In speeches across the state throughout the fall of 1963, Aaron Henry rallied the disfranchised in Mississippi. Henry based his candidacy on the issues of "justice, voting, economics, and education," and though he spoke mostly to black constituents, he tried to show how the white elite used racial segregation to control both black and poor white Mississippians alike. "These politicians," he told an audience in 1963, "have been able to maintain their power by burying Mississippi's problems under a blanket of race hatred."[16] As a self-employed pharmacist, Henry did not have to fear the economic reprisals that kept many from joining the movement, but white supremacists found other ways to stymie his activism. Terrorists firebombed Henry's home and drugstore in Clarksdale several times, and local law enforcement officials repeatedly arrested the NAACP leader on trumped up charges. In an effort to smear him not only as an integrationist but also as a "sex pervert," police accused Henry in 1963 of soliciting sex from a white boy. The charge proved false, but the insinuations had a basis in fact. Though Henry was married, he was also bisexual. According to those who knew him well, Henry felt little discrimination from the local movement because of his sexual orientation, but he hid it much of the time, recognizing that both black and white Mississippians might not understand. It was telling that movement opponents focused on Henry's sexuality as well as his civil rights activism as "proof" of what they saw as the unavoidable connections between "sexual perversion" and integration.[17]

Henry's campaign for governor attracted powerful allies and fresh ideas to the Mississippi movement. Allard Lowenstein, a Stanford professor and political activist, came to Mississippi in 1963 and proposed the idea of bringing white college volunteers into the state to help with the freedom vote. Lowenstein brought a quick mind, an egocentric personality, and most important of all, connections to wealthy white universities. He suggested to Bob Moses that university students could help staff the movement in places where many of the local organizers had been jailed or intimidated. At the urging of Lowenstein, dozens of students, most of them young white men from Yale and Stanford, traveled south to help recruit potential voters for Henry and King. As one volunteer remembered, he and his fellow students were "long on naïve idealism with little real sense of the larger history and risks," but they supplied necessary labor for the freedom vote.[18]

The freedom vote proved a success, tallying more than 80,000 ballots from black citizens across the state. In the spring of 1964, SNCC leaders assessed the lessons of the campaign. The white Democratic candidate, Paul Johnson, had won, but according to SNCC organizer Ivanhoe Donaldson, this was almost beside the point. The freedom vote "showed the Negro population that politics is not just 'white folks' business,'" Donaldson observed, and also that "whites can work [for civil rights] in Mississippi (at least white males)." Recognizing the important contributions of volunteers, Donaldson and others in SNCC still feared that given southern taboos against "miscegenation," the presence of white females would add a volatile ingredient to an already explosive situation in Mississippi. These and other concerns about the volunteers set the stage for a debate over the role of white students in the Mississippi summer project of 1964.[19]

In the wake of the freedom vote, SNCC's small cadre of Mississippi organizers began to plan a much larger campaign for the summer. SNCC then teamed up with the NAACP and other civil rights groups in an alliance called the Council of Federated Organizations (COFO). As the strongest proponents of the summer project, SNCC's Bob Moses and Charlie Cobb argued that student volunteers could staff a massive voter registration campaign and teach summer classes for the state's black children, who attended substandard, segregated schools during the year. Many local organizers, however, worried that the volunteers' educational advantages would overwhelm and intimidate local activists. Yet SNCC staffers and local organizers finally agreed that the skills and financial support that volunteers could bring outweighed the dangers they posed to struggling local movements.

More importantly, such a project would show America that whites and blacks, men and women, northerners and southerners, could work together to heal the deep wounds cut by segregation and disfranchisement.[20]

SNCC struggled to recruit a truly integrated cadre of volunteers for the Mississippi summer project. Many black students simply could not afford to pay their way to Mississippi. The resulting pool of volunteers was integrated but dominated by upper middle-class white students from elite universities outside of the South. Gender, as well as race and class, factored into the composition of the volunteer staff that traveled to Mississippi. As the sociologist Doug McAdam suggests, gender formed a barrier to white women's participation in the summer project as both their parents and SNCC organizers worried about the response of white southerners to the integrated movement. Protective parents often refused to let their daughters go to Mississippi, but because of society's double standard, this was less of an issue for male volunteers, whose parents were more likely to assume that their sons could take care of themselves. SNCC recruiters also felt that the presence of young white men in an integrated movement might be less likely to provoke the wrath of white southerners than the presence of white women. While the societal double standard partially explains the bias against white women volunteers, this was more of a practical response to the sexual and racial taboos of southern culture than an example of chauvinism in SNCC.[21]

The very dangers that restricted white women's participation in the summer project may actually have spurred men's participation. Men were more likely to sign up and be accepted, McAdam observes, because working in the summer project was similar "to any number of other traditional challenges that were available to young men as part of the process of 'becoming a man.'" While this may have been a factor in why young men signed up for the summer project, SNCC organizers rarely used such masculinist rhetoric to recruit volunteers. They wanted to recruit anyone with a true desire to learn about themselves and the South. They wanted people who believed in the beloved community and hoped to bring it to Mississippi.[22]

For the volunteers who joined the summer project, the road to Mississippi led through Oxford, Ohio, where Bob Moses and other movement veterans offered an orientation on racial oppression in the South and a crash course on nonviolence. Traveling in an old, tan Volkswagen van, Donna Howell and two other volunteers subsisted on bread and peanut butter as they trekked from the University of New Mexico to the orientation in Oxford. Along with hundreds of other volunteers, Howell listened to Bob Moses discuss SNCC's allegiance to nonviolence. To volunteers and veteran activists alike, Moses represented the model movement organizer, one who held fast to his ideals through countless beatings. "We don't preach that others carry guns or refrain from carrying them," Moses told the volunteers, "but no COFO workers, staff, or volunteers would be permitted to carry guns." The gentle power of his belief in nonviolence guided the paths of countless activists, yet Moses himself eschewed the leadership role. His soft-spoken demeanor and humility only reinforced the mystique that surrounded him. Volunteers remembered Moses as a "very poetic, sort of a Gandhian-like figure . . . [who] commanded a tremendous amount of respect, [but] didn't have an overtly macho male leadership style." Amzie Moore, the local NAACP leader who originally invited Moses down to Mississippi, admired his young colleague because people followed him even though he never said, "I'm the man, you do this, that, and the other." Like Charles McLaurin and other men in SNCC, Moses was a hard worker, an organizer, and an idealist who represented a new type of militant, nonviolent manhood.[23]

In the midst of a mass meeting during the second orientation week, Moses received word that a group of volunteers who went to Mississippi after the first orientation were missing. A pall of silence fell over the young crowd as Moses related the harrowing tale of three civil rights workers' mysterious disappearance. A veteran white activist, Mickey Schwerner had accompanied James Chaney, a young black activist from Mississippi, and Andrew Goodman, a white college student who had just arrived with the first group of volunteers, to investigate a church bombing in Neshoba County. The three had not returned. Moses told those assembled that the workers were presumed dead. Still reeling from the news of the missing activists, the volunteers and veterans bolstered their courage with freedom songs before boarding buses, trains, and automobiles bound for the Magnolia State.[24]

In anticipation of the integrationist onslaught, state and local officials in Mississippi beefed up law enforcement and passed legislation to prepare for the summer project. Jackson Mayor Allen Thompson proudly showed *Newsweek* photographers his new police battalion decked out in gas masks and riot gear along with an armored vehicle he lovingly dubbed the "Thompson Tank." Governor Paul Johnson ordered the highway patrol to add 200 new officers to the 275 already employed, and he pressed for legislation that outlawed picketing of public facilities. Johnson also received regular reports from the State Sovereignty Commission. One Sovereignty Commission spy attended the Oxford orientation, detailing rumors about "communist infiltration" and interracial sex in secret memos to the governor. "The white girls have been going around with Negro boys, and Negro girls are going with white boys. I have seen these integrated couples going

Civil rights volunteers sing together at the end of the orientation week in Oxford, Ohio, before departing for work in Mississippi during the summer of 1964. Student Nonviolent Coordinating Committee Photograph File, King Center for Nonviolent Social Change.

into the dorms together for extended periods of time," one racy exposé revealed. Unbeknownst to the volunteers, this spy traveled with them from Ohio to Canton, Mississippi, to begin the summer project.[25]

Stepping off the train in Canton, JoAnn Ooiman was one of the earnest volunteers who received a warm welcome from half a dozen COFO staffers and icy stares from angry local whites. A white college student originally from Denver, Ooiman had never been to Mississippi, and her introduction began with a barbeque at a black minister's house. Just as Ooiman and the other volunteers began to dig into the heaping plates of food, police sirens brought the welcome party to a screeching halt. The sheriff hauled the volunteers down to the station, took their mug shots, and then played a taped speech from the district attorney, warning that "the women would be raped by blacks in town and the men would be beaten up." It was a welcome befitting the "closed society."[26]

Despite the warnings of Canton's district attorney, many of the volunteers stayed in the houses of local black families during the summer without incident. In the rituals of everyday life, volunteers and local activists got to know one another as people. "Rise, shine, and give God glory," Ms. Hattie Bell hollered every morning to wake up Ooiman and another volunteer staying in her small house. A domestic worker in white homes for much of her life, Bell had saved up enough money to buy her own place. Since she had retired, she was no longer beholden to whites for income and so was freer to join the movement. She cooked large meals for the young women who stayed with her. Though she grew close to the volunteers over the summer, she never ate with them, abiding the dictates of segregation even in her own home.[27]

As the volunteers and host families soon learned, the careful deconstruction of such racial barriers was an important part of the summer project. For young black men in Mississippi, this was especially difficult given the taboo against their interactions with white women. Explaining her son's reticence to a volunteer, one local woman said, "Jus' one boy touch a white girl's hand, [and] he be in the river in two hours. We raised them up never to even look at one they passes on the street, don't even look, that's the way down here." Veteran activists warned volunteers to be wary of southern white taboos. The SNCC staff sent a few female volunteers home because they began romantic relationships with members of the communities in which they worked.[28]

Volunteers worked on three projects throughout the summer: voter registration drives, "Freedom Schools," and a smaller "white folks" project. The voter registration workers walked some of the same dusty, rural roads traveled earlier by Charles McLaurin. Moving out of the blistering Mississippi sunlight or occasional summer squalls, they climbed up rickety porches and talked to sharecroppers about registering to vote. Black farmers would nod and often agree that they should be allowed to vote. If the canvassers were white, they would say "yessir" or "yes'um," out of deference to the conventions of Mississippi race relations. Some might agree to come to mass meetings. A few might even agree to try to register. But most just listened. "There's a great amount of fear there," said SNCC field secretary Willie Peacock. "They will tell you . . . that they don't want to become registered to hide the pride, which says, 'If I say I'm afraid, then I'm less than a man.' . . . So we've been working on trying to cut through this fear."[29]

Occasionally, organizers used the rhetoric of manhood to push past the fear. When Charles McLaurin led a group of volunteers on a voter registration drive in the small town of Drew, he found many of the local men reluctant to participate. At one mass meeting outside of a small church, McLaurin harangued a crowd of men who looked on in silence. Referring to a group of white police officers who also stood nearby, McLaurin said, "What they're afraid of is that you're gonna rise! That you're gonna say, 'I'm a man! Treat me like a man!' . . . Are you gonna let them see that you're afraid? That you won't join these kids and women?" McLaurin then turned to his supporters and began to chant "Which Side Are You On," an old labor organizing song adapted by the movement. Those at the meeting joined in, shouting in unison:

> Oh people can you stand it,
> Tell me how you can.
> Will you be an Uncle Tom
> Or will you be a man?

At that moment, the police arrested the young organizers. Evidently, they *were* afraid that the men who had remained silent might rise.[30]

At the same time that voter registration work and mass meetings began to cut through adults' fears, the Freedom Schools had a similar effect on the young. As in many southern states, Mississippi's segregated public school system heavily favored white schools over black ones, allocating an average of $81.66 per white student as compared to $21.77 for each black pupil in 1964. Many black Mississippians had grown up attending split-session school years, implemented by white planters to ensure that they had enough additional child labor to plant and harvest their crops. To make up for these educational deficits, SNCC's Charlie Cobb had proposed the Freedom Schools, in which volunteers would teach summer courses in social studies, black history, drama, art, French, English, and nonviolence. Starved of educational opportunity for so long, the students exhibited an insatiable hunger for learning. Yet the schools would not have been possible without the support of parents, many of whom walked their children to classes every day, some as far as seven or eight miles from their homes. By late July, despite arson and bombings, forty-one Freedom Schools enrolled over 2,100 students, testifying to the overwhelming desire for equal education in Mississippi.[31]

Though SNCC valued Freedom School teaching and voter registration work

A Freedom School class meets in Mississippi during the summer of 1964. Student Nonviolent Coordinating Committee Photograph File, King Center for Nonviolent Social Change.

equally, volunteers had preconceived notions of the work they wanted to do, and some questioned the gender breakdown of work assignments. A female volunteer recalled that she felt "shoved to the side" as a teacher, while male volunteers were "being macho men," facing violence out in the field. One male canvasser said that, although teaching was important, "it wasn't the same kind of, if you want, macho adventurism that I was into." Sociologist Doug McAdam used volunteer interviews and staff rosters to estimate that women were nearly twice as likely as men to be assigned to teaching, whereas men dominated the ranks of voter registration workers. At the beginning of the summer, SNCC organizers did make strategic placement decisions. They originally kept white volunteers from doing voter registration work in the extremely dangerous counties and restricted white women's roles in the field for fear that their presence would provoke more hostility from local whites, but as the summer progressed, these restrictions slackened. Many women did work in voter registration even in tough rural counties, and those who worked as teachers also risked violence merely by working in the movement. Regardless of their assignments or their gender, all of the volunteers and staff members "put their bodies on the line." To white Mississippians bent on defending the racial status quo, teachers were no less of a threat than voter registration workers.[32]

No one in the movement was immune to the violence and racism in the Magnolia State. Away from the glare of media cameras, police officers felt no compulsion about beating activists or threatening them with language that revealed the sexual subtext of white male supremacy. Bessie Turner, a black woman from Clarksdale, told SNCC workers about a police officer who took her to jail and made her disrobe and lay face down on the concrete floor while he whipped her with a leather strap. "Turn over and open up your legs," he ordered, "and let me see how you look down there." Then, the officer hit Turner "between the legs with the same leather strap." When Mary Lane, George Johnson, Phillip Moore, and Paul Klein, a black female volunteer and three white male volunteers, went to the police station in Greenwood to report harassment by a local white man, they received similar treatment. Officer Logan (who did not give the volunteers his first name) kept Lane, Johnson, and Klein occupied while Moore spoke to officers in another room. Logan, off duty and out of uniform, asked how the white male volunteers liked "screwing that nigger," referring to Lane. Then he took out a long knife, and as he began to sharpen it, he said, "Sounds like rubbing up on nigger pussy." He brought the sharpened knife to bear on Klein's ribs and asked, "Think it's sharp enough to cut your cock off?" Shaking in fear, Klein and the others must have thought of the three missing civil rights workers, whose eyes probably stared down from wanted posters on the precinct wall. On this day, however, the volunteers were relatively lucky. Officer Logan eventually left them alone, but only after further bullying Lane with a pistol and shoving her to the floor.[33]

Most Mississippi officials opposed the summer "invasion," but few lawmen were as disturbed by civil rights activities as Police Chief Ben Collins from Clarksdale, Aaron Henry's home town. Before the summer began, Collins had coordinated official efforts to squelch Henry's campaign for governor. When Al Lowenstein brought Franklin D. Roosevelt III (the grandson of the former president) to meet Henry, Collins took them all down to the jail for questioning. "Don't you know these white guys ain't fooling around with you but for one reason," Collins warned Henry, "to get your women." Throughout the summer, Collins harassed the civil rights workers in Clarksdale, cutting off their electricity, bringing them in for questioning, and beating those unlucky enough to cross him on a bad day. The chief took a married couple of volunteers down to the station one day, and he tried to goad the husband into a fight, asking, "How many niggers did you sell your wife to last night?" When the male volunteer did not respond, Collins grew angry. "Why don't you stand up like a man?" he demanded. "I'd like to kill you." The chief, whose conception of manhood rested largely on physical power, could not comprehend the volunteer's adherence to the philosophy of nonviolence. Frustrated, he eventually agreed to let the couple go.[34]

By the mid-1960s, some white Mississippians had begun to feel that official opposition to the movement had not been effective enough. Many who had supported the Citizens' Councils as they defended segregation through ostensibly legal means had watched in frustration as the politics of massive resistance failed to thwart the "invasion" of civil rights workers. In 1963 and 1964 these men resurrected the Ku Klux Klan in Mississippi. The first installment of their newsletter, "The Freedom Fighter," published in December of 1963, demanded that white Mississippians listen to the voice of the Klan, because it was "THE VOICE OF MEN!!!" "These men," the newsletter proclaimed, were "too tall to bow down. They are men who have had enough. Enough of the Kennedys, communists, [and] negroes," among other things. Much like the Citizens' Councils before them, the Klan called on white men to join the fight against integration in order to protect their families, yet the organization's unprovoked attacks on African Americans could never have been mistaken for self-defense. In the spring of 1964, Justice Department officials chronicled several beatings of black Mississippians at the hands of Klansmen. On one night early in the summer, the white supremacist group tried to intimidate civil rights activists by burning seventy-one crosses in different parts of the state. Justice Department officials also suspected that the Klan was involved in many of the bombings of black churches and movement offices as well as the disappearance of the three missing civil rights workers, though by the middle of the summer they had few concrete leads.[35]

Though the vast majority of white Mississippians vehemently opposed civil rights, a small group of white moderates in the state has subsequently fallen through the cracks of history. One group of volunteers attempted to organize this silent minority of sympathetic white Mississippians in the "white folks" project. Grenville Whitman, a volunteer from Harvard, began the summer talking to white church and labor leaders in Biloxi, where the presence of federal military installations and a reliance on the tourist trade moderated the harsher aspects of racial oppression. "We were preaching to the choir," Whitman recalled with a wry smile, because these people had already begun to question segregation, but they had little power to sway the majority of their white neighbors. With the exception of vocal movement allies like Ed King and Hodding Carter, most white Mississippians who might have supported the movement were silenced by economic reprisals and social ostracism.[36]

The story of the Heffners from McComb serves as a case in point. Albert "Red" Heffner Jr. lived in a community where other white men formed a militia to defend against demonstrators "creating a disturbance, destroying property, or raping our wives." Heffner was, in many ways, a typical middle-class white Mississippian. He sold insurance and was the proud father of a former Miss Mississippi pageant winner. But Red held a secret in his heart: he sympathized with the civil rights movement. When he invited movement volunteers to dinner just to talk about their reasons for coming south, angry segregationists surrounded his home. "It was beyond my conception that I could be in any danger in my own house," Heffner remembered. Afterwards, his family began to receive bomb threats. Someone poisoned their dog, and Red's insurance business dried up. "People just wouldn't even talk to us on the street," Malva Heffner said. "There's no way to describe the hurt. I had never been put down in my life. I had never been rejected, and it was over something that just wasn't right." Eventually, the Heffners fled to Washington, D.C., to escape the hatred directed at them for one small act of kindness toward the movement.[37]

Opponents of the movement reserved their harshest reprisals for local black activists. Over the summer, SNCC staff chronicled thirty-five shootings, thirty homes bombed, thirty-five churches burned, and eighty beatings. Though movement veterans and volunteers had made a promise to remain nonviolent, local Mississippians made a conscious choice to defend themselves. Guns and hunting were integral parts of rural life in the South, and black men were not about to sit idly by while nightriders shot up their homes. Even though nonviolence had proven effective in the direct action campaigns of the early 1960s, the decision of local people to defend themselves in Mississippi influenced SNCC activists' thinking about passive resistance. "In that kind of environment," remembered one organizer, "it just kind of mutes the whole question of Gandhian philosophy." Over the summer, SNCC veterans began to rethink their allegiance to nonviolence in light of local attitudes toward self-defense. James Forman, the organization's executive secretary in 1964, later wrote that the summer project "confirmed the absolute necessity for armed self-defense," and in a mass meeting at the end of the summer, future SNCC director Stokely Carmichael voiced similar frustrations. "We're not going to stick with this nonviolence forever," he warned.[38]

In fact, 1964 saw the rise of civil rights groups that openly advocated self-defense. The Deacons for Defense and Justice was founded in Louisiana that year to defend black communities from white vigilantes. When the Deacons came to Mississippi to recruit members the following year, one said, "It's time for you men to wake up and be men." This philosophy resonated with some black men, especially veterans. The Deacons eventually expanded to include affiliates in twenty-one cities (seventeen of them in the South). These were predominantly male organizations modeled on black fraternal orders. Roy Burris, one of the Deacons from Bogalusa, Louisiana, explained to a *New York Times* reporter that, when his group fought back against white supremacists, "they finally found out that we really are men." In the tradition of men like Robert Williams and Hartman Turnbow, the Deacons wielded guns to protect themselves, their wives, and their children.[39]

Behind the chivalrous ideal of self-defense, however, lay the reality that women were almost as likely to arm themselves for self-defense as men. While staying in the home of a black woman from Biloxi, Mississippi, during the summer project, Grenville Whitman awoke one night to find the woman guarding the house with a pistol in one hand and a rifle in the other. Hattie Bell, the Canton house mother who woke JoAnn Ooiman up every morning with breakfast and the harmonious call to "rise shine and give God glory," slept with a hatchet under her pillow every night. These stories of women protecting themselves, their families, and the volunteers speak to the reality of self-preservation tactics in rural Mississippi where federal protection for nonviolent protesters was nonexistent. The stories also give a sense of women's strength and courage in the local civil rights movement.[40]

Women showed this strength not just in their willingness to defend themselves and their communities, but also in their untiring activism and leadership. "Women have been the backbone of . . . Mississippi's movement," noted SNCC field secretary Charlie Cobb. Emphasizing the important role that women played in Mississippi before Freedom Summer, sociologist and historian Charles Payne writes that local women were more politically active, attended mass meetings in larger numbers, and attempted to register to vote more often than their male peers. One activist Payne interviewed even dubbed the Delta movement "a woman's war." Though most observers believe that women participated in disproportionately high numbers, few agree on why this was so. Payne offers a variety of explanations, including black women's faith and enthusiasm for the churches that often supported the movement and the possibility that black women may have seemed less threatening than black men.[41]

Both of these factors may have facilitated women's participation in the movement, and yet, it may also be instructive to examine the obstacles to men's involvement. Struggling to explain why it was so difficult to get local black men to join the movement, volunteers were struck by what they perceived as the inability of these men to stand up and fight racism. Segregation has "so smashed and whiplashed" the black community, one volunteer wrote in a letter home, "it makes boys . . . out of men. The men are often so pitifully weak—unable to decide anything." Another wrote of the "absolute castration of the Negro male," who "is trained to be nothing more than a child with his . . . sheepish expression and 'Yessir, yessir' to everything the white man says." Without a deep understanding of the long history of lynching and repression faced by these men, the volunteers callously but perhaps accurately described the crushing fear that crippled many men's ability to participate in the movement. Local women had their own opinions on this issue. Annie Devine, a staunch organizer from Canton who campaigned for Henry during the Freedom Vote of 1963 and later ran for Congress herself, said that she became active in the movement and politics because most men just would not run for office. "Negro men have been pushed around and hounded," she told an interviewer in 1965, so the black man "needs to be reassured that he is a man, and that when he does speak, you know, he'll be looked upon as a man, cause right now he's not, and he hasn't been. He's had no control over his woman; he's had no job to take care of her." Fannie Lou Hamer, who became the most eloquent spokeswoman for the Mississippi movement, explained, "If they beat me almost to death in jail, what do you think would happen to my husband? You have to live in Mississippi as a Negro to understand why it's not more men involved than there is."[42]

Even with the countless obstacles to their participation, many men rose to the challenge and joined the fight against white supremacy in Mississippi. Highlighting women's activism in civil rights studies, scholars have rightly recognized the integral role that women played as the unsung heroes of the movement. But we must also acknowledge the immense courage of local men who, like women activists, were often overlooked in contemporary accounts that focused on articulate national leaders and highly educated volunteers. These supporters could fly home once campaigns ended. Local men and women joined the struggle, knowing that they would have to deal with the white backlash long after others left.

One such local hero was C. O. Chinn. Volunteers would have received no welcome at all when they arrived in Canton if not for men like Chinn, who sacrificed everything for the movement. "He was a powerful man," wrote one movement veteran, "known as 'badass C. O. Chinn' to the Negroes and whites alike. All of the Negroes respected him for standing up and being a man. Most of the whites feared him." Within a week of joining the movement in 1963, Chinn lost his business, but he continued to campaign for the freedom vote, and his personal loss only made him more passionate. He spoke at mass meetings and organized a local boycott against stores owned by members of the Citizens' Councils. Canton police arrested Chinn for trying to convince others to join the boycott—"threatening" them, according to the police—and also for helping SNCC staff prepare for Freedom Summer. At the start of the summer, Chinn was working on the chain gang as a prisoner of the Canton jail. Bone tired at the end of a scorching summer day on the work gang, Chinn would probably have agreed with another local activist who observed that, in Mississippi, the white man "is our friend, as long as we are 'boys.' But when we act as if we are 'mens,' then we're not his friends."[43]

While the role of local men has been overlooked in many accounts of the movement, the gender and sexuality of movement volunteers and SNCC veterans has been the focus of much popular and scholarly attention since the summer itself. The frenzied fear of interracial sex, whipped up by the Citizens' Councils and other proponents of massive resistance, contributed to the sexually charged atmosphere of the summer. From the beginning, SNCC organizers warned volunteers to avoid such interracial liaisons. As a project director in Greenwood, Stokely Carmichael admonished white volunteers to be conscious of the history of white men taking sexual advantage of local black women, and "as far as white girls with Negro boys—of course none of that on the other side of town." Carmichael opposed staff dating, feeling that it would only complicate matters during the summer, but he did not prohibit dating altogether. Given the close quarters of communal living arrangements, the stress and strain of daily organizing, and the young age of most movement volunteers and veterans, it is understandable that civil rights workers formed intimate relationships that summer.[44]

Due to the highly politicized nature of interracial sex, such relationships could both bring activists together and tear them apart. Sociologist Doug McAdam viewed sexual experimentation during Freedom Summer as an inchoate expression of free love, an idea that would appear in full bloom only in the late 1960s. Liberated sexuality also represented the logical extension of SNCC's ideals—a truly free society or "beloved community." The taboos against interracial sex made it that much more enticing. "For black men," historian Sara Evans writes, "sexual access to white women challenged the culture's ultimate symbol of their denied manhood." For white women, who "had experienced a denial of their womanhood in failing to achieve the cheerleader standards" popular at that time, sexual interest from black men was especially empowering. White men and black women also experienced the liberating power of love that summer. But activists found that the personal politics of interracial sex could damage the movement. Black women, at times, grew angry when black men flocked to white women, reinforcing American society's racist standards of beauty. White women may have felt trapped in a Catch-22 of being labeled as racist if they declined black men's advances and opportunistic if they accepted. Despite all of the complications that arose from interracial sex during the movement, it is important to remember that these intimate relationships were born out of a faith in love (both platonic and passionate) and a hope that movement ideals were harbingers of a more egalitarian and open society. As one volunteer wrote in his journal, the people in SNCC "already *have* the 'beloved community' and they rightly see the aim of the movement to be the inclusion of the whole of America into *this* community. . . . Our aim is indeed miscegenation, more profoundly so than they think."[45]

SNCC actually came closest to embodying the utopian ideal of the beloved community before the summer of 1964. The influx of volunteers during the summer project, and the high retention rate of new staff members afterwards, exacerbated what had been relatively minor philosophical differences in the organization. As SNCC attempted to deal with these growing pains, deciding between a highly centralized structure and a more loosely affiliated group of "floating" field secretaries, several female veterans also began to question why they were relegated to what was seen, stereotypically, as "women's work." Executive Secretary Jim Forman remembered that discussions of gender roles had begun before the summer in Atlanta, when women protested assignment to secretarial tasks. Forman suggested that SNCC women stage an office sit-in to protest. The issue cropped up again during Freedom Summer when some women felt that they were assigned to teaching and office work because of their gender. A spy from the Sovereignty Commission, eager to expose divisions within the beloved community, reported, "The 'strong' females on the permanent office staff have told me earlier of a revolution among females, 'the women's fight for equality with men.' . . . I have watched it gain momentum over the past months. There are many male supporters of this new thing."[46]

Among the strong women fingered by the spy was Casey Hayden, a stalwart movement veteran who later coauthored a paper on the position of women in SNCC. In the paper, Hayden and Mary King, another veteran white staffer, compared the oppression of women in the organization to the oppression of African Americans. "The average white person finds it difficult to understand why the Negro resents being called 'boy,'" they wrote, "because the average white person doesn't realize *that he assumes he is superior*. . . . So too the average SNCC worker finds it difficult to discuss the woman problem because of the assumption of male superiority." Initially, the position paper received little serious discussion. It provoked Stokely Carmichael's infamous quip that "the position of women in SNCC is prone." Mary King, who heard Carmichael make this comment, later argued that it was clearly a joke and that he was in fact relatively progressive on gender issues. At the time, such jokes may have deflected the thrust of the women's arguments. Yet Hayden and King's position paper would become an influential document in the history of women's liberation, capturing an epiphany of feminist consciousness that would later burgeon into the women's movement.[47]

The tensions between the egalitarian ideal in SNCC and the reality of gender relations in 1964 led women in the movement to challenge both racism and sexism. Feminism, according to historian Belinda Robnett, "did not evolve from the sexist treatment within SNCC" but from the organization's liberating philosophy and open structure that fostered challenges to authority. The structure of the organization, which was founded on principles of participatory democracy, gave both men and women a voice in decision-making. Martha Prescod Norman, an activist who worked with SNCC in Mississippi and Alabama, remembered that both women and men in the organization inspired her "to be brave, to be smart, to be intellectual—to be all of the things that are stereotypically not female." Empowering women as it did, SNCC was far more progressive than other movement organizations and most parts of American society in 1964. Yet there were times when the civil rights group did reflect society's gender bias in work assignments and formal leadership. Charles Scattergood, a summer volunteer who worked with Charles McLaurin in Sunflower County and stayed in the Delta until 1965, later acknowledged that tension on the local project was due, in part, to sexism. "I saw racism spreading all over Mississippi. But I also saw male chauvinism spreading out pretty bad too," he said. Perhaps Scattergood's experiences in Mississippi led him to question his own gender assumptions, making him more open to the position of the later feminist movement. "I think that women have a definite place in the movement," he later maintained, "not just as secretaries either—as leaders." Such conflicting testimony reveals the complex nature of gender relations in the movement. As Sara Evans originally argued, the women in SNCC experienced both liberation *and* oppression. To acknowledge this paradox is not to single out the organization or its male leaders for special criticism; it merely captures the historical reality of 1964. Despite the pervasiveness and intractability of racism and sexism in America during the mid-1960s, the men and women of SNCC attempted to fashion a movement in which all people could gain personal and political power.[48]

At the end of the summer project, SNCC organizers took this utopian vision to the Democratic National Convention in Atlantic City, where their standard bearer would be the indefatigable local activist, Fannie Lou Hamer. Born the twentieth child of a poor sharecropping family, Hamer joined Charles McLaurin's voter registration drive in Ruleville back in 1962 and traveled with him to the forbidding Indianola courthouse. After trying to register, Hamer lost her job of seventeen years as a timekeeper on a nearby plantation, and her husband Perry, who had worked at the plantation cotton gin for thirty years, was also fired. After losing her job at the plantation, Hamer committed more of her time to organizing a challenge to black disfranchisement, enduring arrests and a vicious beating by police officers in Winona, Mississippi. These blows did not sway Hamer's support for the movement. She housed volunteers over the summer and crisscrossed the state with SNCC organizers to help found the Mississippi Freedom Democratic Party (MFDP) as an alternative to the all-white, segregationist Mississippi Democratic Party. In August, black Mississippians nominated Hamer, Aaron Henry, Ed King, and dozens of other grassroots activists to represent them at the national convention in Atlantic City.[49]

As the MFDP geared up for the election of delegates and the trip to Atlantic City, word came that federal authorities had found the three civil rights workers who had been missing since the beginning of the summer. It turned out that local police in Neshoba County had arrested the activists on Sunday, June 21, 1964, and released them later that night only to inform Klan members of the activists' whereabouts. A posse of vigilantes and sheriff's deputies tracked down the activists. They severely beat James Chaney, the young black man from Mississippi, and then shot the three civil rights workers to death. The posse buried the men beneath a dam of fresh earth and began to spread the rumor that the activists had staged their own disappearance for publicity. In early August, federal officials, who had done little to protect the civil rights activists throughout the summer, finally found the bodies of the three missing men.[50]

When the MFDP delegates traveled to Atlantic City, they brought placards with simple drawings of the murdered activists. These posters of the martyred men were powerful symbols of the struggle for equality in Mississippi, but Fannie Lou Hamer embodied that struggle as well. In challenging the seating of the official Mississippi delegation that unconstitutionally excluded African Americans, Hamer testified before a national television audience about being beaten and jailed simply for trying to vote. "I was beaten until I was exhausted," Hamer testified. "I began to scream, and one white man got up and began to beat me on the head and tell me to hush. . . . All of this on account we wanted to register, to become first class citizens. [If] the Freedom Democratic Party is not seated now, I question America." Fearful that Hamer's powerful testimony would jeopardize white southern support for the Democratic Party and undermine his reelection campaign, President Lyndon Johnson broke into Hamer's testimony with an emergency press conference. No matter, the television networks broadcast her testimony in full on the prime-time news later that night. Millions of Americans heard Hamer's story, which echoed what they had read about the struggles of volunteers and veteran activists all summer long. In order to quell the MFDP's dissent, Johnson and his allies crafted a compromise that would allow Aaron Henry and Ed King to enter the convention as at-large delegates. Henry wanted to accept the compromise, as did national civil rights leaders and some in the MFDP contingent. Hamer and fellow local activist Annie Devine disagreed. Hamer viewed the compromise as a sellout, and she told the other delegates so, exclaiming, "We didn't come all this way for no two seats." One delegate remembered, "I wanted them to accept two seats, but those two women, Mrs. Hamer and Mrs. Devine, shamed me out. . . . I changed my mind right there." In a testament to participatory democracy and the women's leadership, the Mississippi activists voted to reject the compromise.[51]

The MFDP delegation returned from Atlantic City just as many of the summer volunteers went back to their homes and universities. Almost immediately, people began to assess the legacies of the summer project. Using the volunteers as a wedge, SNCC had pried open the state's closed society and made room for moderate white Mississippians such as Hodding Carter to form interracial coalitions that would alter the political landscape of the state. A new generation of black political leaders and community activists came of age in the Mississippi movement. Aaron Henry became a state senator in a biracial coalition of legislators in Jackson. Charles McLaurin returned to Ruleville and eventually became a field organizer for the National Council of Negro Women. He also guided the implementation of Head Start and the Child Development Group of Mississippi in the Delta. Bennie Thompson, a young man who got his start in politics working with MFDP in the late 1960s, went on to represent the Delta in the United States Congress. Student volunteers also came of age politically during the summer project. Many returned home to university campuses and continued the activism that they had begun in Mississippi, struggling for free speech, civil rights, women's liberation, and, later, an end to the war in Vietnam. In addition to developing political maturity and leadership, longtime Mississippi activists Aaron Henry and Amzie Moore believed that the summer project dispelled racist fears of integration and myths about black men circulated by the Citizens' Councils. When volunteers and local activists lived and worked together, they learned about each other as people. If only for one long summer, these young activists exemplified the beloved community that SNCC had envisioned.[52]

In the wake of the summer, however, the utopian vision of the beloved community slowly receded. Klan violence intensified, and as the media lost interest in the local struggles, activists had a tougher time challenging local officials. Jack Wilmore, who headed the U.S. Commission on Civil Rights in Memphis from 1965 to 1967, believed that the movement in the rural South declined after 1965. Based on the testimony he compiled for the civil rights commission, he argued that although the movement had a huge psychological impact on the way white southerners viewed African Americans and the way southern blacks viewed themselves, it had won "few real concessions" and had done little to alter "the black man's socio-economic position" in the rural South. Wilmore felt that the best option for many rural black southerners was to "get the hell out of there" — to leave the rural areas or the South entirely — and seek a better life in cities or the North. Certainly, Wilmore overstated this case. Many of the largest gains in the southern movement came with the political empowerment of African Americans after the Voting Rights Act of 1965, and black migrants who had followed the path of the Great Migration since the 1910s and 1920s found that the road to the "promised land" was littered with its own racial problems that required tough movement remedies.[53]

Yet thousands of African Americans had long believed, as Wilmore did, that migration was the surest and quickest path to equality or, at least, opportunity. For those who felt that coming of age in Mississippi was little more than a pipe dream for black men, there had always been that train ticket to Memphis, Chicago, or New York. In the North, black migrants would find a "man's chance," it was said. In the North, they would find a movement led by men who were willing to fight for their rights "by any means necessary." In the North, they would find a new religion, a new leader, and a new path to manhood.

It seemed to me that Malcolm spoke directly to the emasculation of the black male in particular. And Malcolm wanted to heal that emasculation. He wanted to teach us how, in spite of that, to be men again. So I thought I would like my children and generations to come to know this aspect of Malcolm X. — Ossie Davis, actor/activist/friend of Malcolm X

Chapter Four

God's Angry Men

William Longstreet was born in the tiny town of Coffeeville, Mississippi, in 1940. His parents separated when he was seven, and his mother took him out of the South. Like many black southern migrants, they eventually ended up in Chicago. Longstreet dropped out of school in the tenth grade and joined the Navy, where he became a skilled airplane technician. Receiving an honorable discharge after two years of military service, he searched for a job as an airline mechanic, but found that "color disqualified me from civilian employment in that field." Jobless and depressed, Longstreet brooded over his problems and found what little solace he could, drinking and hanging out with other unemployed men day after day, down on the corner. At night, he came home and fought with his wife. "I was venting my fury on my wife and family," he remembered, "because of my frustrations in attempting to be a man." In 1961 Longstreet joined the Nation of Islam, and his problems seemed to vanish. Through Islam, he found satisfaction in a new job, fulfillment in being a responsible father and husband, and the strength to be a man.[1]

The story of William X Longstreet was one of dozens of conversion testimonials printed in the Nation of Islam's *Muhammad Speaks* in the 1960s. During the early 1960s, the Nation of Islam (NOI) attracted thousands of new converts with its message of community uplift through individual self-help and spiritual purification. In these goals, the Nation was not unlike other fundamentalist religious movements in American history, and more specifically, African American history, but it was unique in two ways. First, the NOI was predicated on the assumption that the only way African Americans could ever be truly free was to separate themselves from the white man, not by going back to Africa, but by carving out sovereign black states in America. Second, NOI was one of the few religious movements among black or white Americans to attract an overwhelming majority of male converts. The Nation won male converts, in part, by telling them that Islam offered the one path to true manhood open to the black man in America. The proof lay in the stories of converts like William X Longstreet and his more famous brother in the faith, Malcolm X.

Malcolm X eloquently advocated the NOI's masculinist liberation theology and its doctrines of separatism, self-defense, and black nationalism that gained wide currency among civil rights activists in the second half of the 1960s. The doctrines espoused by Malcolm and other NOI leaders stood in stark contrast to the nonviolent integrationist philosophy that guided SNCC in the early 1960s. Martin Luther King Jr. and other SCLC ministers had first articulated the nonviolent integrationist philosophy that relied on Christian faith and brotherhood to organize civil rights activists and appeal to America's moral conscience. Though both the SCLC and the NOI used faith as an organizing tool in the struggle for equal rights, NOI ministers consistently portrayed black Christian leaders and nonviolent activists as weak, cowardly, and unmanly. Muslim ministers deliberately constructed public personas of militant manhood as role models for black youth and as a recruiting strategy for the NOI. In the Nation, these ministers argued, a black man could reclaim his manhood and take his rightful position as the head of his household. Black women recruits were promised the respect, protection, and admiration that they deserved as women. The strict separation of gender roles in the NOI formed the foundation of a racial uplift philosophy that linked the struggle for liberation directly to a quest for manhood. Through his fiery eloquence, fierce intelligence, and brutal frankness on the subject of American race relations, Malcolm X brought the Nation's model of militant manhood and message of liberation to thousands of people who might never have considered the Islamic faith. This model of militant masculinity was Malcolm's primary legacy, and it guided the course of the civil rights movement after his death in 1965.

Malcolm X was born Malcolm Little on May 19, 1925, in Omaha, Nebraska. His father was a Baptist minister and an organizer for Marcus Garvey's Universal

Negro Improvement Association (UNIA), a group dedicated to the goals of African repatriation and political self-determination for blacks in the Americas. Under pressure from white supremacists, Malcolm's family fled from Omaha to Lansing, Michigan. Soon after the move, Malcolm's father died under mysterious circumstances. Though the police reported Earl Little's death as an accident, Malcolm believed that his father was attacked by whites, for preaching the UNIA message of black liberation, and then pushed in the path of a streetcar to disguise the murder. One scholar has asserted that this loss of his father at such an early age and the lack of a strong male role model during his formative years spurred Malcolm on a quest for true manhood that eventually made him one of the most powerful speakers of the twentieth century. While his father's untimely death may well have influenced Malcolm's masculinist message and future leadership style, its more immediate effect was to place the Little family in dire straights.[2]

After Earl Little died, Malcolm's mother, Louise Little, had to take care of her eight children alone. Hounded by state welfare officials and weighed down by the strain of caring for so many children with so little support, she was forced to send the children to live with relatives and foster families. Soon after losing her children, she was institutionalized for mental illness. The breakup of the family and the institutionalization of their mother coupled with their father's death might have permanently crippled some children, but Malcolm and his siblings survived. In fact, Malcolm thrived, succeeding socially and academically in schools where he was often the only African American student. These successes did not shield Malcolm from racism or feelings of isolation, however, for as his brother Wilfred remembered, "People saw us as oddballs in the city where we grew up. Whites would describe us as 'those uppity niggers' . . . In those days, the twenties and thirties, it was the same as being in Mississippi." To escape the isolation and racism of the rural Midwest, Malcolm moved to Boston around 1940 to live with an older half-sister.[3]

In Massachusetts, Malcolm entered a new and exciting realm of urban black society that he could only have dreamed of in rural Michigan. Though his half-sister was a member of Boston's black middle class, Malcolm eschewed her social set in favor of the electrifying jazz and youth culture of the Roxbury neighborhood. In bars, pool halls, and dance clubs, the young Malcolm emulated urban hipsters, who bounced to the beat of the era's hottest bebop jazz and Big Band swing. In Boston, and then in New York City, where he later struck out on his own as a hustler in Harlem, Malcolm gave up his education in books and quickly became a studied master of urban street culture. He conked his hair (a painful process of straightening with hot lye solution), donned the flashiest zoot suit he could afford, and lost himself in a subculture of drugs, prostitution, and crime. With his natural intelligence and quick wit, Malcolm thrived in this culture, just as he had in the primary schools of Michigan, but as he would later admit, the cutthroat underworld of stealing and dealing catches up with even the savviest of hustlers. In January 1946, Malcolm was arrested for his involvement in a small-time robbery ring and sentenced to eight-to-ten years in prison.[4]

Malcolm entered prison an avowed atheist, but through correspondence with his siblings in Michigan, he learned about a black religious leader named Elijah Muhammad and the Nation of Islam. Muhammad, who had been incarcerated for evading the draft during World War II because of his religious beliefs, understood that black convicts like Malcolm Little were often highly receptive to his teachings. Muhammad taught that white men were devils and that black men would never be truly free until they separated from whites and formed their own society. A small taste of Muhammad's teachings inspired Malcolm to immerse himself in studies of religion and African American history. His prison studies, correspondences with Muhammad, and debates with fellow inmates strengthened Malcolm's commitment to the Nation of Islam and sharpened his oratorical skills.[5]

When he was released from prison in 1952, Malcolm moved to Detroit and joined the NOI Temple Number One. The Nation claimed thousands of members in the early 1950s, but historians have estimated that fewer than five hundred men and women belonged to the organization when Malcolm joined. Noting Malcolm's oratorical skills, NOI leaders in Detroit soon tapped him for a post as assistant minister at Temple Number One, where the young minister's eloquence won numerous converts for the Nation. One man who heard Malcolm preaching in Detroit during the early 1950s remembered that there were "a number of ministers who had a better background than Malcolm did . . . but Malcolm was the one who was on fire." Malcolm's fiery preaching and his stanch loyalty to Muhammad propelled him rapidly up through the ranks of the NOI hierarchy. He preached in Boston and Philadelphia temples before eventually becoming the minister for Temple Number Seven in New York.[6]

During the mid-1950s, Malcolm confidently strode the same Harlem avenues he had worked as a street hustler a decade before. He quickly became famous for his fervent stepladder preaching on the bustling corner of 125th Street and Seventh Avenue. He also "fished" for converts to Islam in front of black nationalist meetings, where angry men might be amenable to his message about white devils, or outside fundamentalist Christian churches, where devout southern migrants, the majority of them women, might be receptive to the Nation's passionate preaching.[7]

Once Malcolm cajoled the curious men and women into the doors of the Muslim temple, the potential converts heard distinctly gendered messages about race and religion in America. Women and men took seats on different sides of a central temple aisle. Muslim men dressed impeccably in dark suits and the women wore simple, white, floor-length gowns with scarves covering their heads. Malcolm's preaching ran the gamut from the horrors of slavery in America (especially the rape of black women by slave masters) to contemporary race and gender relations in which black manhood had been called into question. "The Honorable Elijah Muhammad teaches us that . . . the black man never will get anybody's respect until he learns to respect his own women! The black man needs today to stand up and throw off the weakness imposed upon him by the slave master white man!"[8]

One of the key tenets of the Nation of Islam was, in fact, that black men should appreciate black women's natural beauty and protect them from white men. Muhammad's teachings directly challenged the defeminization and denigration of black womanhood in mainstream white culture by creating a more positive image of black femininity. Yet the strict gender roles espoused by Muhammad also placed black women on a pedestal not all that different from the one reconstructed for southern white women by segregationists. As with the segregationists, the Muslim conceptions of gender difference, deference, and chivalry thinly veiled a gender hierarchy within the organization. "The true nature of man is to be strong and a woman's true nature is to be weak," Malcolm explained, "and while a man must at all times respect his woman, at the same time he needs to understand that he must control her if he expects to get her respect." Elijah Muhammad added, "There is no nation on earth, that has less respect for and as little control of their women as we so-called Negroes here in America." Though these teachings did appeal to some women who were attracted to the stable (if not egalitarian) relationships in Muslim families, the majority of the converts to the Nation of Islam in the 1950s and 1960s were men who found dignity and power in accepting the traditional position of leadership in their families. In some cities, according to Muhammad, the Nation converted five men to every one woman, a recruiting pattern that stood in stark contrast to southern churches and the southern movement in which the majority of participants were women.[9]

Both women and men who sought entrance into the Nation of Islam began the spiritual journey by giving up many aspects of their former lives. Converts shed their "slave names," which the Muslims argued correctly were often the surnames of former masters, in favor of an X. They were also prohibited from sinful pleasures such as smoking tobacco, drinking alcohol, eating pork, and having sexual relations before marriage. Along with daily ablutions, this ascetic lifestyle was meant to cleanse the body at the same time that Islam cleansed the spirit. Few were more loyal to the NOI strictures than Malcolm, who, by all accounts, was one of the most devout ministers in the Nation.[10]

Once converted, men and women took separate paths on the road to divine acceptance in the Nation, learning different lessons in sex-segregated classes. Men aspired to become members of the Fruit of Islam (FOI), a stern, well-disciplined honor guard for each temple. The FOI members became infamous in media coverage of the Nation because of their training in judo and other self-defense tactics. Yet Malcolm noted that FOI training went far beyond fighting techniques. He claimed that the FOI spent much of their time in "discussions on men [and] learning to be men. They deal with the responsibilities of a husband and father; what to expect of women; the rights of women which are not to be abrogated by the husband; the importance of the father-male image in the strong household," as well as discussing business principles and current events. Women learned of their familial responsibilities in Muslim Girls Training classes. In these classes, Muslim women learned "how to keep homes, how to rear children, how to care for husbands, how to cook, sew, [and] how to act [as] . . . a good Muslim sister and mother and wife." In fact, the Muslim Girls Training classes resembled the home economics courses taken by countless black and white women in schools across the country during the 1950s and early 1960s. As radical as the Nation's nationalist rhetoric could be, its vision of gender relations was cut from traditional family values advocated by many conservative, middle-class Americans, black and white.[11]

For Malcolm, this traditional ideal of family life became a reality not long after Sister Betty X joined Temple Number Seven. Born and raised in Detroit, Michigan, Betty Sanders had begun her college career as an education major at Tuskegee University in Alabama. She joined the Nation of Islam and met Malcolm in 1956 after moving to New York to attend nursing school. Gradually, it became apparent that Malcolm and Betty were attracted to one another, but formal dating was out of the question. "I never 'dated' Malcolm as we think of it because at the time single men and women in the Muslims did not 'fraternize,' as they called it." Instead, the two would go out with groups of young people from the Temple. Even in this highly chaperoned courtship, Malcolm's noble bearing, charm, and broad smile won Betty's heart. When the two traveled to Detroit, Betty's Methodist parents were impressed with her "friend" the Muslim minister, but a blessing for marriage was out of the question. This and Malcolm's distaste for "Hollywood" romance led to a simple, civil ceremony early in 1958.[12]

In an interview with *Essence* magazine more than thirty years after she married Malcolm, Betty candidly talked about their evolving relationship. Malcolm had initially warned his bride-to-be that it would be hard for him to keep her updated on his frequent travel plans as one of the most sought after spokesmen for the NOI. "It was basically that fear of a woman having control," Betty remembered. "So when we got married, I never asked his whereabouts." Yet as he grew closer to Betty, Malcolm made sure that he was always in touch with his wife, wherever his many travels took him. Another early sticking point in their relationship was Betty's desire to work outside of the home. "I thought Malcolm was a little too strict with me," she told the interviewers. "He was possessive from the beginning to the end, though I think he learned to control it. . . . He didn't want anybody to have any influence over me that could in any way compete with his." Betty did eventually convince her husband to let her continue doing volunteer work, teaching Muslim Girls Training classes at the Temple when she was not taking care of their growing family. Aside from some serious disagreements about her desire to work and his frequent travels, Betty fondly recalled their relationship as a happy one. Her love and support at home made Malcolm's successful career possible, reflecting the traditional gender norms then endorsed by the NOI and much of American society.[13]

If the gender ideology of the NOI did not draw the attention of the mainstream news media, the organization's claim that white men were devils and its demand for land in America to create sovereign black states did. When Louis Lomax and Mike Wallace, journalists for CBS News in New York, heard about the Nation's teachings and growing popularity, they asked Elijah Muhammad and Malcolm X for permission to record NOI meetings and interviews with Muslim leaders. The resulting documentary, *The Hate that Hate Produced*, exposed the NOI to thousands of viewers outside of Harlem, who had never imagined such a group existed. Asked if he hated all whites, Malcolm responded, "For the white man to ask the black man, 'do you hate me' is just like the rapist asking the raped or the wolf asking the sheep 'do you love me.'" White viewers were shocked by such a blunt retort to a question about race, but black viewers exhibited a range of responses to Malcolm's withering indictment of white racism. According to the writer Alex Haley, who would later coauthor Malcolm's autobiography, some African Americans were initially horrified by Malcolm's rhetoric, fearing that it would jeopardize the movement for racial integration that was beginning to make progress in the 1950s. Others, however, deeply admired Malcolm, because he had "the courage to say aloud, publicly, things which they had felt" in their hearts for many years about white racism in America.[14]

In the opening of *The Hate that Hate Produced*, Mike Wallace observed that the "gospel of hate" preached by the Nation would have "set off a federal investigation if it were preached by southern whites." In fact, Malcolm's preaching and the Muslim movement had already set off such an investigation. The Federal Bureau of Investigation had been following Malcolm's career since the mid-1950s. Agents learned that he had dodged the draft during World War II by pretending to be insane. Malcolm later claimed that he told military psychologists in the 1940s, "I want to get sent down South. Organize them nigger soldiers, you dig? Steal us some guns, and kill up some crackers!" While Malcolm's criminal record and his conduct during World War II caught the attention of federal investigators, the Bureau was much more interested in Malcolm's success in converting African Americans to Muhammad's brand of Islam. One FBI informant in New York dubbed Malcolm a "very convincing speaker," and after seeing him speak in Charlotte, North Carolina, another agent grudgingly admired "how Malcolm X unites the individuals into an emotional entity . . . [and] uses his skill as a speaker to direct emotions and hatreds of his audience toward white people."[15]

Seeing the attention that resulted from *The Hate that Hate Produced*, NOI leaders decided that they needed their own publication to combat biased coverage, not only of their teachings, but also of current events that pertained to African Americans. Malcolm had cut his teeth in the newspaper business with a column entitled "God's Angry Men," which was first printed in 1957 in the *Los Angeles Herald Dispatch* and the *New York Amsterdam News*. By the early 1960s, the NOI had the resources to begin publishing their own paper, *Muhammad Speaks*. Under Malcolm's initial direction, *Muhammad Speaks* quickly became the Nation's primary voice and a major source of funds and publicity. The publication of *Muhammad Speaks* increased the visibility of the Nation in more ways than one, as NOI men were required to pound the pavement selling the paper for several hours a day in order to meet high individual sales quotas. If a Muslim man did not sell the required number of papers, one former member of the NOI from Chicago remembered, "they [would] give you the loving Fruit of Islam," which was a "beating with a strap." Although this did not happen every time a young brother missed his quota, it was indicative of the tough and sometimes brutal militaristic regimens that hardened male recruits in the Nation. The quotas and punishments undoubtedly drove up sales of *Muhammad Speaks*, further spreading the word of Elijah Muhammad.[16]

"We Must Have Some Land!" "We Must Control Our Neighborhoods!" "We

Must Protect Our Women!" These were the banner headlines in many of the early issues of *Muhammad Speaks*. Malcolm explained the Nation's desire to "leave a land of bondage and go to a land of our own . . . [in] several states here on American soil, where those of us who wish to can go and set up our own government, our own economic system, our own civilization." Malcolm and Muhammad also demanded that the U.S. government finance the first twenty-five years of this endeavor in return for nearly 300 years of unpaid slave labor. In the eyes of NOI leaders, separation was the ultimate form of protection for black women and control of black destiny. "Separation and some good earth that we can call our own is a must! The woman is the man's field to produce his nation. If he does not keep the enemy out of his field, he won't produce a good nation." Though the Nation's leaders demanded complete separation in black states, they were not about to wait until that day came to begin instituting their programs. Members of the Nation began black farming collectives in rural areas and opened restaurants, laundries, groceries, and other retail establishments near temples in urban areas. These black-owned institutions brought pride and revenue to the Muslim community, and they would later be held up as models of self-sufficiency by Black Power advocates in the second half of the 1960s.[17]

In addition to promoting black entrepreneurship and community control, each issue of *Muhammad Speaks* dedicated several articles to "The Women in Islam." The NOI attacked what they saw as the racist American beauty aesthetic that idealized blond white women as the ultimate model of attractiveness. Eldridge Cleaver, a young Muslim who was incarcerated in San Quentin prison in the early 1960s and would later become the Minister of Information for the Black Panther Party, wrote an article that asked why "'the official standard of beauty' is that of the Caucasian peoples?" Cleaver argued that the American beauty aesthetic was "one of the cornerstones of White Supremacy" as he and other NOI writers railed against skin bleaching creams and hair straightening agents used by black women and men. Although their attacks on the restrictive and exclusionist American beauty standards presaged similar social criticisms leveled later by feminists, the NOI gender strictures were no less rigid than the ones they sought to replace. The Nation, in fact, forbade women to wear cosmetics of any sort. *Muhammad Speaks* asked, "Should women wear pants or dresses?" in one column and answered this rhetorical question by chastising women for "wearing the clothes and acquiring the actions of a man." Men wore the pants in Muslim families, just as they did in many middle-class American families at this time, but distinctive anxieties about gender relations and class status also fueled the Nation's rhetoric about the family. The Muslims ministered primarily to members of poor, urban households:

men who often lacked the economic wherewithal to support their spouses as homemakers and women who worked outside of the home, sharing or sometimes shouldering the breadwinner burden. In other words, low wages, unemployment, and underemployment made it difficult for many men in these families to achieve the ideal of patriarchal manhood that typified middle-class American culture in the 1950s and early 1960s. To compensate for this, Muslim teachings urged women to take on more subservient, domestic roles associated with traditional femininity. *Muhammad Speaks* constantly reiterated, "The woman provides a man a means of raising himself," and thus, "the so-called Negro woman must return to femininity," so that the black male can reclaim his manhood. The Muslims were not alone in calling for women to return to femininity and domesticity; Madison Avenue advertising campaigns used a similar logic to hawk an assortment of appliances and other household goods during this period. Instead of the labor-saving devices touted by Madison Avenue as solutions to the difficulties of domestic work, *Muhammad Speaks* assured readers that their faith could serve this function. Echoing ads for products that claimed to make housework more "fun" and efficient, the paper printed a testimonial from one Muslim woman who said that after her conversion to Islam, sewing, cooking, and other household chores "suddenly took on more meaning and actually became easier."[18]

Even as the Nation's leaders demanded domestic conformity of "their" women, *Muhammad Speaks* looked abroad to recognize the role of revolutionary women in international freedom struggles. Articles championed the advocacy of women's rights by Egyptians, citing experts from the Middle East who argued, "The Koran warns women against falling into the pitfalls of sin, but does not prohibit social and political freedom." Women in the Nation responded to external criticisms of gender discrimination among Islamic cultures. When critics pointed to the practice of women wearing veils in Islamic societies as an indication of their inferior status, Tynnetta Deanar, a regular NOI columnist, urged readers to understand that a "respect and concern for women's welfare amidst strangers . . . initiated this practice." Discussions such as this in *Muhammad Speaks* reveal a complicated picture of NOI gender ideology, one that espoused both liberation and subordination. Yet a definite hierarchy existed within the Nation's organizational structure and within the families of African American Muslims. The protection and admiration offered to women in the NOI were part and parcel of a rigid patriarchy that Muhammad and Malcolm saw as a crucial foundation for true manhood.[19]

As the struggle for integration gained momentum in the early 1960s, both women and men in the Nation leveled scathing attacks on the leaders of the movement, often challenging their manhood as well as their tactics and goals. Tynnetta Deanar, for instance, suggested that the civil rights movement evidenced "the gradual weakening of our men to the state of cowards, flinching before the demands of the White Race." NOI members and ministers dubbed civil rights leaders unmanly cowards and Uncle Toms, in large part because of their allegiance to the philosophy of nonviolence. Discussing the student sit-ins that swept across the South in 1960 and inspired the formation of SNCC, Malcolm X told reporters, "Anybody can sit. An old woman can sit. A coward can sit. . . . It takes a man to stand." Likewise, when Martin Luther King led a nonviolent civil rights campaign in Birmingham, Alabama, Malcolm questioned his recruitment of women and children for marches. "Real men don't put their children on the firing line," Malcolm scoffed, concluding, "Martin Luther King is a chump, not a champ."[20]

More to Malcolm's liking were southern rebels like Robert Williams and Hartman Turnbow who advocated armed self-defense. Like these men, Malcolm and other ministers in the Nation articulated their support for self-defense in terms of protecting womanhood. "You've got Klansmen knocking Black women down in front of a camera and that poor Black man standing on the sidelines because he's nonviolent," Malcolm said, scolding those who "turned the other cheek." To bring this critique of nonviolence home, Malcolm invited Robert Williams to speak in New York's Temple Number Seven, introducing him as "the only fighting man we got" down in the South, and urging his congregation "to help him so he can stay down there." Malcolm and other leading Harlemites raised money to buy some of the weapons Williams used to defend his home in Monroe, North Carolina.[21]

Malcolm could only offer financial and moral support to Robert Williams, however, because Elijah Muhammad dictated that Muslims, especially Muslim ministers, were prohibited from intervening in politics or political movements. According to Muhammad, this was a necessary first step in separation from white America, but for activist-minded Muslims like Malcolm, it was a bitter pill to swallow during the heady movement days of the 1960s. Though he absolutely forbade any members of his congregation to participate in the March on Washington in 1963, Malcolm himself traveled to the nation's capitol to observe the protest. Dubbing the event the "farce on Washington," Malcolm demanded, "Whoever heard of angry revolutionists swinging their bare feet together with their oppressors" and singing "with gospels and guitars?" Later, Malcolm added, "You don't do that in a revolution. You don't do any singing; you're too busy swinging." To Malcolm, the dream of an integrated, egalitarian society that Martin Luther

King spoke of during his famous speech on the steps of the Lincoln Memorial was an American nightmare of racial oppression. Malcolm and King were both, in a sense, "God's angry men," but the two charismatic ministers could not have been further apart philosophically than they were that day. King's faith in Christian love and nonviolent protest seemed unstoppable at that moment, possibly the zenith of the southern civil rights movement. This contrasted dramatically with Malcolm's equally zealous faith in complete racial separation, the Nation of Islam, and the divine guidance of Elijah Muhammad.[22]

By 1963 the surge of new recruits inspired by Malcolm X, the success of Muslim-owned shops and business enterprises, and the increased revenue from paper sales had made the upper echelons of the NOI quite wealthy. Elijah Muhammad and his family benefited the most from the Nation's growth. One writer who visited Muhammad at this time noted that the Messenger of Islam lived with his wife in a "stately mansion on Chicago's South Side." Though he preached thrift for his followers, Muhammad himself lived a lush life. Members of the Nation, including Malcolm X, who subsisted on little more money than was absolutely necessary, did not begrudge the Messenger his wealth. It was a tangible symbol of the Nation's success and proved the truth of its message. In 1963, however, Malcolm learned from Muhammad's own son that the Messenger was partaking of other earthly pleasures strictly forbidden to Muslims. Several of Muhammad's secretaries, Malcolm learned, had become pregnant out of wedlock under mysterious circumstances. As it turned out, Muhammad was having affairs with these women. Perhaps Muhammad viewed these affairs as his prerogative, a logical extension of the patriarchy he preached, but there was little doubt that these transgressions were not sanctioned by the Nation's strict moral code. Though Malcolm claimed to have continued his steadfast support of Muhammad despite these adulterous affairs, the faith of the Nation's most eloquent minister had been shaken.[23]

The exposure of Muhammad's affairs created a small rift between Malcolm and the Messenger that widened over the next few years. When President John F. Kennedy was assassinated in late 1963, Malcolm observed wryly that this was little more than "the chickens coming home to roost." Afterwards, Malcolm explained what he meant, saying that a country that allowed "white people to kill and brutalize those they don't like" should not be surprised when this atmosphere of violence and hatred led to the assassination of one of its favorite sons. Muhammad, who had warned his ministers not to make disparaging comments about Kennedy's death, reprimanded Malcolm with a ninety-day suspension, during which he was to make no statements to the press. Some have speculated

Though both Martin Luther King Jr. and Malcolm X became spiritual leaders of the movement, Malcolm often criticized King's nonviolent approach as unmanly. Photograph by Marion Trikosko, 1964. U.S. News & World Report Magazine Collection, Prints and Photographs Division (LC-U9-11696, frame 16), Library of Congress.

that the suspension was an attempt to rein in Malcolm, because he was beginning to overshadow Muhammad as the public face of the Nation. Whether or not this was so, Malcolm accepted the punishment and turned his attention to shepherding a new star into the faith.[24]

During his suspension, Malcolm bided his time, accompanying his friend, the young boxer Cassius Clay, to Miami, where Clay was training for a shot at the world heavyweight title. Clay had grown up in Louisville, Kentucky, where there were few if any Muslims, but his amateur boxing career took him all over the country for Golden Gloves tournaments. During a tournament in Chicago in the late 1950s, Clay learned of the Nation of Islam, and when he returned to Kentucky, he tried to write a high school report on the organization. His teacher rejected the topic, but Clay's interest in the Nation was not diminished. He met Malcolm X on a visit to Detroit in the early 1960s, and Malcolm became both a friend and mentor to the young fighter. Like Malcolm, Clay embodied a new model of black manhood. With his brash and arrogant style, Clay defied the expectations of the boxing world that black fighters should behave with self-effacing deference to white reporters, managers, and commentators. Wielding a wit that was even quicker than his fists, he mocked these racist expectations. During one spoken word performance in 1963 entitled "I Am the Greatest," Clay boasted that he was a perfect role model. "I am the greatest! . . . I'm good looking, clean living, and I am modest," he joked. With the crowd already reeling, Clay delivered the KO: "My only fault is that I don't realize how great I really am." Years later, he would look back on his career and remark with pride, "I had to prove you could be a new kind of black man. I had to show the world."[25]

Despite the speed with which he delivered both punches and jokes, Clay faced a potentially brutal bout in his first challenge for the heavyweight title in 1964, and he needed all the help he could get. He welcomed Malcolm's presence in the training room, where the Muslim minister served as the contender's spiritual adviser as he prepared to challenge Sonny Liston for the title. Before the fight, few sportswriters gave Clay a chance of beating Liston, but Malcolm knew better. Sitting in seat number seven at ringside, he watched as Clay stunned the boxing world with a victory. Shortly after the bout, the new champion announced his faith in the Nation of Islam and took the name Muhammad Ali, conferred upon him by Elijah Muhammad.[26]

In Ali, Elijah Muhammad found a new champion and, in the words of one historian, a replacement for Malcolm "as the leading symbol of black masculinity" in the Nation. Ali's intelligence, grace, and strength beamed from the front pages of *Muhammad Speaks* for months after his championship as the paper's coverage of Malcolm gradually degenerated into slander and libel. At the end of his ninety-day suspension in March 1964, Muhammad refused to reinstate Malcolm. After years of faithfully following the Messenger's orders, Malcolm decided that the time had come for him to branch out on his own. Realizing full well that there could be dangerous repercussions to his actions, the young minister broke with the NOI and founded the independent Muslim Mosque Incorporated.[27]

"I have reached the conclusion," Malcolm said at a press conference in March 1964, "that I can best spread Mr. Muhammad's message by staying out of the Nation of Islam." The immediate reasons for his departure from the NOI may have been the ninety-day suspension and tensions between Malcolm and Muhammad, but Malcolm's break from the Nation was also indicative of his own intellectual growth in this period. He had no qualms with the masculinist theology of racial uplift espoused by the Nation, but Malcolm believed that he could continue to preach this message and weave it into broader concerns about human rights while also become more active in the movement once he struck out on his own. In later interviews, Malcolm's friends and associates suggested that the ideological confines of the Nation, especially the strict prohibition against political action, restrained his boundless intellectual curiosity and activist bent. Once out of the Nation, Malcolm was free to join with other civil rights leaders in expanding his movement philosophy. He demanded improvements in education, housing, and jobs and called for African Americans to use the power of the ballot to effect change. Accepting these reformist tactics as important means to an end, Malcolm was no less militant after his break with the NOI. He advocated black nationalism as both a "political concept and form of social action against oppression." Although his political ideology remained vague immediately after he broke from the Nation, he reiterated his staunch advocacy of self-defense for black activists, saying, "Every Negro ought to have a weapon in his house, a rifle or a shotgun. Any Negro who is attacked should fight back; if necessary, he should be prepared to die like a man." Malcolm even called for the organization of black gun clubs, but few would heed this call until the Panthers recapitulated it in the late-1960s.[28]

Upon leaving the Nation of Islam, Malcolm planned a religious pilgrimage to the Middle East. The journey to Mecca, known in the Muslim world as the hajj, served several purposes for Malcolm. First, it allowed him to escape the firestorm of criticism that was beginning to rain down upon him from his former brothers and sisters inside the Nation. Second, it afforded him the opportunity to learn more about his chosen faith from theologians and practitioners outside of the Nation. Most important in the eyes of white observers and integrationists, it was on this trip that Malcolm first acknowledged the possibility of interracial fellowship within the faith of Islam. In Mecca, Malcolm prayed, slept, ate, and communed with Muslims of different races and nationalities. "They were of all colors," Malcolm wrote of his fellow pilgrims, "from blue-eyed blonds to black-skinned Africans, . . . displaying a spirit of unity and brotherhood my experiences in America had led me to believe never could exist between the white and the non-white." Malcolm had known that white Muslims existed before his hajj, but this public epiphany was certainly newsworthy back in the States. Few could believe that this man who had preached fire and brimstone against the "white devils" for twelve years as a Muslim minister had begun to acknowledge the humanity of whites. Yet Malcolm's associates remember that this was not as much of a sea change in his thinking as it appeared to be. Malcolm himself cautioned that the "Muslims of 'white' complexions who had changed my opinions were men who . . . practiced true brotherhood," but he reiterated that "any American white man with a genuine brotherhood for a black man was hard to find, no matter how much he grinned."[29]

After his hajj to Mecca, Malcolm traveled to Africa where he met several political and religious leaders who impressed upon him the need for African American solidarity with African anticolonial struggles. One such episode involved a meeting between Malcolm and a light-skinned Algerian revolutionary who had become the ambassador to Ghana after his country won its independence from France. When the Algerian ambassador asked Malcolm about his current ideology and future plans, Malcolm began to discuss black nationalism. Puzzled, the ambassador asked how he fit into such a strategy as "a Muslim brother and a revolutionary" who was not "black." Malcolm was uncharacteristically speechless, but the answer soon became clear. In the U.S., Malcolm would continue to preach black nationalism, but internationally, he advocated a type of Pan-Africanism that allowed for alliances with anticolonial movements throughout the Third World, where conceptions of race were often quite different from those in the U.S.[30]

Returning home to New York, Malcolm continued to expand his original masculinist liberation theology to include this new international focus, and he also began to make overtures to more mainstream civil rights leaders. He founded the Organization of Afro-American Unity (OAAU), modeled on the Organization of African Unity, a group of leaders from several independent African nations. In the OAAU, Malcolm began to press for a hearing in front of the United Nations in which he would charge the United States with violating the international charter on human rights. On the domestic front, Malcolm began looking for ways that the OAAU could form alliances with other movement groups, even with traditional civil rights leaders that he had once blasted as unmanly cowards and Uncle Toms. When one former Muslim asked Malcolm whether he should volunteer for SNCC's Freedom Summer campaign in Mississippi, Malcolm said that he should, if that was what he wanted to do, but warned him against getting tied to any one civil rights organization. Malcolm offered to assist King during SCLC's protest movement in St. Augustine, Florida, volunteering to "dispatch some of our brothers there to organize self-defense units among our people" to give the Ku Klux Klan "a taste of its own medicine." Not surprisingly, King did not accept this offer.[31]

Despite their differences with Malcolm, King and other mainstream civil rights leaders realized that the former Muslim minister could play an important role in the movement if only as a threat of what might happen if nonviolence did not succeed. During the campaign for voting rights in Selma, Alabama, in early 1965, Malcolm journeyed southward to share a podium with Coretta Scott King. Malcolm told the audience and the reporters assembled in Selma, "The white man had better be glad that Dr. King is leading a nonviolent revolution. There are those of us who are waiting for him to fail. Then the real revolution will begin." Behind the scenes, the actor/activist Ossie Davis and others arranged meetings between Malcolm and representatives of the Urban League, SCLC, and other mainstream civil rights organizations. Davis recalls that these meetings were an attempt by Malcolm to "get on board with the regular civil rights leaders but at the same time retain enough threat to serve his old purpose . . . saying, 'Look if you don't deal with them, you're going to have to deal with me.'" In public, civil rights leaders kept their distance from Malcolm. King told the press, for instance, that Malcolm's break with the NOI had little relevance for the civil rights movement, but he warned, "If sizable tangible gains are not made soon all across the country, we must honestly face the prospect that some Negroes might be tempted to accept some oblique paths such as [those] Malcolm X proposes."[32]

Malcolm's relationship to mainstream civil rights leaders was downright collegial compared to his growing estrangement from the Nation of Islam. Venom spewed from the pages of *Muhammad Speaks* as NOI leaders trotted out nearly every loyal minister they could find to denounce Malcolm as a heretic. Philbert X, Malcolm's own brother, questioned his sibling's sanity, saying, "I am aware of the great mental illness which . . . beset my mother whom I love and one of my brothers and may now have taken another victim, my brother Malcolm." Though Philbert would later renounce this statement, he was not alone among Muslim ministers in casting aspersions on Malcolm. Louis X, the minister of the NOI temple in Boston, penned a long, scathing indictment of Malcolm that questioned his ability to provide for his family as a husband and father since he was still living in a house that technically belonged to the Nation. Louis also challenged Malcolm for "using women" to undercut Elijah Muhammad's divinely sanctioned position as the Messenger of Allah, as if this indirect attack were somehow less manly than a direct confrontation that was settled *mano a mano*. Muhammad, speaking in a less cryptic manner than usual, warned Malcolm and others who "speak evil against me that they might be playing with fire and a very hot fire at that." Malcolm fought back, arguing that he lost respect for Muhammad when he refused to admit to his adultery. "You can't take nine teenage women and seduce them and give them babies and . . . then tell me you're moral," Malcolm said of Muhammad in a 1965 speech. "You could do it if you admitted you did it and admitted that the babies were yours. I'd shake your hand and call you a man. And a good one too. [Audience laughs] But when you seduce teenage girls and . . . make them hide your crimes, why you're not even a man, much less a divine man."[33]

By this point in early 1965, Malcolm had obviously traveled a great distance from his position as the Messenger's right-hand man in the Nation of Islam. Biographers of Malcolm agree that his thinking changed more in the ten months after he left the Nation than it had during his entire twelve-year career as Muhammad's most eloquent minister. Yet one thing that had not changed was Malcolm's reliance on the rhetoric of manhood to win supporters. "I'm the man you think you are," Malcolm told one audience member who asked in early 1965 what Malcolm would do in the wake of civil rights legislation. "It doesn't take legislation to make you a man and get your rights recognized," Malcolm said, "and if you want to know what I'll do, figure out what you'll do. I'll do the same thing—only more of it." Malcolm's distinctly gendered rhetoric leveled opponents who were unwilling, in his eyes, to take a bold stance against the Man.[34]

Malcolm's followers have testified to the fact that his manly rhetoric had a powerful psychological appeal for them. Many listeners—especially, but not exclusively, young men—were drawn to him as a father figure, because of his self-styled image of militant manhood. Herman Ferguson, one of Malcolm's followers, who joined him in the OAAU, idolized "the quiet kind of strength that came with this man . . . just the way he carried himself, this was a different black man." Comparing Malcolm to other civil rights leaders and even his own father, Ferguson continued, "I could never agree with Martin Luther King. You do protect yourself and defend yourself when you have to. I have seen my father not turn away from a physical encounter, but turn away from a verbal encounter so that it wouldn't lead to something physical. . . . It did something to me, because . . . a boy thinks his father is the greatest thing in the world." Ferguson followed Malcolm because he was a different kind of man than King or his father had been, and he was not alone. The poet and civil rights activist Sonia Sanchez worked with CORE in Harlem during the early 1960s, and she admired Malcolm for speaking in "this very manly fashion" what African Americans had been thinking for many years but had been afraid to say. There were other facets to his appeal. Malcolm was a handsome man, and like other Muslim ministers, he dressed immaculately in simple, elegant, dark suits that conveyed respectability and a seriousness of purpose. This image only reinforced his preaching about men's responsibilities as husbands and fathers, which also appealed to women. According to Sanchez, Malcolm "assumed the responsibility of father, brother, lover, man. . . . He became the man that most African American women have wanted their man to be: strong."[35]

There is evidence that in the months after he left the Nation, Malcolm was beginning to soften his masculinist rhetoric in favor of a more inclusive vision of women's roles in the movement. Malcolm assigned several leadership roles in the OAAU to women, and one biographer notes that Malcolm's "new position on women" after his break with the NOI "was that they be treated as equals." When Malcolm shared a Harlem podium with Fannie Lou Hamer late in 1964, he introduced her as "the country's number one freedom fighting woman," explaining, "You don't have to be a man to fight for freedom. All you have to do is be an intelligent human being." After returning from trips abroad, Malcolm said, "One thing I noticed both in the Middle East and Africa, in every country that was progressive, the women were progressive. In every country that was underdeveloped and backward it was the same degree that the women were undeveloped, or underdeveloped, and backward." With this recognition came regret. "I taught the brothers that the sisters were standing in their way; in the way of the Messenger, in the way of progress, in the way of God Himself," Malcolm explained in early 1965 in a letter to a relative. "I did these things brother. I must undo them." Yet despite his change of heart about the position of women in society, Malcolm continued to contrast the "inherent" weakness of femininity with the strength and militancy of manhood. In the last full speech of his life, Malcolm suggested that an influx of former Muslims like himself into the ranks of mainstream civil rights organizations would make "Uncle Tom Negro leaders stand up and fight like men instead of running around here nonviolently acting like women."[36]

Though he wanted to take a more active role in the struggle for civil rights as a charismatic spokesman for militant action, Malcolm would not get a chance.

His life was cut short by NOI assassins' bullets on February 21, 1965. Twenty-two thousand people queued up in the slow, respectful line of mourners that passed by Malcolm's casket in the public viewing ceremony. Later, in his eulogy to the slain leader at the memorial service, Ossie Davis summed up what would become Malcolm's most enduring legacy. "Malcolm was our manhood," he said, "our living, black manhood! This was his meaning to his people. And in honoring him, we honor the best in ourselves."[37]

Malcolm X had embodied militancy and manhood during his life, and these would be his primary legacies to the movement after his death in 1965. Wallace D. Muhammad, Elijah Muhammad's son, remembered that from the very beginning of Malcolm's ministry in the Nation, "We were attracted to Malcolm. He automatically became like a leader for us, a role model. He was an inspiration, a great inspiration for the young men and boys of the Nation of Islam." In the way Malcolm told his own story to countless converts in the Nation and then later to Alex Haley, the coauthor of his autobiography, he highlighted his own passage into manhood through a fearless confrontation with the truth about racism in America. In this, he would serve as a model for a new generation of militants in the latter half of the 1960s, young men and women in groups like the Black Panthers who dubbed themselves the "heirs of Malcolm X."[38]

The connection that Malcolm X and other ministers from the Nation of Islam drew between racial uplift and the quest for manhood also fed into a very different stream of thought in the civil rights movement. As the movement shifted in the mid-1960s, demanding economic equality as well as social justice, scholars and federal officials attempted to untangle the threads of poverty, race, and gender. Much of this scholarship began to focus on black manhood and black family structure, recurring themes in many of Malcolm's sermons. Preaching to impoverished black men, Malcolm demanded, "Get off the welfare. Get out of that compensation line. Be a man. Earn what you need for your own family. Then your family respects you. . . . So husband means you are taking care of your wife. Father means you are taking care of your children. You are accepting the responsibilities of manhood." Social scientists investigating Harlem and other urban black communities in the 1960s drew similar conclusions, arguing that black men needed to take charge of their lives and their families to halt the cycle of poverty that gripped the nation's "ghettos." Coming from Malcolm X, this was a call to arms for black men, but when such analysis came from white social scientists and federal policymakers, it sounded like just another white challenge to black manhood.[39]

When you deprive a man of a job, you deprive him of his manhood, deprive him of the authority of fatherhood, place him in a situation which controls his political life and denies his children adequate education and health services, forcing his wife to live on welfare in a dilapidated dwelling, you have a systematic pattern of humiliation which is as immoral as slavery and a lot more crippling than southern segregation.

— Martin Luther King Jr., speech at the University of Chicago (January 1966)

Chapter Five

The Moynihan Report

ess than one month after Malcolm X's assassination in February 1965, Daniel Patrick Moynihan, Assistant Secretary of Labor for Policy Planning and Research, completed a report on minority male unemployment and the breakdown of the black family in America's inner cities. In May, Secretary of Labor Willard Wirtz forwarded an abridged version to President Lyndon Johnson. Impressed by Moynihan's arguments, Johnson included them in a major civil rights speech at Howard University. Civil rights leaders initially applauded the president's frank willingness to address the problems of inner city poverty, but as policy proposals based on the study began to crystallize, debate about its real meaning heated up. When it was finally released to the public at the end of the summer as urban uprisings took place in California, a firestorm of controversy exploded in the media, bringing issues of masculinity to the forefront of debates about civil rights and poverty policy in America. "The attached Memorandum is nine pages of dynamite about the Negro situation," Wirtz had written in introducing the original memorandum to the president. Unlike thousands of documents produced by the federal bureaucracy each day, this report lived up to Wirtz's claim. It certainly was "dynamite."[1]

Moynihan argued that providing equal opportunity for African Americans was not enough; the government had a responsibility to provide equal results in jobs, housing, and education. Acknowledging that the black middle class was closing racial employment and income gaps, Moynihan nonetheless emphasized that, among the black poor, "the master problem is that the Negro family structure is crumbling." He detailed statistics about high rates of "illegitimate" births of black children in the nation's cities, but focused primarily on the "systematic weakening of the position of the Negro male" in American society. A history of emasculation in slavery and Reconstruction, dispersion in urban migration, and severe unemployment, Moynihan argued, had heavily strained black families and black men in particular. Believing that the breakdown of the black family was "the principal cause" of urban violence and other forms of delinquency in the ghetto, Moynihan proposed a national policy to "bring the structure of the Negro family into line with the rest of our society." Among his policy recommendations, Moynihan proposed a welfare allowance for families with both parents present, full employment for black men ("even if we have to displace some females" from the workforce), family housing for African Americans in the suburbs, more opportunities for black men to serve in the armed forces, and wider public dissemination of birth control materials. Though these specific policy recommendations were not included in the published version of Moynihan's report, formally titled *The Negro Family: The Case for National Action*, the key issues of that paper were covered in this memorandum to Johnson.[2]

The Moynihan Report and the controversy that surrounded its publication represented an attempt by the federal government, the academy, and the mainstream news media to address the intersections of race, gender, and poverty in America. Widely publicized in the wake of a massive uprising in the Watts area of Los Angeles, California, Moynihan's report came to be viewed as the Johnson administration's official analysis of the urban "riots" that rocked the nation in the late 1960s. Many of the "rioters" were young black men, frustrated with the slow pace of change brought about by the civil rights movement. Like Malcolm X, Moynihan believed that obstacles to black manhood lay at the heart of the "race problem" in America, and both men saw a reduction of welfare dependency and black men's acceptance of family leadership as solutions to that problem. Whereas Malcolm spoke directly to black men, demanding that they take on the responsibilities of manhood, Moynihan spoke to policymakers, arguing that the federal government had a responsibility to help black males attain the manhood that white society had long denied them. Some mainstream civil rights leaders, including Martin Luther King, agreed with Moynihan's analysis of the problem, but few concurred with his proposed solutions. The controversy sparked by Moynihan's report distracted the Johnson administration, which was already shifting resources from the War on Poverty to the war in Vietnam, and undermined attempts by the federal government to address the demands of the civil rights movement in the second half of the 1960s.

In the movie *Nothing But a Man*, which opened in December 1964, Duff Anderson (Ivan Dixon) struggles against the odds to become a man, a father, and a responsible husband. As the film begins, a lonely blues harp lopes along on the soundtrack behind the pounding jackhammers of Anderson's railroad gang in rural Alabama. Migratory railroad work provided Anderson with a good living, but when he decides to marry the local preacher's daughter, Josie Dawson (Abbey Lincoln), he must forgo the carefree life of an itinerant railroad man and settle down as a low-paid sawmill laborer. Duff Anderson refuses to be "half a man" like his father-in-law, the preacher, who, according to Duff, has "been stooping so long [he doesn't] know how to stand up straight," so he tries to organize a union at the sawmill. The white foreman fires and blacklists him so that he can get few other jobs around town. At the end of the day, he returns home frustrated by futile attempts to find a new job and takes his anger out on his wife, Josie. As a relatively well-paid schoolteacher, Josie tells Duff that he does not have to work, because her salary can support the family for a while. "You're not a man because of a job, Duff," Josie says. A tortured Anderson replies, "You don't know nothing about it." At the conclusion of the film, Duff remains unemployed, but he accepts the responsibility of raising his son and settles down with Josie. Jobless, but determined to raise a family, Anderson comes to terms with the fact that he may be "nothing but a man," but at least he is a good one.[3]

Nothing But a Man provides a fictional account of the difficulties faced by unemployed black men who struggled to fulfill the role of breadwinner expected of fathers and husbands in the 1960s. The film was one of the few movies that Malcolm X liked, because it mirrored the reality that spurred much of his masculinist rhetoric. During 1964, 29 percent of black males in the workforce were unemployed for some portion of the year, and half of these men were unemployed for fifteen weeks or more. For black men in the inner cities between the ages of eighteen and twenty-four, the unemployment rate was five times higher than the rate of joblessness for young white men. Falling through the cracks of the capitalist economy these men found it nearly impossible to live up to a standard of manhood that required them to earn enough money to support their families.[4]

With the nation's attention focused on the problems of race and racism by the civil rights movement, officials at the Department of Labor (DOL) grew increasingly concerned about the high rate of minority male unemployment in the mid-1960s. Just as *Nothing But a Man* opened in theaters, staffers at the DOL Office of Policy Planning and Research began an investigation of the effects of unemployment on black men and black family structure. After ninety days of intensive research and writing, Assistant Secretary of Labor Daniel Patrick Moynihan completed the final draft of a report entitled *The Negro Family: The Case for National Action*. Ellen Broderick and Paul Barton, members of Moynihan's Policy Planning staff at the DOL, conducted the majority of the research for the report. Barton, who cowrote a preliminary outline of the report with Moynihan, remembered that few other governmental officials were involved. "We basically didn't tell anyone [about it]," he said. Ellen Broderick noted that the only person outside the Labor Department allowed to see the report before its publication had to read it in Moynihan's office because "the paper was kept under such tight wraps during the entire period of its research and preparation." Perhaps this secrecy was due to the controversial subject matter and analysis. Once Moynihan finished the report, the DOL printed one hundred copies. Ninety-nine of them went into a safe, and one went to Bill Moyers, the White House press secretary. Recognizing the report's importance, Moyers requested an abridged version for the president.[5]

It is impossible to understand the Moynihan Report without first examining the life of its primary author and the political environment in which he wrote the document. Daniel Patrick Moynihan was born in 1927, the grandson of an Irish immigrant. Until he was ten, he lived in comfortable suburban neighborhoods in New Jersey and Queens. Moynihan's father, John, had a good job as an advertising copywriter in the city, but he also had problems with drinking and gambling. After racking up debts at the racetrack, John Moynihan left his family and fled to the West Coast in 1937. With the country still languishing in the Great Depression and without support from her husband, Margaret Moynihan struggled to make ends meet for her family. They went on welfare for a time and moved to various apartments in New York City and the surrounding area until finally settling in the tough, working-class Irish neighborhood known as Hell's Kitchen. Moynihan shined shoes and worked on the docks as a teenager to help support the family. Looking back on his young adulthood Moynihan later remarked with characteristic dramatic flare, "I've lived much of my life in a jungle of broken families, watching them tear out each other's minds, watching them feast on each other's hearts." A stint in the navy and graduate work at Tufts University served as his tickets out of poverty. In the early 1960s, he moved to Washington to work for the Department of Labor in the young, energetic Kennedy administration, where he could address the problems of poverty and fatherlessness that he had seen firsthand.[6]

The first half of the 1960s was a time of great optimism in Washington. There was a sense that the government could actually do something to alleviate poverty and strengthen all Americans' civil rights. In 1964 Moynihan had just completed a stint on the taskforce with Sargent Shriver that outlined the Johnson administration's ambitious proposals for the War on Poverty. Among the members of Moynihan's Policy and Planning staff at this time was a young iconoclast named Ralph Nader, who would later become a radical consumer advocate, environmental reformer, and presidential hopeful. There was a refreshing "lack of cynicism about what the federal government could do," according to Moynihan's research assistant Paul Barton, "and a belief that the Policy Planning staff could actually make a big difference." Seeking to understand how economic factors such as unemployment affected the social structure of poor urban communities, the members of the Policy Planning and Research staff analyzed statistical data on poverty, race, and family stability. The fruit of their labors was Moynihan's report.[7]

After acknowledging the gains of the civil rights movement and especially the progress of the black middle class, Moynihan argued that the "fundamental problem" was one of family breakdown in the impoverished black communities of the nation's inner cities. Among the indicators of family breakdown cited in the report were the proportion of babies born to unmarried couples in black and white communities (24 percent and 3 percent respectively in 1963) and the percentage of black and white families headed by women (21 percent and 9 percent respectively in 1960). Longitudinal data indicated that these trends and racial gaps were worsening. Moynihan also noted that this breakdown of family structure had led to "a startling increase in welfare dependency." With fewer husbands present in black families, he argued, more black women were turning to Aid to Families with Dependent Children (AFDC), a type of welfare created in 1935 that covered families where one or both of the parents was absent or incapacitated. In fact, one implication of the report was that AFDC had provided an incentive for many unemployed men to desert their families, so that the women and children could receive welfare.[8]

Beginning with this statement of the problem, Moynihan then proceeded to investigate the historical and contemporary causes of family breakdown. Throughout the period of slavery and segregation, the report noted, "the Negro male, particularly in the South, became an object of intense hostility," and he suffered more from racism than black women, which "worked against the emergence of a strong father figure." Migration to urban centers also placed a strain on family structure. In the cities, according to the 1960 census, women headed 23 percent of African American families as opposed to 11 percent in rural black farming communities. For support of this thesis, Moynihan quoted liberally from the distinguished black sociologist E. Franklin Frasier whose 1939 work entitled *The Negro Family in the United States* chronicled the effects of black migration to the "City of Destruction." The final causal factor highlighted by Moynihan was the effect of unemployment on black men and their families. For decades, black male unemployment and separations or desertions among black couples rose and fell together. DOL researchers saw this correlation breaking down in the mid-1960s, suggesting that poor, minority families might continue to split up even if male employment rose again, because researchers believed the culture of poverty was beginning to make family breakdown self-perpetuating. Based on this analysis, Moynihan concluded that the government should focus its attention on both unemployment and poor black families.[9]

Moynihan wrote that these strains on the black family created a "tangle of pathology," a phrase he borrowed from the black sociologist Kenneth Clark. One of the most distressing knots in this tangle of pathology for Moynihan was the "matriarchal" family structure that resulted from unemployed or underpaid black family men. To his credit, Moynihan recognized that there was "no special reason why a society in which males are dominant in family relationships is to be preferred to a matriarchal arrangement," but he argued that the matriarchal structure of poorer black families was "so out of line with the rest of American society [that it] seriously retards the progress of the group as a whole, and imposes a crushing burden upon the Negro male and, in consequence, on a great many Negro women as well." Black women attained more education than black men, and they worked in greater numbers than their white female counterparts. When combined with black male unemployment and low wages, Moynihan believed that these factors undermined traditional male authority in working-class black couples' relationships and more importantly contributed to the number of couples that split apart. Though unemployment, low wages, and historical oppression may have undermined the black family structure, Moynihan warned that the cycle of family breakdown would begin to feed on itself if the federal government did nothing to bolster the position of the black man. Without strong male role models, black children (especially black boys) would be less likely to succeed in school and more likely to sink into delinquency. As they matured, these young men would again be less likely to attain good jobs and more likely to desert their own families, tightening the "tangle of pathology."[10]

The Negro Family avoided specific policy recommendations other than the general (albeit emphatic) conclusion that a concerted effort by the federal government was needed to support African American families. Yet within the report, there were hints of policy proposals, especially for increasing black male employment in the armed forces. Before writing *The Negro Family*, Moynihan and the Policy Planning staff had penned a report entitled *One-Third of a Nation*, which focused on the high rate of rejection for poor men (especially poor black men) called up for the draft by selective service. Moynihan had argued that the armed forces could and should provide special training for these men. In *The Negro Family*, he explained why. African Americans constituted only 8 percent of the armed forces in 1964, yet they made up 11.8 percent of the United States' population. Moynihan noted that if the military recruited enough black men to get proportionate representation in the armed services, black male unemployment would drop substantially. The greatest gain, according to Moynihan, would be a psychological one, because black men would find less racial discrimination in the military than in the society at large and they would also find an "utterly masculine world . . . away from the strains of the disorganized and matrifocal family life in which so many Negro youth come of age." For those who died in combat, Moynihan admitted that the cost was "inestimable," but he felt that the risk was worth it, for, in quoting the words of an armed forces recruitment campaign, Moynihan argued, "In the U.S. Army you get to know what it means to feel like a man."[11]

President Johnson learned of this report in early May 1965, a time when he was especially receptive to new ideas about the future direction of federal involvement in the civil rights movement. Johnson had just won a landslide victory in the election of 1964, and though he had squashed the challenge of the Mississippi Freedom Democratic Party delegation at the Democratic national convention in Atlantic City, he took his general election victory as a mandate to enact civil rights and antipoverty legislation. Moynihan's analysis of the connection between black male unemployment and persistent racial inequality in America struck a sympathetic cord with the president.[12]

As a southern politician, Lyndon Johnson had walked a fine line over the course of his long career in public service between conservative support for the racial status quo and moderate pressure for racial progress. When he was a young man, Johnson taught at a small segregated school for Mexican Americans in Cotulla, Texas. Later, as administrator of the New Deal's National Youth Administration (NYA) state office in Austin, Johnson administered segregated youth programs, but ensured that black NYA facilities received ample funds. As a con-

In *The Negro Family: A Case for National Action*, Daniel Patrick Moynihan argued, among other things, that poor minority men who lacked male role models could benefit from service in the armed forces. Moynihan is shown here with Ralph Abernathy, president of the Southern Christian Leadership Conference, talking to reporters outside of the White House in 1969. Photograph by Warren K. Leffler. U.S. News & World Report Magazine Collection, Prints and Photographs Division (LC-U9-21046, frame 6), Library of Congress.

gressman and then senator from Texas, Johnson initially opposed national civil rights bills, voting against the Fair Employment Practices Commission in 1948, for instance, arguing, "If a man can tell you who you must hire, he can tell you whom you can't hire." Yet, in the 1950s, he defied the Citizens' Councils as the only senator from the old Confederacy who did not sign the so-called Southern Manifesto, which admonished the Supreme Court for usurping state authority in outlawing segregation. Clearly, Johnson was aiming for a wider constituency than the South as Senate Majority Leader after 1954, but a close investigation of his racial voting record suggests that Johnson's support of civil rights bills after 1957 did not reflect simple political expediency. Instead, it represented Johnson's growing personal commitment to civil rights for all Americans.[13]

Having shepherded the Civil Rights Act of 1964 through Congress in the wake of Kennedy's assassination, Johnson turned his eyes to the Voting Rights Act of 1965 and an arsenal of new programs being developed for a War on Poverty. In the late spring of 1965, after learning of Moynihan's report, Johnson asked him to cowrite a presidential address for the graduation ceremonies at Howard University, one of the most prestigious historically black colleges in the country. Moynihan wrote the first draft of the speech and then revised it with White House wordsmith Richard Goodwin before running it by NAACP president Roy Wilkins and Urban League president Whitney Young.[14]

In the Howard speech, delivered on June 4, 1965, President Johnson lauded the victories already won by the civil rights movement, but he observed that freedom was not enough. "You do not take a person who, for years, has been hobbled by chains and liberate him," the president said, "bring him up to the starting line of a race and then say, 'You are free to compete with all the others.'" Johnson argued, as had Moynihan, that equal opportunity must yield an equality of results before it could be said that Americans of all races were truly free. The president concluded, "It is not enough to open the gates of opportunity. All our citizens must have the ability to walk through those gates." While noting that middle-class African Americans had made much progress, Johnson pointed to the breakdown of the family in low-income black communities as perhaps the "most important" indicator of what remained to be done in the civil rights revolution. The breakdown of the black family, he observed, "flows from centuries of oppression and persecution of the Negro man. It flows from the long years of degradation and discrimination, which have attacked his dignity and assaulted his ability to provide for his family." Acknowledging that there was no single answer to this problem, Johnson believed that jobs for black men, better housing, welfare programs for two-parent families, and innovative health care initiatives constituted parts of the answer. He concluded his speech with a call to "scholars, and experts, and outstanding Negro leaders—men of both races—and officials of Government" to attend a White House conference that would fashion concrete solutions to the problems faced by African Americans.[15]

Letters of support flooded into the White House in the days and months following the Howard speech. "Never before," wrote Martin Luther King Jr., "has a President articulated the depths and dimensions of the problem more eloquently and profoundly." Representative John Conyers echoed King's sentiment, lauding the speech as "one of the greatest statements ever made by a President of the United States about the desperate struggle of Negro Americans to achieve their rightful place in American society." Aminda Wilkins, the spouse of NAACP president Roy Wilkins, focused on the family in her response. "Through the years, I have talked and worried about the deterioration of the Negro family life and the failure of organized groups to do anything about it. . . . To know that our President has identified the problem and its causal factors, spoken out on them and

plans action is beyond our greatest hopes and dreams." In addition to these letters from African American leaders and luminaries, Johnson received hundreds
of letters of support from everyday people like Jessie R. Shipp, who wrote, "You
really spells out the plain truth. I think you are great. We need mens in times like
these like you. With fervent will their part to play." In one of his few responses to
this outpouring of support, Johnson admitted to Aminda Wilkins, "There was,
of course, some apprehension that so frank a discussion of a somewhat sensitive
issue might be misunderstood. However, I am pleased to report to you that the
reception has been uniformly positive."[16]

Although a few newspaper stories in June and July 1965 traced the impetus
for the president's speech at Howard back to a report done by the Department
of Labor, most Americans knew nothing of *The Negro Family*. Moynihan, who
resigned from the Labor Department during the summer to campaign for the
presidency of New York's city council, had left Washington by the time his report
garnered wide publicity in late August. At that point, journalists began citing the
report as an explanation of the urban uprisings that would continue to rock the
nation in the second half of the 1960s.[17]

The summer of 1964 had witnessed explosive racial unrest in New York City,
but the spark of the "long hot summers" that burned throughout the late 1960s
caught fire in the Watts area of Los Angeles, California, in August 1965. California Highway Patrol officer Lee Minikus pulled over Marquette Frye and his
brother on suspicion of drunk driving in what started out as a routine traffic stop
in the predominantly African American neighborhood of Watts. A crowd of onlookers gathered after another squad car pulled up, and Frye's mother emerged
from the group of spectators to harangue the white police officers for stopping
her son. Rumors spread quickly about the fracas that ensued between white police and black bystanders. Some said that the police assaulted Mrs. Frye after
dragging her down to the station house, and others reported seeing a pregnant
woman in the crowd beaten by white officers. Though these rumors were never
substantiated, tensions between the LAPD and black residents sparked eight-days
of looting and violence in Watts during which thirty-four people died, approximately 1,000 were injured, and 4,000 were arrested out of an estimated 35,000
who actively participated in the uprising. Official estimates of property damage
ranged upwards of $200 million. Noting, as many commentators have, that the
majority of the participants were young black men, historian Gerald Horne offers
one analysis of the gender implications of the Watts uprising. "The black nationalism that ultimately detonated in Watts was . . . [in part] a reaction against the
historic and stereotypical notion that blacks were the 'female' of the races: sub-

ordinated, subordinate, dominated, and timid. Through black nationalism a slice of race cum gender privilege could be reclaimed by means of a sometimes brutal masculinity." The rumors that touched off the uprising, according to Horne, reveal that one impetus may have been a response by black men to the myth arising from slavery that they "could not protect their families and 'their' women."[18]

Though a significant minority of the participants in the Watts uprising were women, contemporary analysts focused on explaining the men's actions, and they believed that they found the answer in the theory of family breakdown cited in Moynihan's report. The *Los Angeles Times*, under the headline "Racial Unrest Tied to Negro Family Failure," characterized the "typical" juvenile arrested in the uprising as a seventeen-year-old "male Negro with little or no previous contact with the police," who was usually from a "broken home." The California governor's commission that later investigated the causes of the Watts uprising likewise attributed unrest to minority family instability, fatherlessness, and problems within the welfare system. Moynihan remembers that Bill Moyers, the White House press secretary, gave copies of *The Negro Family* to the press on August 17, 1965, when journalists began "demanding to know what was happening in California," but other federal officials suspect that Moynihan himself leaked the report, knowing the additional attention it would receive in the wake of the riots. Conservative Washington columnists Roland Evans and Robert Novak wrote an article in mid-August that, in the eyes of some scholars, was "the most influential news story connecting the report with the post-riot atmosphere." Evans and Novak downplayed Moynihan's discussion of unemployment and the historical causes of family breakdown and highlighted the causal nature of the breakdown itself in spurring violence. Evans and Novak also exposed a debate raging in the administration over whether to move forward with Moynihan's family policy recommendations. This debate, Evans and Novak argued, "may determine whether this country is doomed to succeeding summers of guerilla warfare in our cities."[19]

Considering that Moynihan completed his report five months before the Watts uprising, it may have been unfair for journalists to connect his thesis to the racial unrest in California, but Moynihan himself contributed to such analysis. "From the wild Irish slums of the 19th century Eastern seaboard to the riot-torn suburbs of Los Angeles, there is one unmistakable lesson in American history," he wrote; "a community that allows a large number of men to grow up in broken families, dominated by women, never acquiring any stable relationship to male authority . . . that community asks for and gets chaos." Though Moynihan used this thesis to argue once again that the government had an obligation to ensure that all men had the jobs and wages necessary to provide adequately for their families, his hyperbole veered closer and closer to a position that would be taken by many as "blaming the victim."[20]

In the wake of Watts, civil rights activists and their allies recognized possible problems in the public perceptions of the report, especially a potential for manipulation of the family breakdown theory by movement opponents. William F. Ryan, a psychologist who had worked with the Congress of Racial Equality (CORE) in Boston, observed that the perception of Moynihan's report created by press coverage fed into the argument that "the present unequal status of the Negro in America results not from the obvious causes of discrimination and segregation, but rather from . . . the 'instability' of the Negro family." Department of Labor officials had shied away from releasing the report for this very reason, fearing that it would "be picked up by the segregationists and used against the Negro." When the government began disseminating copies of the report late in the summer, these fears proved justified. The Citizens' Councils praised Moynihan's report in the pages of the *Citizen* and offered to sell copies to segregationists inclined to find out more about the "tangle of pathology" in black communities.[21]

As segregationists and other conservative pundits coopted the report to support their own political ends, a backlash against Moynihan's thesis began to grow in movement circles and within the government itself. Many of the report's conservative proponents and liberal critics had not read the document itself, but instead based their opinions on summaries or excerpts printed in the press. A case in point was a scathing indictment penned by Dr. Benjamin Payton, the director of the Protestant Council of New York City's Office of Church and Race. "The symmetry of the report is flawed," Payton wrote, "only by the simplistic logic which holds it together, the inadequate empirical evidence it utilizes, and the erroneous premise upon which it is based." Citing only newspaper articles, including the essay written by Evans and Novak, Payton argued that matriarchy and illegitimacy were symptoms of deeper problems — "insufficient jobs and job training programs, inferior segregated education, and inadequate and unsafe housing conditions" — points that Moynihan himself would have wholeheartedly seconded.[22]

Payton ended up unwittingly agreeing with much that Moynihan had actually written, but more informed critics targeted the report's questionable implications for women and federal civil rights policy. Mary Dublin Keyserling, director of the Women's Bureau in the Labor Department, agreed with Moynihan that family breakdown and minority unemployment were serious problems, but she challenged some of his basic assumptions regarding women's roles. In an article published just months after his report was released, Moynihan argued, "It is in the perspective of the underemployment of the Negro father that we must regard the Negro mother as being *overemployed*." Keyserling disagreed, citing a 19 percent higher rate of unemployment among nonwhite women than nonwhite men in 1964. She went on to argue that both minority men and women were discriminated against in the labor force, noting the high proportion of low-wage and unskilled jobs many of them held. Keyserling believed that the federal government had a responsibility to improve the quantity and quality of employment for black men *and* women. Civil rights leaders pointed out three other problems with the report. First, SNCC leaders argued that Moynihan's report and Johnson's Howard speech presumed too much in suggesting that the movement had already won equality of opportunity. Working in grassroots organizing every day, these activists could testify to the fact that civil rights and antipoverty legislation had barely scratched the surface of problems in the rural South and urban North by 1965. Second, many believed, as did Bayard Rustin, an organizer of the March on Washington, that female-headed families in poor black communities might be a "healthy adaptation" to the problems of poverty and racism that besieged the family in urban ghettos. Finally, the Urban League's Whitney Young suggested that like their black peers, poor whites in the nation's cities also struggled with obstacles to family stability.[23]

Yet despite these criticisms, some civil rights activists initially believed that Moynihan's analysis might offer a new impetus for the government to address racism and poverty in America. No one more eloquently stated this position than Martin Luther King Jr. "The flames of Watts," King said, "have illuminated more than the western skies — they lit up the agony of the ghetto." He concurred with Moynihan's thesis that "the progress in civil rights [could] be negated by the dissolving of family structure" in these ghettos, and he traced the difficulties of family stability back to the horrors of the middle passage and slavery, as had Moynihan. King also suggested that the availability of domestic jobs in the cities made black women more employable than men, positioning them to be heads of households, so that "the Negro male existed in a larger society which was patriarchal while he was the subordinate in a matriarchy." Following the lead of Malcolm X, Moynihan, and others, King was beginning to articulate the gender implications of economic discrimination and racism in America's inner cities. Yet there were still real differences between these civil rights leaders and policymakers. Even though King accepted much that Moynihan had posited in *The Negro Family*, he also highlighted the history of strength and resilience that allowed black families to survive through troubled times. "No one in all history had to fight against so many physical and psychological horrors to have a family life," King preached. "The fight was never lost: victory was always delayed, but the spirit persisted and the final triumph is as sure as the rising sun." The increasing public awareness of obstacles to family stability, according to King, represented both dangers and opportunities. The danger was that opponents of the movement would attribute family instability in poor black communities to "innate Negro weakness," but there was also an opportunity for the nation to "deal fully rather than haphazardly with the problems as a whole—to see it as a social catastrophe and meet it . . . with an adequacy of resources."[24]

The federal government attempted to take full advantage of this opportunity with the White House conference "To Fulfill These Rights," which Johnson had proposed during his speech at Howard University. Civil rights activists, scholars, and government officials met in Washington in November 1965 to plan the larger conference for the following spring. In confidential meetings with federal officials, prominent civil rights leaders agreed in late October that the White House conference should focus on family stability as well as "economic security for the Negro family head," protection of civil rights workers in the South, and enforcement of the 1964 civil rights act. Yet others, like sociologist Herbert Gans, worried that the focus on the family would reinforce an "overly paternalistic" way of dealing with civil rights and might "deflect attention away from the economic causes of the Negro problem." Because of these conflicting opinions and the maelstrom of controversy surrounding Moynihan's report, the issue of the family was buried in one of eight sessions in the planning meeting; the others dealt with more traditional civil rights issues such as voting, education, and employment. As the meeting opened, one official downplayed Moynihan's role by joking, "I have been reliably informed that no such person as Daniel Patrick Moynihan exists." Rendered an invisible man, Moynihan quietly attended the early sessions on the family.[25]

Moderated by NAACP Legal Defense stalwart Constance Motley and presided over by the sociologist Hylan Lewis, the family session convened in the Washington Hilton. Though its official purpose was to plan for the upcoming civil rights conference, the meeting became a free-form discussion of the problems faced by black families. At first, session participants focused on the economic underpinnings of family instability, but the conversation branched out into the need for male role models and the problems of matriarchy in poor black communities. Dorothy Height, president of the National Council of Negro Women, addressed these criticisms of female-headed families, arguing that scholars needed to recognize "the tremendous contribution made through the years by the Negro woman in the family." For Height, neither matriarchy nor patriarchy was the ideal. Instead, she advocated "building up a sense of partnership and interrelatedness within the family." Few observers focused on Height's thoughtful comments, however, because on the second day, Moynihan responded to the acerbic criticisms leveled against him by Benjamin Payton regarding his supposed ignorance of the economic causes of family breakdown. "Do you see that the object of this report was not to say that jobs don't matter," Moynihan beseeched those in attendance, "but to say that jobs do matter in the most fundamental way? That housing matters in a profound way. . . . [and that] we can measure our success or failure as a society, not in terms of the gross national product, not in terms of income level, . . . but in the health, and the living, loving reality of the family in our society." Payton responded by quoting the report itself as having argued that the breakdown of the black family is "the fundamental source of weakness of the Negro community at the present time." This debate about the wording of Moynihan's argument distracted from the substantive issues that his report had raised and led participants to disregard Dorothy Height's proposal of federal support for spousal partnerships rather than either patriarchal or matriarchal families. The debate was far from over, but for all intents and purposes, the planning session for the White House civil rights conference was.[26]

Official reports and unofficial accounts of the planning meetings left the impression that the scholars, civil rights activists, and government officials in attendance had accomplished very little. As chair of the family session, Hylan Lewis penned the recommendations that the federal government implement a national family policy, which included providing jobs for all men. But Lewis was careful to argue that once families were guaranteed an economic foundation for success, they "should have the right to evolve in directions of their own choosing." The vague consensus cobbled together by Lewis is a testament to the fact that few concrete plans were laid out for the larger White House civil rights conference the following spring or future administration policy regarding the family. One participant felt that the conference did little but "consolidate and intensify the dissatisfaction, frustrations and militancy of the Negro leadership," and another observed wryly, "It may be that the Hilton Hotel is not fertile ground for the planning of a revolution."[27]

The revolution was going on in the streets, far from the posh conference rooms of the Washington Hilton and the rarified air of policy discussions about the family. Realizing this, the U.S. Commission on Civil Rights traveled to cities across the nation to collect testimony from residents of the urban ghettos. One of the first places the commission visited in 1966 was the Hough area of Cleveland,

Ohio, where 39 percent of the families lived below the poverty line and 32 percent had female heads of households. Looming at an astonishing 15.6 percent, male unemployment in the neighborhood was nearly quadruple the national rate by late 1966, and Department of Labor staffers who visited Hough insisted that this official count seriously *under*estimated true unemployment in the area.[28]

The stories collected by the commission revealed the strains that unemployment and poverty placed on low-income black families. "Our whole attitude and idea about a man's worth is where he works," one man who counseled youth in the neighborhood told the commission. "Naturally, a lot of kids are not only trying to find some way of making a living, but they are trying to gain some dignity, some type of recognition, and being able to be men." One-fifth of the families in the Hough area survived only with help from AFDC, which stipulated that no able-bodied man could reside in the home. This rule spurred some unemployed men to desert their families because, as one woman noted, "a man doesn't want to feel that he is going to take bread out of his child's mouth if he is really a man . . . [so] if he is not able to support his family adequately, he usually leaves." Reverend Walter Grevatt Jr., a minister in the neighborhood, found it very difficult to counsel his unemployed male parishioners not to leave their wives and children, because he knew that this would deprive the families of much needed assistance. The solutions offered by the local people who testified before the commission included striking down the "man-in-the-house" rule that restricted AFDC payments to single parent households and the institution of public child care that would allow parents to take jobs to support their families.[29]

The testimony compiled by the U.S. Civil Rights Commission in 1966 articulated the needs of poor families quite eloquently, but when the White House civil rights conference "To Fulfill These Rights" convened a few months after the Cleveland hearings, consensus and concrete proposals seemed frustratingly elusive. As the conference approached, some activists and movement groups reconsidered their involvement in such a top-down approach to civil rights. "No More 'Cullud' Leaders and 'White Experts' On Us" read a placard carried by demonstrators from the District of Columbia who gathered to protest at the conference site. Stokely Carmichael, the new head of SNCC, withdrew his organization from the conference, saying, "The White House conference, especially with its original focus on the Negro family as the main problem with which America must deal, accentuates [the] process of shifting the burden of the problem" from the oppressor to the oppressed. By 1966 Carmichael and many of the other SNCC activists who had come of age in Mississippi had grown completely disillusioned with the federal government's role in the struggle for black equality. Black Power and community self-help were their new mantras, and their speeches echoed Malcolm's militant rhetoric. Other civil rights activists, however, had not given up hope for government intervention. Speaking at the beginning of the meeting, African American labor leader A. Philip Randolph did broach the subject of the family, which had become almost taboo in government circles by June 1966. "The man of the family is supposed to be the protector and support of the family. But if he is denied education and employment, if he cannot play his role as a husband or a father, the family breaks down," Randolph concluded, echoing Moynihan's report. Few other speakers addressed the family at all. In fact, the vast majority of conference participants navigated a wide course around this volatile issue. To address unemployment and welfare restrictions that Moynihan and others believed undermined family stability, the conference proposed the creation of metropolitan job councils, affirmative action by public and private employers in hiring minorities, and reform of AFDC with a guaranteed income for all families.[30]

The modest recommendations that resulted from the conference had little or no impact on federal policy in the final years of the Johnson administration. The president and the public at large had seemingly lost the political will to enact major civil rights legislation. Frustrated by the waning popular support for civil rights, Harlem's congressional representative, Adam Clayton Powell, belittled the conference as a place where black and white leaders met "to whisper words of futility into the hurricane of massive indifference." Presidential assistant Harry McPherson described resistance to serious reform within the government itself, warning Johnson's cabinet members that each federal agency had a responsibility to act upon the proposals of the White House conference. "It will not do," he said, "to drop these recommendations into the still waters of the bureaucracy." Despite McPherson's warning, the conference recommendations made barely a ripple as they sank to the bottoms of file drawers in the various departments. Federal agencies should not shoulder the only responsibility for inaction on civil rights, however. The president himself was increasingly distracted from domestic issues by the escalation of the Vietnam War, and without his support, federal civil rights and antipoverty policy began to suffer.[31]

The shift in resources from the War on Poverty to the war in Southeast Asia had serious implications for federal policies resulting from the Moynihan report. Noting the disparity between $14 billion in federal allocations for the war in Vietnam and $1.5 billion spent in the War on Poverty, activists in CORE had joined their SNCC comrades in refusing to participate in the 1966 White House civil rights conference. CORE leaders observed that military action had "called

Angered by policy debates that emerged in the wake the Moynihan Report, demonstrators picket outside of the White House conference "To Fulfill These Rights" in June 1966. Photograph by Warren K. Leffler. U.S. News & World Report Magazine Collection, Prints and Photographs Division (LC-U9-15971, frame 30), Library of Congress.

the government's attention away from the vigorous efforts to enforce the law and preserve the rights of Negroes in this country." The growing emphasis on military spending dovetailed with one of the implicit policy recommendations in Moynihan's report, namely the increased recruitment of minority men into the armed forces. The resulting federal program, Project 100,000, seemed to offer the Johnson administration a unique opportunity to fight a two-front war on poverty at home and communism abroad.[32]

Though it may not have been directly inspired by *The Negro Family*, Project 100,000's efforts to address unemployment and military manpower demands by recruiting low-income and minority men into the armed forces in 1966 certainly fit Moynihan's model. In a July 1965 memorandum for White House aide Harry McPherson, Moynihan had argued that minority unemployment might drop by as much as 5 percent "if 100,000 nonwhite men were added to the Armed Forces." "Above all things," Moynihan suggested, "the down-and-out Negro boy needs to be inducted into the male, American society." African Americans were underrepresented in the military as a whole in 1965, comprising only about 9 percent of the armed forces as opposed to 11 percent of the population, but much higher percentages of African American troops fought and died in Vietnam that year. In 1965, 15 percent of the Army's troops in Vietnam were black, and black soldiers made up 22 percent of the Army's enlisted casualties in Southeast Asia between 1961 and 1965. As the numbers of American troops in Vietnam increased the African American proportion of casualties dropped, but by 1967 it still topped 15 percent. A low-income, minority recruitment program such as Project 100,000 could receive bipartisan support in a time when civilian public works projects and civil rights initiatives were declining in popularity. Yet one of the same factors that made Project 100,000 politically expedient—mobilization for the war—also made it a tragedy. A sign held by one demonstrator outside the White House conference targeted this tragic irony, asking the rhetorical question: "Vietnam: Final Solution to Black Unemployment?" In an interview more than thirty years later, Paul Barton, one of Moynihan's assistants at the Department of Labor, explained regretfully, "We saw some very good things about the kinds of jobs that blacks had in the military. On the other hand, we were beginning to see the Vietnam War was heating up and later, [we realized], 'You're not helping them a lot by making them cannon fodder.'"[33]

The shift of federal resources to the war in Vietnam signaled the waning of government interest in civil rights, poverty, and the black family, but the controversy over *The Negro Family* touched off an avalanche of academic scholarship on these topics. In the second half of the 1960s and throughout the 1970s, more than fifty books and five hundred journal articles addressed the effects of poverty and discrimination on black families. In the first few years after the release of *The Negro Family*, scholars seemed to support much of what the report had suggested. Though they carefully distanced themselves from Moynihan, the psychologists William Grier and Price Cobbs actually furthered *The Negro Family* thesis in their 1968 explanation of *Black Rage*. With chapters on "Achieving Womanhood" and "Acquiring Manhood," Grier and Cobbs argued that "a great many of the problems of black people in America can be traced back to the widespread crumbling of the family structure." Like Moynihan, they linked this phenomenon to slavery, when the black man was "psychologically emasculated," but also found contemporary obstacles to black manhood in economic injustice. "In a capitalist society economic wealth is inextricably woven with manhood," Grier and Cobbs wrote. "Closely allied is power—power to control and direct other men, power to influence the course of one's own and others' lives. . . . It is this power both individually and collectively, which has been denied black men." For Grier and Cobbs, as for Moynihan, part of the answer lay in providing black men the economic foundation to exercise patriarchal power in their families and political power in the society.[34]

By the early 1970s, however, the growing influence of the feminist movement generated fierce academic and popular critiques of this thesis. Robert Staples, Angela Davis, Carol Stack, Deborah White, Herbert Gutman and other distinguished scholars challenged the thesis of *The Negro Family* with research that highlighted the black family's resiliency under the strains of slavery and poverty. Recognizing the existence of a matrifocal family structure that Moynihan had pointed to as an indication of family breakdown, these scholars argued, as had early critics of the report from the civil rights movement, that alternative family structures in low-income black communities were healthy adaptations rather than signs of pathology. They also targeted the thesis about overwhelming obstacles to the attainment of black manhood. "Stereotypes of the black male as psychologically impotent and castrated," wrote Robert Staples, "have been perpetuated not only by social scientists but through mass media and accepted by both blacks and whites alike. This assault on black masculinity is made *precisely because black males are men*; not because they are impotent." In other words, Staples argued that the power inherent in black men's gender identity was an implicit threat to white male dominance of society. This threat had engendered both physical attacks on black manhood and intellectual attacks in the social sciences, according to Staples. Yet even though he argued that a racist political ideology underlay social science analyses of the black family and black manhood in the 1960s, Staples agreed that low income levels and unemployment for black men in America's inner cities formed a "major impediment" to black familial relationships. Like most scholars who critiqued *The Negro Family*, Staples' difficulty was not with the problems Moynihan had analyzed, but with the solutions he offered. The real solutions, Staples and others argued, lay not in government support for black male patriarchy or intervention in black family structure, but in addressing basic social and economic inequalities that continued to plague American society.[35]

Poets were just as incensed by Moynihan's policy proposals as their social science colleagues. June Jordan was, like Moynihan, the product of a poor upbringing in New York City, and she too had worked her way out of poverty by becoming a wordsmith. While Moynihan's medium was the policy report, Jordan's was poetry. Many of her poems described the gritty reality of life in New York's impoverished neighborhoods and the strength of the women—especially black women, like her mother—who had to struggle simply to survive and raise their children. When she first learned of *The Negro Family* report, Jordan "didn't have the time for Mr. Moynihan or any other Mr. Man's theories," because she was busy demonstrating in the movement, raising her son, and working. But she did eventually find time to pen "Memo to Daniel Pretty Moynihan." "Don't you liberate me / from my female black pathology," she warned him, and as for a solution to the problem of black matriarchy, she offered the "simple proposition" that he "take over my position." Sonia Sanchez was only slightly more charitable in "Queens of the Universe," calling out the "cracker," who "done superimposed on our minds myths about ourselves . . . [as] matriarchs and no good bums." She continued, "i ain't sayen that some of that might not be," but there were reasons why minority men could not support their families ("like no gigs") or why women headed some black households ("like bruthus cuttin' out cuz this was the cooooooollLL thing to do or becuz the sistuhs made more bread than the bruthus"). In the view of professors and poets, Moynihan may have seen a real problem, but he remained blind to its causes and solutions. As June Jordan later wrote, she and others would not "willingly submit to the flagrantly popular, illogical, and misogynist [suggestion] that the solution to the impoverishment of Black women/Black mothers is the enablement of everybody else."[36]

The negative response to *The Negro Family* in the civil rights community, the academy, and the federal government left Moynihan feeling misunderstood and embittered. Appearing on the television program "Meet the Press" in late 1965, Moynihan pleaded for understanding. "I was trying to show," he explained, "that unemployment statistics, which are so dull . . . nonetheless ended up with orphaned children, with abandoned mothers, with men living furtive lives without even an address: that unemployment had flesh and blood and it could bleed." The harsh realities that *The Negro Family* addressed, according to Moynihan, did not reflect badly on the people in the nation's slums, but on the society that continued to allow those slums to exist. He had hoped that the focus on the family would enlist conservative support for full employment and other antipoverty initiatives in a way that traditional civil rights bills could not and also in a way that would not engender a backlash among the white working class. He did not foresee the negative response from the movement itself or the rapid decline in support within the Johnson administration. Feeling stabbed in the back by an administration that quickly distanced itself from him during the controversy, Moynihan complained to a White House aide in 1966, "If my head were sticking on a pike at the South West Gate to the White House grounds the impression would hardly be greater."[37]

With a changing of the guard at the White House two years later, Moynihan climbed down from this political pike at the South West Gate and moved into the West Wing as the chief domestic advisor for President Richard Nixon. Seen variously as the "house liberal" in Nixon's administration or as a "neoconservative," depending on one's point of view, Moynihan pushed for a form of guaranteed income with the Family Assistance Plan and tacitly approved Nixon's efforts to decrease unemployment through support of "black entrepreneurship" and corporate tax breaks for minority training programs. In the Nixon administration, Moynihan proved once again a magnet for controversy when a memo he wrote to the president regarding civil rights was leaked to the press in the spring of 1970. Given the "extraordinary progress" made by the civil rights movement and also the increasing tenor of radicalism in the more militant sections of the black community, Moynihan proposed that "the time may have come when the issue of race could benefit from a period of 'benign neglect.'" The fury of civil rights leaders exploded in the press, and "benign neglect" became a symbol of how little the federal government had accomplished in the area of civil rights since the mid-1960s.[38]

The Moynihan report and the controversy after its release brought many of the issues surrounding black masculinity that Malcolm X had addressed in the early 1960s to the forefront of mainstream American consciousness in the second half of the decade. Never before had so many social critics and commentators in the government, the media, the movement, and the academy addressed the relationships between race, poverty, and gender. Moynihan's belief that an increase in black male employment could bolster black men's position as patriarchs and stabilize the family structure in poor urban communities struck Johnson and others in his administration as an innovative approach to antipoverty policy. Given the assumptions about race and gender roles that dominated American society in the mid-1960s, this should come as no surprise. "Well, in 1964 there was still the general pattern and the general expectation that the male was the breadwinner," Moynihan's assistant Paul Barton remembers. "We were very much interested in upgrading the economic status of the black male," he explains, "so that they could become the breadwinners and change this trend toward children not having fathers, not being raised by . . . successful fathers in the economy as role models for socialization." Like Moynihan, Barton had been raised by a single mother, and though both men hewed closely to the principle of objectivity in their social science research, their life experiences may have influenced their analysis of the family in unconscious ways. Their backgrounds, their research, and the society in which they lived led them to assume that reestablishing a patriarchal family structure in poor communities would provide a solid socioeconomic foundation for the progress of the civil rights movement. This thesis proved more controversial than its authors could ever have anticipated. The controversy kicked up by *The Negro Family* report clouded the government's civil rights initiatives at a time when they might have been most effective and also served as a smokescreen for a shift in federal funds away from the fight to vanquish poverty in America toward efforts to combat communism in Southeast Asia.[39]

In the long term, Moynihan's report on the black family had even more unintended and wide-ranging consequences. The hope that a focus on the family and manhood would enlist bipartisan support for full employment and antipoverty programs in the 1960s disappeared as feminist critics began to challenge the patriarchal assumptions on which the report was based and as radicalized movement activists grew increasingly jaded about potential government action on behalf of poor families. At the same time that it lost support from liberals, however, Moynihan's thesis about the importance of the family gained credence in more conservative circles. As Richard Nixon, Ronald Reagan, and other Republican leaders in the 1970s, 1980s, and early 1990s began pressing for welfare reform and touting family values, Moynihan's ideas gained a new lease on life, albeit in a modified form. In 1992, President George H. W. Bush echoed Moynihan's thesis in a speech at Notre Dame University. "At the heart of the problems facing our country stands an institution under siege. That institution is the American family. Whatever form our most pressing problems may take, ultimately, all are related to the disintegration of the American family." Rather than helping black men in America's inner cities gain the economic means to become patriarchs or supporting black family stability with federal programs as Moynihan had once suggested, conservative politicians focused on the connections between race, gender, and poverty to attack and stereotype "deadbeat dads" and "welfare queens." Attributing this shift to Moynihan would be unfair. A shift in American political culture began just as his report was released in the mid-to-late 1960s, leading to a gradual rollback of the interventionist welfare state. Though conservative politicians made rhetorical allusions to poverty, race, and gender, their main concern was extracting the federal government from the "tangle of pathology" that Moynihan and others observed.[40]

As the federal government began to swing its focus away from the connections among poverty, race, and gender, activists in the civil rights and labor movements refused to let Americans forget these issues. In Memphis, Tennessee, hundreds of male African American sanitation workers marched with Martin Luther King Jr. in 1968 to demand union recognition and higher wages so that they could provide for their families. When these men strode through the streets of Memphis, protesting the racist paternalism of city officials, they wore signs that demanded recognition, not only of their union and civil rights, but of their manhood as well.

And this hell was, simply, that he never in his life owned anything, not his wife, not his house, not his child, which could not, at any instant, be taken from him by the power of white people. This is what paternalism means. — James Baldwin, *Nobody Knows My Name* (1961)

Chapter Six

I Am a Man!
The Memphis Sanitation Strike

On March 28, 1968, Martin Luther King Jr. directed a march of thousands of African American protesters down Beale Street in Memphis, Tennessee. King's plane landed late that morning, and the crowd was already on the verge of conflict with the police when he and other members of the SCLC took their places at the head of the march. The marchers were demonstrating their support for 1,300 striking sanitation workers, many of whom wore placards that proclaimed, "I AM a Man." As the throng advanced down Beale Street, some of the younger strike supporters ripped the protest signs off of the wooden sticks that they carried. These young men, none of whom were sanitation workers, used the sticks to smash glass storefronts on both sides of the street. Looting led to violent police retaliation. Troopers lobbed tear gas into groups of protesters and sprayed mace at demonstrators unlucky enough to be in range. High above the fray in city hall, Mayor Henry Loeb sat in his office, confident that the strike was illegal, and that law and order would be maintained in Memphis.[1]

In one sense, the "I AM a Man" placards worn by the sanitation workers represented a demand for recognition of the dignity and humanity of all African Americans in Memphis. This demand caught white Memphians by surprise because they had always taken pride in being racially progressive. Token integration had quietly replaced public segregation in Memphis in the mid-1960s without the level of demonstrations and unrest that accompanied desegregation in other southern cities. However, the 1967 mayoral elections revealed the true colors of the conservative Memphis electorate, as segregationist candidate Henry Loeb rode a wave of white backlash against the movement into office. Loeb took his election as a mandate to maintain "law and order," a phrase popular in the political parlance of the late 1960s, often equated to suppression of civil rights protest and defense of the racial status quo. The mayor still referred publicly to black Memphians as "his Negroes," and observers characterized his vision of race relations as reminiscent of a "plantation mentality." Strike leaders focused much of their rhetoric on Loeb's paternalism and denial of the strikers' manhood. These were working men, fighting for higher wages so that they could support their families and fulfill the traditional breadwinner role of men in a capitalist society. Though their goals may have been traditional, their struggle was not. By challenging white men's paternalism and power in Memphis, the strikers and their allies questioned what had been a monolithic (and monochromatic) model of masculinity, creating new possibilities for working-class black men, black youth, and others to define their own identities. In this sense, the "I *AM* a Man" slogan and the sanitation strike represented a dispute over what it meant to be a man.[2]

As the civil rights movement expanded from a struggle for social and political rights into a campaign for economic justice, competing visions of manhood emerged based on the age and class of movement participants. The young men who ripped the signs off of their sticks during the march, for instance, were contesting not only white constructions of manhood, but also the manhood espoused by older black leaders. The sanitation workers were members of an urban working class that had a long history of activism in Memphis, but had very little input into the decision-making process and direction of the civil rights movement in the early 1960s. King was trying to bring these men into the movement in the second half of the decade. To do this, he had begun to address not only their financial situation, but also the way that economic oppression affected them as men. Although the "I *AM* a Man" slogan and the sanitation workers' demands dealt explicitly only with the impact of low wages and poverty on working-class black men, the campaign also raised questions about the position of women in Memphis society and in the movement. The struggle for manhood in Memphis resists a simple black and white model of gender identity. Instead, the sanitation workers' protest illuminates a spectrum of meanings for manhood and womanhood in both the black and white communities, and it offers a chance to investigate the ways in which gender and race shape assumptions about work and workers' rights.[3]

The racial composition of the Memphis labor force began to shift around the turn of the century when increased mechanization of agricultural production and new urban job opportunities encouraged black migration from farms in the Mississippi Delta to the cities. This migration exacerbated tensions between black and white urban residents that erupted in periodic outbreaks of violence and lynchings.[4] Blacks, who once worked the land as sharecroppers, now competed with whites for manufacturing jobs in Memphis. This exacerbated racial divisions within the city's working class. Most attempts to organize interracial alliances among workers in the South failed, and the majority of the Memphis labor unions that survived remained segregated. When white workers fought for raises, they usually demanded higher wages for whites only. As W. E. B. Du Bois suggested, white supremacy in the workplace offered higher "psychological wages" for poor white workers, but in general, racial segregation kept wages relatively low across the board in the region.[5] Though integrated unions would have allowed a unified working class to demand higher wages for all workers, working-class whites often resisted alliances with black coworkers for fear that this would jeopardize their social status in the strict racial hierarchy of southern society.[6]

Low wages and poor working conditions in the Memphis Public Works Department of the 1950s and 1960s were a direct result of racial divisions in the workplace. White supervisors openly discriminated against black employees in job assignments, pay scales, and advancement. Black sanitation workers in Memphis earned so little money at this time that 40 percent of the men still qualified for welfare even though many worked second jobs. In addition to paying miniscule wages, the city attempted to save money by refusing to modernize ancient equipment used by black workers. Until the public works commissioner grudgingly purchased pushcarts and trucks with mechanical packers in the mid-1960s, workers had to haul huge garbage cans on their backs, frequently enduring painful injuries to remain on the job. "Back then," remembers sanitation worker Taylor Rogers, "everybody had a 50-gallon drum in the backyard. . . . You carried those tubs on your head and shoulders. Most of the tubs were leakin' and that stuff was fallin' all over you. You got home you had to take your clothes off at the door 'cause you didn't want to bring all that filth in the house." To cut costs further, supervisors often sent "nonessential" public works employees home on rainy days. While he and other black workers were the first to lose shifts when it rained, L. C. Reed bitterly observed, "white men worked shine, rain, sleet, or snow. Them supervisors just sit there till four o'clock and then get up and go home ever since I been here. This is not the way to do things."[7]

Although they realized that they would have little support from their white coworkers, black sanitation workers united in the 1960s to fight for better wages and working conditions and against racial discrimination in the Public Works Department. Their first attempt to strike in 1963 failed because of inadequate organization. Former sanitation worker, T. O. Jones, helped his disgruntled coworkers form Local 1733 of the American Federation of State, County, and Municipal Employees (AFSCME) in 1964, but city officials refused to recognize the union. Another walk out in 1966 also failed to achieve union recognition, but it did win new recruits. "I joined Mr. T. O. Jones and the union in 1966 cause we just wasn't getting justice," said Ed Gillis. These false starts prepared the public works employees for a longer struggle that began in earnest in 1968 after an old garbage truck malfunctioned, killing two black workers. The *Commercial Appeal*, one of two white dailies in Memphis, reported that the workers had been "ground up like garbage." The sanitation department paid the workers' families an additional month's salary and $500 for the funeral expenses, but no city representatives attended the funerals, and no further compensation ever reached the families.[8]

On February 12, 1968, the sanitation workers' union met to discuss the deaths of their coworkers and the partial pay that they had received when forced to go home early on rainy days. These incidents pushed the workers beyond the breaking point. Even though they knew that a sanitation strike would have been more effective during summer months when uncollected garbage would have festered in the streets and led to much worse sanitary conditions, these men voted unanimously to walk off the job. They demanded higher wages, dues checkoff, time-and-a-half for overtime, safety measures, and back pay for rainy days when they had been asked to go home.[9]

All of the sanitation workers were men, but at least one woman attended that seminal meeting, and her speech concerning racial discrimination in the city of Memphis helped spur the men to action and focus their attention on the civil rights dimensions of the strike. Cornelia Crenshaw reminded the sanitation workers that, despite some union leaders' claims that this was a simple labor dispute, the "real" issue was race. While labor leaders tried to downplay the issue of race in the beginning of the strike, Crenshaw and the Reverend Ezekial Bell made sure that the issue of racial discrimination in wage rates and raises remained central to the workers' demands. Bell labeled Crenshaw a "lady well-known as a civic and political leader," but other public figures denigrated her role in the strike. Gwen Awsumb, the only (white) woman on the City Council, said that Crenshaw "had a chip on her shoulder" after she was fired from the Memphis Housing Authority. Like other women who were involved in the strike from the beginning, Crenshaw logged long hours, often working until one or two o'clock in the morning, drumming up donations and making sure that the needs of the strikers were met. This was especially important early on, before national civil rights leaders got involved. Crenshaw's behind-the-scenes work was business as usual for women in the movement, but her outspoken leadership early in the strike was exceptional. Black ministers and white labor leaders quickly overshadowed her public role in the strike as the media cameras and local citizens focused their attention on the male leaders of the labor and civil rights movements.[10]

At the insistence of Mayor Henry Loeb, television crews filmed the strike negotiations from the beginning. Loeb knew how to manipulate the local media, and he came out of the early negotiations looking relatively calm and polite when compared to the brash national union representative P. J. Ciampa. Ciampa's blunt negotiating style pushed many moderate Memphians into Loeb's corner. Soon after televised negotiations began, some white Memphians showed their disdain for Ciampa with bumper stickers that read, "Ciampa Go Home." National AFSCME President Jerry Wurf decided at this point that he needed to step in and deal with Loeb directly.[11]

By February 20 Ciampa and Wurf had worked with local union leaders to revise the strikers' list of demands. The new list included union recognition through a written contract, a grievance procedure, a 10 percent wage increase, fair promotion policies, sick leave, pension programs, health insurance, and payroll deduction of union dues. Mayor Loeb continued to refuse union recognition and dues checkoff from wages because he believed that this would set a bad precedent for unionization of municipal employees in "his" city. He argued that the sanitation workers were being duped by AFSCME officials ("outsiders"), who only wanted to line their pockets with the hard-earned money of local Memphians. Loeb saw himself as the sanitation workers' keeper. He vowed throughout the strike that he would not abandon his "moral obligation" to protect them from union officials. To the sanitation workers and local black leaders, this kind of rhetoric smacked of paternalism. The workers felt more than capable of making their own decisions about the intentions of the national union. After all, they were not children, but men.[12]

Gradually, the strike leaders began articulating their demands in the gendered language of claiming manhood. Addressing the men at a union meeting in the first week of the strike, Bill Lucy, the highest-ranking black official in the national AFSCME office, blasted Loeb's paternalism. "The honorable Mayor . . . is going to take care of you," Lucy observed with biting sarcasm. "He's treating you like children, and this day is over because you are men and must stand together as men and demand what you want." The strikers cheered in agreement. They boiled down this sentiment into a simple slogan of pride and defiance: "I AM a Man."[13]

The "I AM a Man" slogan resonated with the sanitation workers, in part because it echoed a theme of the Delta blues that had pumped out of Beale Street clubs and juke joints since before World War II. Blues music had followed the migration of black sharecroppers from the farms and plantations of the Mississippi Delta to manufacturing and service jobs in cities like Memphis and Chicago. Blues guitar players like B. B. King and Muddy Waters thrilled African American urban audiences in the 1950s with a new amplified version of the acoustic blues that they had learned growing up in the Delta. Although King set the tempo for the Beale Street beat, Waters's Chicago blues recordings first popularized the genre nationwide and dealt directly with African American manhood.

The title of Waters's song "Mannish Boy," first recorded in 1955, captured the ambiguous position of black men in America. This slow blues ballad began with a black mother telling her five-year-old son that he would one day be "the greatest man alive," but at the age of twenty-one, the son realized that though he felt like a man, people continued to perceive him as a boy. The proof of manhood in "Mannish Boy"—as in many blues songs from this era—was the narrator's sexual prowess. With the chorus, Waters refuted those who questioned black manhood, belting out, "I'm a Man, spelled M-A-N!" and punctuating each line with instrumental breaks and a responsive chorus sung by female vocalists. The macho swagger of Waters's song challenged racially exclusive constructions of manhood in the 1950s. Perhaps, it laid the cultural foundations for later demands of political activists during the 1960s. Drawing on some of the same gender and racial dilemmas that concerned Waters, the "I AM a Man" slogan galvanized the sanitation workers in support of a challenge to white economic and political hegemony in Memphis.[14]

In mid-February, seven hundred sanitation workers sat-in at a public works committee meeting held by the city council. Fred Davis, one of only three black councilmen, presided over the meeting that began amicably enough but ended in an angry demonstration by the union. Local black ministers gave speeches and led the workers in freedom songs. Reverend Ezekial Bell fired up the crowd when he said that he would not care if somebody tore the city seal down off the wall of the meeting hall. After listening to this rousing rhetoric, the sanitation workers refused to leave the hall until the committee finally agreed that a full council meeting would address a resolution about the strike. The committee recommended that the council support union recognition and dues checkoff, but the resolution passed by the council the following day said nothing about either proposal. Instead, it recognized the mayor as the sole spokesperson for the city.[15]

The striking workers felt betrayed by the council. The ministers and union leaders realized that they needed to come up with a nonviolent way for the workers to protest these injustices and release their frustrations. "The men were angry," union president Jerry Wurf remembered. "They were tired, beaten men, making a struggle that before they died they would stand up and be men. They were not bomb throwers. . . . But they were really worked up, and when that kind of guy gets worked up, he's worked up. And I was scared." The police agreed that the sanitation workers could march to Mason Temple Church of God in Christ as long as they stayed on one side of the street. Led by union organizers and ministers, the strikers and their supporters marched until a police cruiser reportedly crossed the center line and ran over a female demonstrator's foot. Some of the men in the march began rocking the police car to protect the female marcher, and the police retaliated by spraying the entire procession with mace, hitting ministers, union leaders, and federal civil rights officials. Shocked and dismayed that they had been maced while wearing their clerical collars, the ministers recognized that the sanitation strike held significance for the entire black community. At a meeting immediately after the march, Reverend Ralph Jackson preached, "I am sick and tired of Negroes getting on their knees and begging the great white father for the crumbs that fall from his table."[16]

The day after the march, February 24, one hundred and fifty black ministers met to form an organization to support the strikers. This group eventually took the name Community on the Move for Equality (COME). COME called for an economic boycott against downtown businesses and against the two white daily papers in Memphis, the *Commercial Appeal* and *Press-Scimitar*, which they believed printed biased accounts of the strike. Preaching from their pulpits every Sunday about the struggle, the ministers helped organize the black community behind the sanitation workers. What had begun as a strike of 1,300 black sanitation workers had expanded into a citywide civil rights campaign. The COME strategy committee, headed by Reverend James Lawson, soon realized that they could bring more pressure on the Loeb administration by inviting national civil rights leaders to Memphis.[17]

When NAACP president Roy Wilkins came to Memphis along with national labor leader Bayard Rustin on March 14, 1968, to address a crowd of over 9,100, they articulated the sanitation workers' fight as a struggle to get a living wage, one that would allow them to support their families. Wilkins chastised city leaders for paying the sanitation workers so little that they could not fulfill their roles as breadwinners. This minimum level of acceptable wages was often called a "family wage." "If I were the mayor of this city," Wilkins said, "I would be ashamed. I wouldn't want these men not to be able to feed their families on the lousy pittance they are paid." With higher wages, Wilkins argued that the workers could fulfill their traditional role as men by taking care of their family's financial needs. When Martin Luther King Jr. came to speak in Memphis four days later, he reiterated this call for recognition of the strikers' manhood through payment of a living wage.[18]

Local leaders brought King in to speak because they knew that he would bring national media attention to the strike that might force Mayor Loeb to reconsider his position, but King also offered his own analysis of the gender implications of the strike. Speaking to a crowd of over 10,000 people, King preached, "We are tired of our men being emasculated so that our wives and daughters have to go out and work in the white lady's kitchen, leaving us unable to be with our children and give them the time and attention that they need." King went on to join the chorus against Loeb's paternalism, saying, "Don't let anybody tell you to go back on the job and paternalistically say, 'Now, you are my men, and I'm going to do the right thing for you.'" King ended his speech with a promise that he would return to lead a massive, nonviolent march in Memphis to support the sanitation workers.[19]

King's involvement in the Memphis strike reflected a commitment to economic justice that he recognized was integral to the fight against racial discrimination, but he also understood on a personal level the demand for recognition of black manhood that had become the rallying cry for the sanitation workers. As a young child, King saw his father, the Reverend Martin Luther King Sr., battle such discrimination in Atlanta. One day, when the two were driving together, a white traffic cop pulled them over and demanded of King's father, "Boy, show me your license." "Do you see this child here," King's father replied defiantly, referring to his son. "That's a *boy*. I'm a *man*. I'm Reverend King." Later, Martin's father explained the incident to his son in order to teach him a lesson that he

Martin Luther King Jr. speaks to supporters of the Memphis sanitation strike in March 1968, less than one month before he was assassinated. *Memphis Press-Scimitar* photograph. Special Collections, University of Memphis Libraries.

would never forget: "When I stand up, I want everyone to know that a *man* is standing."[20]

In his first speech to the sanitation strikers, King had equated low pay and racist treatment with the tradition of white emasculation of black workers that stretched back to the times of slavery. King's primary motive for addressing the emasculation of black men was to attack the dehumanizing effects of paternalistic racism and low pay. This was, in part, a response to discussions of black male joblessness, poverty, and family stability raised by Daniel Patrick Moynihan in the mid-1960s. Like Moynihan, King not only addressed the effect of economic discrimination on men, he also showed how attempts to emasculate black men affected the status of black women and black families. When he said that emasculation of black men forced "our wives and daughters . . . to go out and work in the white lady's kitchen, leaving us unable to be with our children," he observed that the denial of black manhood affected the ability of black parents to care for their children. Inherent in this was an implicit assumption that denial of a family wage to black men left black women unable to fulfill what King saw as their true role, as mothers.[21] King accepted a patriarchal ordering of the black family in his call for higher wages and status for black men. He argued that black women should not have to work as domestic servants in white homes but assumed that they would accept domestic duties in their own households. At the very least, King believed that all families, regardless of race, should have enough income to allow women a choice of whether to work inside or outside the home.

The male domination of the SCLC and the patriarchal order of American society in the 1960s bolstered King's support for male-headed households and also his rhetoric of manhood. King's support for black patriarchy reflected the gender hierarchy within the black church and SCLC. SCLC's direct action campaigns, nonviolent philosophy, and faith-based inspiration had won countless women supporters and staffers for the organization, but the organization's leadership ranks remained dominated by men. These were preachers, accustomed to a world of congregations and choruses where women predominated, but men led. Ella Baker, a strong independent activist who had guided the creation of SNCC, chafed at the male domination of SCLC, as did Septima Clark and other women in the organization. If King's rhetoric reflected the gender hierarchy in his organization and the black church, it also echoed the patriarchal assumptions of many Americans at this time, assumptions shared by men as different as Malcolm X and Daniel Patrick Moynihan, Robert Williams and Lyndon Johnson. Even the language mirrored this cultural bias, so it was easy for civil rights leaders and politicians to equate the rights of all humanity with the rights of "mankind." At various times in the course of the Memphis campaign, however, labor and civil rights leaders articulated the various meanings of the "I *AM* a Man" slogan in both gendered calls for manhood and gender "neutral" calls for human rights.[22]

Civil rights and labor leaders responded to the lack of white respect for black humanity and also the attempts by white men to emasculate black men. Reverend Lawson told the press that the mayor "treats the workers as though they are not men, [and] that's a racist point of view. . . . For at the heart of racism is the idea that a man is not a man, that a person is not a person." In this instance, Lawson was simply saying that racism precluded full recognition of African American humanity. At other times during the Memphis movement, however, strike leaders defined "I *AM* a Man" in the strict sense of men's rights rather than the broader construction of human rights. When King addressed the emasculation of black men in Memphis, he alluded to what many participants and observers believed was the crux of the "I *AM* a Man" slogan. White men and women had referred to black men in Memphis and throughout the South as "boys" since slavery. This verbal infantilization paralleled the physical emasculation of black men in slave beatings, Redemption-era lynchings, and twentieth-century KKK retaliations for

In 1968 striking sanitation workers in Memphis demanded higher wages, union recognition, and respect as men. *Memphis Press-Scimitar* photograph, March 1968. Special Collections, University of Memphis Libraries.

civil rights activities. The sanitation workers' slogan was a direct response to the verbal and physical emasculation of black men. Some strikers and their leaders believed that a nonviolent struggle against the paternalism of the city "fathers" was the best way to contest this emasculation, but by the second half of the 1960s, there was a strong, outspoken contingent of black men who, like Malcolm X, saw nonviolence as obsolete.[23]

One organization that advocated an alternative style of civil rights struggle in Memphis was a group of young militants known as the Invaders. Most of the Invaders were black males in their late teens and twenties, who viewed themselves as the radical arm of the civil rights movement in Memphis. Charles Cabbage and Coby Smith organized the Invaders in 1967 as the "security" wing of a student group called the Black Organization Project (BOP). Members of COME had made some attempts to include this group of young militants in their organizing efforts, but relations between the two groups were strained. The Invaders advocated Black Power, and their rhetoric often included calls for violent resistance to the city's white power structure. This rhetoric contradicted COME's strategy of nonviolent direct action.[24]

In 1968 Calvin Taylor was a senior at Memphis State University, an intern for the *Commercial Appeal*, and a member of the Invaders. Taylor's supervisors at the newspaper did not know of his ties to the Invaders, and he attended many of the strike demonstrations as both a participant and observer. Press reports about the Invaders angered Taylor. "It's kind of cute that they call us Black Power boys," he noted sarcastically. "White people just can't get that out of their head, 'boy.'"[25]

Like many young men on the cusp of adulthood, the Invaders were preoccupied with the rite of passage into manhood. Taylor intimated this when describing the Invader recruitment strategies to an interviewer. "A black boy, when he's fourteen, isn't really a boy, he's a man—'cause he knows what the world is all about," Taylor argued. "So we decided we'd go a step further—and we'd get people in high school . . . and people who [were] freshmen and sophomores in college—to make up this Invader group." Mainstream American rites of passage into manhood at this time included getting a job, starting a family, going to college, or joining the military, but the Invaders argued that simply learning to live in racist society and having the courage to confront bigotry served as a rite of passage for young black men. Like the young activists in SNCC, the Invaders were coming of age in the movement.[26]

If the Invaders' definitions of black manhood contrasted with traditional white definitions, they also contradicted definitions espoused by older, more conservative black leaders. One Invader, who defined himself as a "radical," stepped up to the microphone at a mass meeting and blasted the advocates of nonviolence. "Preaching and money raising are fine," he said. "Somebody has to do it. But there are some *men* out there. We've got to do some *fighting*. Not marching —fighting! And when you talk about fighting a city with as many cops as this city's got, you better have some guns! You're gonna need 'em before it's over!" (emphasis in original) As staunch advocates of the philosophy of nonviolence, Martin Luther King Jr. and James Lawson certainly did not agree with this construction of manhood that defined men by their willingness to fight the city power structure with violence. When Taylor talked about his conversion from a belief in nonviolence to a strategy based on violence or self-defense he said, "It used to be, 'Man . . . okay . . . we got beat last night. I got hit over the head five times. Beautiful thing.' You know. 'We're doing this for the brothers!' After a few knocks . . . you get kind of tired." Frustration drove Taylor and other Invaders to seek new forms of brotherhood and new definitions of manhood that accepted or even required participation in violent protest.[27]

On March 28 Taylor and the other Invaders got a chance to participate in a violent protest. That was the day that King returned to Memphis to lead the ill-fated march down Beale Street that culminated in a police riot. Although most Invader leaders did not actively participate in the looting and violence, their rhetoric stirred up younger demonstrators and provided a cover for onlookers who came to the march with an agenda that included more than just nonviolent protest. Young protesters held up hand-painted signs with slogans like: "Loeb's Black Day," "Loeb Eat Shit," and most subtle of all, "Fuck You Mayor Loeb!" Few observers could tell who started the looting at the time of the march, but Reverend Lawson remembered that the looters were "chiefly men, chiefly male, under thirty, I suspect." These young men altered the character of the sanitation strike by rejecting King's calls for nonviolence. After the march degenerated into violence, King felt compelled to remain involved in the Memphis campaign until he could prove the viability of nonviolent protest.[28]

Between 1965 and 1968, King and other civil rights leaders of his generation struggled to convince the new generation of militant activists not only that nonviolence was the best way to combat the violence and prejudice in America, but also that it could be a manly way. King understood the frustration and anger that drove younger activists to demand Black Power and to back up their demands with threats of violence. "Black Power is a psychological call to manhood," he wrote in 1967, but he also knew that "the job of arousing manhood within a people that have been taught for so many centuries that they are nobody is not easy." For King, the key to this process was cultural education not violent confrontation. Knowledge of the proud African American heritage and history in this country would, he argued, impart a profound sense of dignity much more lasting than the ephemeral euphoria of violent struggle. While he sympathized with those who called for Black Power, he disagreed with their methods of attaining dignity and manhood. King still believed that the most effective strategy of protest was nonviolence, and he was not alone in this belief. The debates about violent protest and manhood in the sanitation workers' strike reached California where the Chicano labor leader César Chávez was facing similar challenges to his nonviolent strategies in the United Farm Workers strikes against grape growers. In March 1968, Chávez echoed King's movement philosophy, explaining to his followers why he was fasting rather than fighting: "I am convinced that the truest act of courage, the strongest act of manliness, is to sacrifice ourselves for others in a totally nonviolent struggle for justice. To be a man is to suffer for others. God help us to be men!"[29]

As eloquent as these older leaders were, their words and exemplary actions did not seem to be enough to stem younger activists' increasing disillusionment with the tactics of nonviolence. King, Chávez, and a few other leaders had a deep, philosophical commitment to nonviolence, but many of their followers saw this simply as a tactic, not a way of life. The story of the Invaders in Memphis suggests that increased willingness to rebel violently was, in part, a result of the generation gap in the movement. Yet the allegiance of Hartman Turnbow, Robert Williams, Malcolm X and other veteran activists to armed self-defense complicates this thesis. Nonviolence and armed resistance had coexisted in the movement from the beginning, but the younger generation of activists that came of age in the late 1960s was more willing to accept the latter as both a tactic and a philosophy. The willingness of the young to embrace armed resistance brought this same militant sentiment, an understandable reaction to racist violence, out in older activists as well. The Invaders were not the only people involved in the Memphis uprising. They were not the only ones who could be driven to violence by police brutality. They were not alone in their frustrations with the slow pace of change in the movement. James Robinson, one of the striking workers, remembered that when the men found out that there was a police informant secretly attending their meetings "he about got beat to death." Such incidents occurred, but they were rare. James Lawson, who had worked as a missionary in India and studied Gandhian forms of nonviolent protest, admitted, "It has never been that everyone [in the movement] was a nonviolent person. . . . I don't pretend, for example, that the sanitation workers were nonviolent. I mean, however, some did get the idea and tried to use it well."[30]

For the most part, the sanitation workers did remain true to the strategy, if not the philosophy, of nonviolence throughout the strike, but they were not the only ones whose manhood and commitment to nonviolence were tested by the confrontations with police. Middle-class black Memphians who supported the struggle were also dragged into the fray. During a mass arrest of strikers and their supporters after a sit-in at city hall, a police officer told Reverend Henry Starks to "get along, boy. Go on, boy. Move it, boy," and Starks fired back, "I'm not a boy. I'm the Reverend Mr. Henry Starks and if you call me 'boy' just one more time you are going to have to arrest me for assault." Other well-to-do members of the black community also responded militantly to racist police rhetoric during the sanitation strike. On the day of the march and mini-riot, Harold Whalum, president of a local insurance company, was standing outside of the NAACP offices with Executive Secretary Maxine Smith and a few other women when a police officer walked by and said, "Get in there you black motherfucker!" Whalum replied, "Is it necessary, do you have to talk to the ladies like this?" The policeman called Whalum a "Black SOB" and knocked him to the ground.[31]

Black and white newspaper coverage of strike violence and police brutality highlighted the struggle for manhood in the sanitation strike. The *Tri-State Defender*, the largest black weekly newspaper in Memphis, questioned the actions of national guardsmen who maintained "law and order" during the strike. The black paper portrayed the predominantly white guardsmen as trigger-happy cowboys, whose unruly conduct disrespected and endangered the lives of law-abiding African American ladies. According to the *Tri-State Defender*, the guardsmen were "waving their shotguns out the window and rudely spitting tobacco on the streets where Negro women are standing." One of the major white dailies, the *Commercial Appeal* concentrated its attacks on King, who, at the insistence of advisers, had left the Beale Street demonstrations when the march turned violent. The *Commercial Appeal* dubbed King's "flight" from the disturbance "Chicken a la King." If King was a coward or a chicken, as the newspaper portrayed him, he certainly could not have been a "true" man.[32]

The white newspapers were not alone in questioning King's manliness. Members of the Invaders viewed his nonviolent philosophy as less than manly, even though they held him in high esteem. When King met with Invader leaders after the march debacle, Calvin Taylor observed, "For a man he had very soft looking skin. . . . But this man actually lived and believed nonviolence. This was one of the reasons he looked so soft to me." King's presence awed Taylor, but the young Invader remained critical of the older civil rights leader's methods.[33]

King realized that he had to put these and other questions about nonviolence to rest. After violent incidents erupted in the first march, he vowed that he would come back to Memphis and lead a successful nonviolent march before he traveled to Washington for the Poor People's Campaign. He returned to Memphis on April 3, two days before the second march. That night, Ralph Abernathy convinced King to go to Mason Temple to speak to the three or four thousand Memphians who had braved inclement weather to attend the mass meeting. King accepted Abernathy's invitation and gave his now famous "Mountaintop" speech, the last public address of his life. During this speech, King recalled his victorious Birmingham campaign. Given his assessment of white attempts to emasculate black men in his first Memphis speech, his choice of metaphor in his second speech was telling. King reminisced, "And there was a power [in Birmingham] which Bull Connor couldn't adjust to; and so we ended up transforming Bull into a steer [a castrated bull], and we won our struggle."[34] Here, King reiterated the power that nonviolence had had earlier in the movement when it had neutralized the violence upon which white male supremacy rested in the South. As he concluded his speech, he addressed the issue of manhood that had been raised by the sanitation strike, but summed up the goal of the sanitation strike and the upcoming Poor People's campaign in broader terms, saying, "And that's what this whole thing is about. . . . We are saying that we are determined to be men. We are determined to be people."[35]

King would not be in Washington to lead the Poor People's campaign, however. James Earl Ray gunned him down the day after the "Mountaintop" speech on April 4, 1968. With King's assassination, the eyes of the nation focused on Memphis and the sanitation strike. Civil rights leaders across the country warned white Americans that they had lost the person most likely to bring about a peaceful reconciliation between the races. Former SNCC leader, Stokely Carmichael, predicted a "violent struggle in which black people would stand up on our feet and die like men. If that's our only act of manhood, then Goddammit we're going to die." Clarence Coe, a black Memphis trade unionist, said that after he learned of King's assassination, "I just expected to go to war." There was violent social upheaval in many cities throughout the United States in the wake of King's death, but Memphis remained relatively quiet.[36]

In the wake of King's death, black and white Memphians came together to find meaning in the tragedy. A biracial, multidenominational contingent of ministers had earlier scheduled a meeting with Mayor Loeb for April 5 to call for a strike settlement, but the meeting took on new importance in light of the assassination and national coverage of the strike. In a prepared statement, the ministers eulogized King as an "eminent preacher of peace, advocate of the power of nonviolent love, promoter and practitioner of true manhood."[37] The ministers used this public forum to throw their support behind King's nonviolent definition of manhood, but many white Memphians still opposed King and what he had stood for. Conservative white city council members felt that they faithfully represented these constituents throughout the strike in their general opposition to the strike.

During the month of March, the city council had met on a weekly basis and continued to support Mayor Loeb. While the three African American members of the city council backed the strikers in varying degrees, they stood against a strong majority of white council members that endorsed the mayor's position. Tom Todd, one of the leaders of the council's white majority, resented the pressure that union leaders placed on the council with sit-ins. Todd offered a conservative analysis of the struggle, suggesting, "It would have made it a lot easier if these creatures [union leaders] had come down here and acted as men and not . . . as gangsters." One of the other white council members observed, "You couldn't have negotiated with any of them any more than you could negotiate with the devil."[38]

I AM A MAN!

When other white council members began to reconsider their opposition to the strike, conservative white Memphians branded them as race traitors. Jerred Blanchard swung his vote behind union recognition before any of the other white council members. To some angry white constituents, "I became the fourth 'nigger' on the Council," Blanchard remembered. "That was the night the phone started ringing." Blanchard was not the only one who received calls from irate white Memphians after he altered his strike position. When the papers misquoted councilwoman Gwen Awsumb as suggesting that it was time for the mayor to compromise, she received calls from many of the white citizens that had helped elect her. One woman screamed, "I voted for you and now you are doing things for those niggers. You are nothing but a cigarette smoking bitch." Awsumb had merely observed that it might be time for the mayor to reconsider his position on the strike, but any breaking of ranks in the sanitation strike was seen as the worst form of treachery in certain parts of the white community. If some white Memphians recognized African American humanity and equality, then what would it mean to be white? In much the same way that the segregationists in the Citizens' Councils had wielded racial loyalty as a weapon to enforce southern political unity during the 1950s, conservative white Memphians attacked white moderates in the late 1960s because they realized that a divided white electorate might lead to black political power. Once again, the types of attacks reveal gender anxieties underlying this political and racial struggle.[39]

White women who actively supported the strikers, or who had husbands who did, received the brunt of such attacks. Reverend Richard Moon, a white minister who went on a hunger strike outside Mayor Loeb's office after King's assassination, said that his wife received the most offensive calls. Both women and men "would express themselves in very vivid terms about how my wife had had sexual intercourse with blacks, . . . and that there were probably certain parts of her anatomy that were black," he later recalled. The sexual nature of this attack reveals the extent to which white male supremacy rested on control of white women's and black men's sexuality. Criticisms of Moon and Awsumb highlight the degree of gender and racial conformity expected of southern white women during this period of social upheaval.[40]

The role of black women in supporting the Memphis sanitation strike raised different questions about the city's social and economic relations than did the activities of white women. Many of the sanitation workers' wives and female supporters worked double shifts out of necessity before and during the strike. They cooked and cleaned for white families during the day and performed these chores again for their own families at night. For these women, the struggle for black equality was more than just a campaign to attain an equal footing with the white women for whom they worked. It was a fight for liberation from the double burden they bore because of their race and gender. While white women were learning from Betty Friedan about the "feminine mystique" and the stifling seclusion of the domestic sphere, black female domestics left their own domestic sphere only to enter another one in the white community. They faced an entirely different mystique from their white "sisters."[41]

During the 1968 school year, white teachers at St. Mary's Episcopal School for Girls in Memphis asked their students to write essays about their black maids. The girls' essays reveal how members of the white community learned the "proper" place for black women in southern society. One student said that Catherine, the black woman who worked in her house, was "very modern, but . . . still as loyal and kind as the old plantation mammies." She went on to thank "those Dutch traders that brought such a valuable commodity to America." This student recognized a difference between "modern" and "traditional" attitudes in black women, but still, it was telling that she viewed African Americans as "commodities" rather than people. Other students echoed these sentiments in their praise of "loyal maids" and criticism of "uppity" ones. One student saw that black maids could allow white women to break out of the role of homemaker. "I feel that a mother should not be required to stay at home because society feels it is good for her children," she said. "There are so many things that they have to do today that a maid can ease the burden." Questioning "traditional" gender roles for white women, this student completely accepted older roles for black servants. She recognized, without a hint of irony, that black women's labor played a key role in white women's liberation.[42]

Black women advocated civil rights because southern society tied their status to their race. They certainly recognized the broader implications of the sanitation workers' strike and their claims to manhood. Hazel McGhee had just finished a strike with other laundry workers in Memphis when her husband walked off the job at the sanitation department. One day, early in the sanitation strike, her husband called home from the union hall. He was not sure whether he could or should go on. "After I done been out seven months and two weeks, and he done went out and stayed a couple of days," if he had quit the strike, she said, "that would make me feel that he wasn't like the slogan, a *man*." Higher wages for black men meant the possibility of freedom from the double burden borne by black women. Black women supported the sanitation strikers' calls for manhood and higher wages because recognition of African American manhood would lead to recognition of African American humanity and broader freedom for both black men *and* women. Mrs. L. C. Reed, the wife of one of the strikers, summed up her view of the strike in yet another bitter critique Loeb's position: "He was telling them like some little child, like you tell a little child, 'Go on back to work, I'll give you some candy.' . . . You can't treat them like little children, you know, anybody. Mens are mens these days, no matter what color they are."[43]

As a mother and the executive secretary of the Memphis chapter of the NAACP, Maxine Smith also recognized the salience of gender roles in the sanitation strike. It was tough to raise a child while being active in the movement, but nothing was going to keep her from fighting for her rights and instilling the same passion for justice in her young son. When asked if she thought she had "failed" her child by taking him to demonstrations and "not teaching him to respect police," she grew irritated, saying, "I didn't have to teach him," because his "first confrontation with police was a very negative one." Like many mothers, Smith was expected to take care of her child before she joined the demonstrations, but she had other ideas of maternal responsibilities. These included ample doses of protest as well as loving care.[44]

Union and civil rights leaders knew that, without the assistance and participation of black women, their movement would have ground to a halt. Taylor Rogers, one of the sanitation workers, went to his family at the very beginning of the strike "to tell them what the situation was and what they might have to go through by me walking off the job." Rogers's family assured him, "Whatever help we can give, we'll work together and try to make things work." This support was crucial for everyone on strike, according to Rogers: "I guess all the other men talked with their families the same way and we just got together, and we decided to stand up and be men, and that's what we did." But this couldn't happen without the support of women from the community, who marched and attended the mass meetings just as frequently as men. The women's actions often spoke louder than the words of male leaders quoted in the daily papers. During one march to city hall, the leaders consciously placed the women in the front of the crowd as a shield. One minister remembered that "some of the men decided . . . , 'Well, they're not going to hurt the women, so put [them] out in front.'" These leaders borrowed this strategy from King's Birmingham campaign in which public opinion had swung against Bull Connor when he turned fire hoses on women and children. Conflict between armed male authorities and unarmed female protesters served SCLC well in news coverage of demonstrations in Birmingham, Memphis, and later Charleston. But women were not limited to silent roles in these civil rights campaigns. During a mass meeting toward the end of the strike, one observer noted, "In a large place like Mason Temple, women set up nuclei around the hall and sang their own variations on the sermon coming out of the loudspeakers."[45]

The continued mass meetings at Mason Temple, pressure from local merchants and federal officials, as well as the specter of King's assassination weighed heavily on Loeb and other city officials during the first half of the month of April. On April 16 city and union officials finally got together to formalize a strike settlement. The agreement included a fifteen-cent hourly wage increase, a "memorandum of understanding" concerning the existence of the union, dues checkoff, strictly merit-based promotion, and an end to racial discrimination in the work place. The union had not received official recognition as the sole bargaining agent for the workers, but the memorandum of understanding allowed both sides to exit the dispute claiming victory. Loeb believed that nothing had really changed in Memphis due to the sanitation strike, but strikers and their supporters felt differently. Local union official Robert Beasley proclaimed twenty years later, "I am a man; I guess that really did mean something. Didn't it?" SCLC staffer Hosea Williams elaborated on Beasley's statement, explaining that the strike altered the relationship between white and black men in Memphis. The goal at least was to replace paternalism with partnership. "White folks, and particularly white southerners, have addressed African-Americans as 'boy', and a boy is someone controlled by a parent," Williams said. "But a man is someone [who] makes his or her own decisions, . . . so what they were saying to the city [was] . . . 'We are no longer your children. We are men, and men make decisions for themselves.'" James Robinson, who worked in the Memphis public works department for thirty-three years, put it more simply. To him, "I *AM* a Man" meant that the sanitation workers just "weren't gonna take that shit no more."[46]

The strikers fought hard for recognition of their manhood and their union, but both struggles ended inconclusively. The struggles for human dignity and new definitions of manhood do not end in the tangible victories or defeats that are usually found in studies of civil rights and labor conflicts. Gender and racial identities are constantly being reconstructed and contested. The sanitation workers won higher wages and challenged the mayor's paternalism. For a time, their local, AFSCME 1733, became the largest single union in the city with almost 6,000 members, the vast majority of whom were black. And beyond the Memphis city limits, the strike, according to union official Bill Lucy, won "a new kind of respect and a new kind of recognition" for sanitation workers across the country. In short, the strikers gained pride and dignity — for themselves, for their families, and for working-class black men and women in Memphis and the rest of the nation. For over a year after the sanitation strike, black employees who attempting to organize other city departments in Memphis wore "I *AM* a Man" signs, and when African American auto workers in Michigan formed the Dodge Revolutionary Union Movement (DRUM) in 1968, they chanted:

> For hours and years with sweat and tears
> Trying to break our chain . . .
> We broke our backs and died in packs
> To find our manhood slain . . .
> But now we stand for DRUM's at hand
> To lead our freedom fight,
> And now til then we'll unite like men
> For now we know our might.[47]

The revolutionary fervor of DRUM was indicative of the radical path taken by both the labor and civil rights movements at the end of the 1960s and in the early 1970s. The self-proclaimed "vanguard" of this new revolution, the Black Panther Party, framed the terms of the debate more than any other movement organization. The Panthers and the radical white student groups that followed them down a revolutionary path used ideals of manhood to recruit new supporters, but they would eventually realize that this masculinist movement philosophy contained internal contradictions that could cripple their revolution.

> We shall have our manhood. We shall have it or the earth will be leveled by our attempt to gain it.
> — Eldridge Cleaver, *Soul on Ice* (1968)

Chapter Seven

"The Baddest Motherfuckers Ever to Set Foot Inside of History"

Three carloads of Black Panthers glided to a stop on the dimly lit Oakland street. Eldridge Cleaver, the party's minister of information, had ordered the lead car to pull over. Among the Panthers in the caravan that night was "Lil' Bobby" Hutton, age seventeen. Even though Hutton was young when he joined the party, the Panthers welcomed him because, according to party cofounder Bobby Seale, "Everyone from sixteen years of age and up was treated like a man. If he wasn't a man, he could get out of the Party." Hutton, who had been on many Panther patrols before the night he joined Cleaver's caravan, had undoubtedly proven himself worthy of Panther membership.[1]

There was a palpable tension in Oakland's black community that night. Two days earlier, on April 4, 1968, James Earl Ray had assassinated Martin Luther King Jr. in Memphis. The Panthers opposed King's philosophy of nonviolence, and they derided him for expecting anything other than "murder, brutality, degradation, and castration" from the white power structure. Despite their philosophical disagreements with King, party leaders were infuriated when Ray gunned down the civil rights leader in cold blood. Fearing that unfocused rioting and rebellion in the wake of King's death would only harm the black community, the Panthers publicly urged Oakland residents to remain calm, and the city escaped much of the violence that erupted in other urban areas immediately after the assassination. Privately, however, anger seethed in the Panther ranks as party leaders plotted a more focused retaliatory strike.[2]

After hearing of King's death, Cleaver wanted to "just go out and shoot up the town," but he cooled his heels until two days after the assassination when he joined several other Panthers in the night patrol. Though most Panther patrols were strictly defensive in nature, designed to check police brutality in black neighborhoods, the Panthers in the caravan on April 6 had a different agenda. "We basically went out to ambush the cops," Cleaver told an interviewer in the late 1980s, "but it was an aborted ambush, because the cops showed up too soon." Most of the Panthers in Cleaver's caravan, including Bobby Hutton, were armed. As the three Panther cars pulled over, a fourth car inched down the deserted street toward them. Suddenly, a bright beam of light trained on Cleaver, and a policeman's voice called from the darkness, "Hey, you, walk out into the middle of the street with your hands up, quick."[3]

In earlier speeches, Cleaver had goaded the police, saying, "We know you cowardly punks. You're not brave men. If you were brave men, if you were even a man, you would not be able to [brutalize our community]." But on this night Cleaver checked his bravado and complied with the policeman's order. Suddenly, as Cleaver moved past the front of his car, gunshots shattered the stillness of the night. Within minutes, police backup arrived on the scene. "Scatter! Let's get out of here," one of the Panthers yelled as they fled into the surrounding neighborhood. Cleaver jumped a fence and landed on Bobby Hutton in a tiny alleyway. Bullets streaked into the tight enclosure as the two slipped through a small window into a nearby basement. According to Cleaver, he could "taste death" on his tongue.[4]

The basement that had appeared to be a safe haven from the firefight above became a death trap in minutes. Police bullets and tear gas canisters ripped into the room. Armed with a rifle, Hutton returned fire as long as he could, but a police bullet eventually pierced Cleaver's leg and a gas canister hit him in the chest. As the building burst into flames, Cleaver and Hutton surrendered. Supporting the wounded Cleaver and choking from the tear gas, Hutton staggered out of the burning basement toward the police line. Two officers had been shot during the melee, and the police, who would later count 157 bullet holes in the first squad car on the scene, were enraged. Despite Cleaver's wounds, they ordered the two captured Panthers to run to the nearest police car. Hutton stumbled, and in an instant, he was dead, felled by the police officers' bullets.[5]

One year later, the Panther paper eulogized Hutton, arguing that his "manhood was accelerated" by his participation in the struggle. Hutton, the paper continued, had been "forced to do what those who call themselves men and act like Negroes would not do." In other words, he had earned his own manhood when he picked up the gun and aimed it at "The Man"—the cops and the white power structure. Bobby Hutton's tragic death transformed him into a martyr for the party cause, and in the eyes of many Panthers, he became a model for revolutionary manhood. Hutton had died trying to emulate his hero, Huey Newton, the cofounder of the Black Panther Party and a man whom Eldridge Cleaver dubbed "the baddest motherfucker ever to set foot inside of history."[6]

A history of masculinity in the civil rights movement, or any history of American manhood, would be incomplete without an analysis of the Black Panther Party. Like the Nation of Islam, the party made bold and explicit claims to manhood as the basis for its struggles against racial and economic oppression. Unlike their Muslim brothers, however, the Panthers did not subscribe to Elijah Muhammad's eccentric reading of Islam. The party's ideology was instead a mix of demands for self-determination and revolutionary international socialism. While their evolving ideology heightened race and class consciousness in America's inner cities, the most strident message from Panther leaders in the early years of the party was their clarion call for black males to stand up and "be men," to stand up and be revolutionaries.[7] The Panthers also influenced and won the support of white movement groups such as Students for a Democratic Society (SDS) and the Weather Underground, in part because of their emphasis on militancy, manhood, and armed self-defense. A masculinist liberation ideology helped the Panthers win recruits and allies, but it also spurred many men in the movement to use violence to prove their manhood rather than to further a progressive political agenda. The revolution that the Panthers envisioned never came to pass, but their models of manhood and radical activism remain among the most visible and controversial legacies of the civil rights movement.

In October 1966, Bobby Seale and Huey Newton worked in the North Oakland Anti-Poverty Center where they discussed the problems that faced the Bay Area's black community. Out of these discussions emerged a set of demands that became the Ten Point Platform for the Black Panther Party for Self-Defense. Among the platform's demands were full employment, decent housing, adequate education that included black history, exemptions for black men from military service, freedom for black prisoners, and an end to police brutality against minorities. Seale's wife and Newton's girlfriend typed the platform in the antipoverty center office, and the Black Panther Party was born.[8]

Newton and Seale wanted to attract both women and men to the party, but they were especially interested in recruiting young, working-class black men. Newton believed that a lack of employable skills and education made these men feel powerless to change their environment. He further argued that a young black man in this position often believes "that he is something less than a man, as is evident in his conversation: the white man is 'THE MAN,' he gets everything and he knows everything." Newton understood this as a sarcastic term intended to mock what white men felt was their exclusive prerogative over power and masculinity, but he also knew that the term cut both ways, reminding young black men that they often *were* less powerful than "THE MAN" that they ridiculed. Newton and Seale hoped to serve as role models and organizers for young men who had been frustrated by, rather than included in, the earlier civil rights movement. They wanted to show young black men in America's inner cities that they too could be "THE MAN," that they too could have power.[9]

The cofounders of the Black Panther Party for Self-Defense were themselves members of Oakland's black working class. Newton and Seale were both born in the South, but their families had migrated to California in search of job opportunities and freedom from harsh racial repression. Neither of these things was easy to come by in Oakland during the 1950s and 1960s. Growing up "on the block" was a struggle for Newton, who was relatively light skinned and slight of build with boyish good looks. As a teenager, Huey and his friends would wrap their hands in towels and box each other for sport. "Fighting has always been a big part of my life, as it is in the lives of most poor people," Newton recalled in his autobiography. "I was too young to realize that we were really trying to affirm our masculinity and dignity using force in reaction to social pressures extended against us." With few good job prospects, Newton decided to try college, despite the fact that a high school guidance counselor had told him that he would never make it. At Oakland's Merritt College, Newton met party cofounder Bobby Seale, who had similarly struggled to find his way as a young man, working odd jobs as a carpenter, comedian, and drummer after serving in the air force. Newton and Seale understood the problems of Oakland's black community because they had seen these problems firsthand. When they organized the Panthers, the two men began by addressing the immediate concerns of their community, starting with police brutality.[10]

Despite police efforts to recruit minorities in the Bay Area, African Americans accounted for less than three percent of the Oakland force in 1966, and many of the white officers had reputations for using derogatory language and unnecessary

"THE BADDEST MOTHERFUCKERS"

force against black residents. The Panthers first garnered support in the Oakland black community when they began following police officers on their patrols to ensure that they did not brutalize African American residents. When they observed police patrols, the Panthers displayed their weapons openly in accordance with California law. During one patrol of an Oakland neighborhood, a police officer questioned Newton about the weapon he was carrying. Newton, who had studied the California gun laws, turned the question back to the white officer and asked him what gave him the right to carry his gun in the black community. "Who in the hell do you think you are," the officer demanded of Newton. "Who in the hell do you think *you* are?" Newton replied, dropping a round into the chamber of his gun for emphasis. By this point, a crowd of onlookers had gathered. Newton told them to watch and make sure that the police did not retaliate against the Panthers. The white police officers backed away slowly and left the neighborhood.[11]

These demonstrations against police brutality attracted recruits and local publicity for the party, but the Panthers gained national notoriety when they marched into the California State Assembly in May 1967 to protest a gun control bill that would have curtailed their police patrols. Reporters, who were covering an appearance by Governor Ronald Reagan at the Capitol, swarmed around the Panthers. Cameras clicked and whirred as the armed Panthers stood in steely silence while Seale issued the first official party statement. Seale told onlookers to take note that the "racist California Legislature" was attempting to keep black people "disarmed and powerless," and he called for African Americans to "arm themselves against terror before it's too late."[12]

Six women and twenty-four men took part in the Sacramento demonstration, but media coverage invariably focused on the men. Photos of Seale, Bobby Hutton, and other Panther men in their black berets, leather jackets, and dark sun glasses made good copy for newspapers across the country. This emphasis on black men with guns, as terrifying and tantalizing as it was to media moguls, was not merely a construction of white journalists. The Panthers consciously wielded this image as an organizing tool. Eldridge Cleaver, a writer, ex-convict, and former Muslim who had joined the party earlier in 1967, told one interviewer, "For the young black male, the Black Panther Party supplies very badly needed standards of manhood." As one of the party's most articulate spokespeople, Cleaver did much to fashion the party's image of manhood, but he was not alone in highlighting this aspect of the Panthers appeal. Sonia Sanchez, an African American poet teaching classes at San Francisco State College in the late 1960s, compared the Panthers' assertions of manhood to sentiments expressed by Malcolm X.

"The Panther Party was probably a manifestation of Malcolm on many levels," she observed, because it "gave a sense of 'We are men and not boys . . . Don't call us boys. Call us young men.'"[13]

As the party grew beyond the Bay Area, this gendered aspect of its image continued to be a powerful drawing card for new recruits, both men and women. One of the first branches of the party outside of Oakland sprang up in Los Angeles amidst the smoldering embers of Watts. Alprentice "Bunchy" Carter, Eldridge Cleaver's prison mate in the early 1960s and also a follower of Malcolm X, founded the party chapter in Los Angeles. "The Man is a beast," Carter told Panther recruits in southern California, "and he is armed against us. The only thing that will deal with the Man is the gun, and men who are willing to use the gun." Elaine Brown, who eventually became a party leader after her initial recruitment in the Los Angeles chapter, was blown away by the strength, self-confidence, and radical ideas embodied by Carter and the Panthers. "Here were men who were saying, 'Listen, we are willing to take charge of our lives. We are willing to stand up,'" Brown later said, explaining what drew her to the party. "It was the appeal that Malcolm had in many ways, [an] appeal to my psyche and my emotional need to say, 'Yes, there were men in this world — black men — who cared about the community, wanted to do something and were willing to take it to the last degree.'" Brown was one of the few early recruits, however, as the Los Angeles chapter grew very slowly until a confrontation with the police in northern California gave the party a central cause to rally behind. In October 1967 a shootout between Panther leader Huey Newton and members of the Oakland police department left Newton wounded and one police officer dead. The death of Officer John Frey resulted in a series of trials that sent Newton to jail but offered the Panthers a wide forum for critiquing racism in the American criminal justice system and organizing black militants. At a speech shortly after Newton's arrest, Carter urged African Americans in Los Angeles to join the Panthers and follow Newton because he has "shown us that we too must deal with the pig [police] if we are to call ourselves men."[14]

Before Newton went to prison in 1967, fewer than fifty men and women worked for the party's two chapters in Oakland and Los Angeles. When Newton emerged from prison in 1970, there were over thirty Panther chapters across the country with about five thousand members who sold approximately 125,000 copies of the *Black Panther* newspaper per week and operated community service programs that reached thousands more. The Panthers' newspaper and community service initiatives such as the Free Breakfast Program, which provided hot meals for poor children before school each day, became the bread and butter outreach of the party. Panthers did not just theorize about a revolution that would help the poor; they actually worked to improve the lives of the poor every day. This garnered respect and recruits for the party in black communities across the country. Much of the explosion of membership was due to the organizing skills of Chief of Staff David Hilliard, the publicity generated by Eldridge Cleaver and Bobby Seale, and the hard work of thousands of grassroots activists, women and men. Yet the Panther's public campaign focused on Newton and the image of a strong black man waging a lonely struggle against a racist system.[15]

Among Panther leaders, Cleaver most eloquently lionized Newton and codi-fied the gender ideology of the party in his writing and speeches. Before Newton went to jail, Cleaver had him pose for a photograph in full Panther uniform with a shotgun in one hand, a spear in the other, and African shields lying at his feet. Few pictures better captured the warrior pose and militant masculinity embod-ied in the carefully constructed Panther image. Though Newton claimed to find the photo embarrassing, the massive popularity of the "Free Huey" campaign en-sured that this poster was plastered on the walls of radical students' dorm rooms and Panther offices all over the country. This was the period when Cleaver called Newton "the baddest motherfucker ever to set foot inside of history," arguing that Newton "had set a standard of what it means to be a man" in his shootout with the police.[16]

Such claims rested on a masculinist liberation ideology explicated most fully in Cleaver's collection of prison essays entitled *Soul on Ice*. Published in February 1968, *Soul on Ice* sought to explain how racism split gender identities, creating schizophrenic racial types of manhood and womanhood. According to Cleaver, black and white men were "supermasculine menials" and "omnipotent adminis-trators" respectively, while black and white women were "Amazons" and "ultra feminines." In other words, men and women of both races were constantly striv-ing for the "true" manhood and womanhood that their racial opposites appeared to embody. Cleaver believed, for example, that white women envied black wom-en's strength, while black women longed to be "feminine," closer to the Ameri-can racist standards of beauty embodied by white women. As a former Muslim, Cleaver had made this argument before, but his analysis of race and masculinity in *Soul on Ice* was more original and complicated. White male "omnipotent ad-ministrators," he argued, had disassociated themselves from the physical body, relegating this (and most menial labor) to black men, while seeking to retain sole custody of cognition and intellect. This perceived loss of physicality bred insecurity in the white male psyche just as the restricted access to education (and professional positions) handicapped the black male psyche. Because white men had power, they compensated for their feelings of insecurity by controlling black male bodies. White men became the ultimate arbiters of sexuality by denying black men access to white women and white women access to black men, while placing few societal restrictions on their own relations with black women.[17]

In *Soul on Ice*, Cleaver admitted with regret that as a younger man he had used rape as an "insurrectionary act" in a twisted revolt against this gender and sexual hierarchy. But by the late 1960s, he understood that there were different paths to manhood for "supermasculine menial" men. For these men, Cleaver explained, revolutionary violence appeared to be the only recourse. "Self-conscious black men curse their own cowardice," he wrote, "and [they] stare at their rifles . . . laid out on tables before them trembling as they wish for the manly impulse to . . . send them screaming mad into the streets shooting from the hip." Influenced by the psychologist Frantz Fanon, Cleaver hoped that the party could harness this rebellious impulse as it had been used in the Algerian revolution. Fanon, an Algerian who studied psychology in Paris, had returned to his native country to counsel men involved in the anticolonial uprising against the French. Fanon's psychological case studies, subsequently published in *The Wretched of the Earth*, revealed that anticolonial rebellion had a cathartic effect on men in a colonized country, many of whom had internalized an inferiority complex as a result of racist colonial propaganda. Cleaver cited Fanon's work to show that African men had been able "to achieve their manhood" through revolutionary violence, and he used such psychological theories to explain how the Panthers' claims to manhood could channel the frustrations of working-class black men into a movement for revolutionary social change. Unlike the earlier civil rights movement, when armed self-defense had been just one alternative to nonviolent direct action, in the latter stages of the movement many young militants would come to view armed struggle as the only effective means of confronting the white power structure.[18]

From jail, Newton articulated an intellectual side of the struggle for man-hood based on Cleaver's theories. Newton critiqued the use of the term "the Man" to refer to white men in positions of power because, he argued, this epithet implicitly denied nonwhite manhood. This was why the Panthers referred to police officers as "pigs," to show that they were "less than a man." Newton also understood that political education was necessary to add substance and depth to the claims of Panther manhood. The intellectual aspects of party training that he instituted allowed the Panthers to "regain their mind and their manhood."[19]

The party leadership took Newton's proclamations to heart, requiring regular political education classes in all branches. According to one Panther who joined around 1968, these classes attracted "people who were much more oriented to-

The militant manhood embodied by the Black Panther Party is captured in this 1968 photograph of Captain George "Baby D" Gaines (fifth from right, with the beard) and several Panther recruits undergoing weapons training in Marin City, California. Courtesy of Pirkle Jones.

ward reading and studying and understanding revolution, as opposed to just being angry and mad." At first, the political education classes focused on an understanding of the Ten Point Platform, but as the party grew, discussions expanded to include *The Autobiography of Malcolm X*, Mao Zedong's treatise on Chinese communism, and Fanon's *The Wretched of the Earth*. These books mirrored a shift in the Panther's political ideology from black nationalism to international socialism as the Panthers began to view themselves as allies of anti-colonial revolutionaries around the world. This internationalism inspired a more elaborate analysis of domestic power relations, which sprang from the Panthers' original protest against police brutality. Panther classes taught that police entered the black community only to protect private property, not to protect and serve the people. Socialism, party ideologues argued, would not only achieve equality by eliminating private property, it would also end oppressive police brutality. Armed with the strategy of self-defense, the ideal of revolutionary manhood, and an emerging socialist ideology, the Panthers hoped to radicalize the working class, especially working-class black men.[20]

If the addition of new recruits had been the only result of the Panthers' masculinist liberation ideology, the movement might have advanced unhindered. But the ideals of manhood espoused by Cleaver and other Black Power leaders had serious negative implications for men who did not fit his model and also for women, who, unsurprisingly, had difficulty achieving ideals of manhood in any form. Cleaver's vision of "true" manhood, for example, could never include gay men because he viewed homosexuality as a "sickness" akin to "baby rape." Though he claimed to be friends with fellow writer and civil rights activist James Baldwin, Cleaver thought that Baldwin, being gay, should keep quiet about his sexuality. Homosexuality, Cleaver argued, was "not something [Baldwin] should be projecting out as a model for black manhood." Other Black Power pundits hammered away at similar themes. Amiri Baraka, an intellectual leader of the Black Power movement, argued that straight black men were the only true men in American society, because "most white men are trained to be fags. For this reason it is no wonder their faces are weak and blank . . . [with] those silky blue faggot eyes."[21]

Homophobia became one of the chief weapons wielded by movement partici-pants during the Black Power era even though gay men had played crucial roles earlier in the struggle. In the first half of the 1960s, the movement benefited from the participation and leadership of many activists who also happened to be gay, men like James Baldwin, Aaron Henry, Al Lowenstein, and Bayard Rustin. This is not to say that the earlier movement was free from homophobia or that sexuality did not affect the ability of these men to participate. Many gay movement activ-ists downplayed or denied their sexuality for fear of the negative consequences for personal and professional relationships. Such fears were not unfounded. Rustin, for example, had to resign from the Fellowship of Reconciliation after a convic-tion on "morals charges" stemming from an arrest for homosexual activity in the early 1950s, and his relationship with Martin Luther King's SCLC was strained, in part, because many of the ministers viewed Rustin's homosexuality as a sin and a public relations liability. Yet King supported Rustin as a director of the March on Washington in 1963, just as SNCC stood by Aaron Henry after his arrest for "sexual perversion" in Mississippi, and these men made invaluable contributions to the movement in the first half of the 1960s.[22]

By contrast, the masculinist liberation ideologies that guided many movement groups in the second half of the decade encouraged antigay rhetoric and senti-ment. From 1966–1970, the Panthers and other militant groups flung a stream of homophobic epithets against their opponents and the politically apathetic. Party leaders ridiculed conservative whites and black moderates alike as "sissies" and "punks," and they derided the police as "faggots" and "whores." Though many

Panthers brandished heterosexism in this way, Cleaver was the most outspoken proponent of this tactic. When Governor Ronald Reagan barred him from teaching at the University of California at Berkeley, Cleaver called Reagan a punk, a sissy, and a "dickless motherfucker" before challenging him to several duels. Luckily for the future president, Cleaver never got "satisfaction." Though the Panthers did not explicitly exclude gay men from their ranks in the late 1960s, such strident statements fostered intense homophobia in Panther offices and black communities across the country. In attempting to refashion a powerful identity for black men, the Panthers accepted negative stereotypes of gay men as "weak," and they used homophobia to seal chinks in the armor of their manly image.[23]

The Panthers' ideas about manhood similarly complicated gender relations in the party. From the beginning, party leaders had recruited both men and women. The image of strength and confidence projected by male Panther leaders had a powerful, sensual appeal for many female recruits. Though this was by no means the only reason that women joined the party, it did not hurt recruitment. Once they entered the party, female recruits, like their male counterparts, learned to handle weapons at the same time they studied revolutionary theory. Panther leaders understood that the ever-present threat of conflict with the police made it prudent to train both men and women in self-defense. As one woman remembered, "We learned to clean and break down guns. . . . I was good, too. I got up to marksman level. In the Party, men and women pretty much got the same training." Despite this training and an official position that "there are no sexual roles in the Black Panther Party," Panther men often relegated women to administrative positions, occasionally dubbing them "Pantherettes." The traditional ideals of manhood espoused by the Panthers in the early years of the organization required that women submit to the dictates of men who dominated the party's leadership positions at that time. The national leadership position garnered by Kathleen Cleaver was the exception that proved this rule since she was also the wife of the Minister of Information. As she later explained, the traditional gender breakdown in the party ironically reflected white male power in the dominant culture that the Panthers struggled against. "Black men were seeking to be more assertive and more in control. Self-determination, Black Power, community empowerment all mean black men are not submissive to the dominant white man, or to the police," Cleaver said. In that situation, she concluded, "It's very tricky to create something that's not totally male dominated."[24]

The primary ideal for women in the party during this period was as revolutionary mothers and helpmates for men. Elaine Brown remembers that in southern California, the women separated from the male Panthers to learn about their

Women in the Black Panther Party received similar training to that of men, though they were not always treated as equals, especially in the party's early years. This Panther recruit attends a 1968 weapons training class in Marin City, California. Courtesy of Pirkle Jones.

special role in the party. "Our gender was but another weapon, another tool of the revolution," she writes. Women in the party "had the task of producing children, progeny of the revolution." Writing in the *Black Panther* in 1968, another Panther captured the dual, often contradictory role of women in the party as both "military" and "domestic." "As women, we are expected to be by our men's sides, gun in hand to help them carry on," she wrote, but then added that, "we MUST reproduce warriors so that there will be future generations to carry on the revolution, [and do] household duties, such as cleaning, caring for family, sewing, and cooking, etc." Though this was a very traditional breakdown of gender roles, one that women in the party would later challenge, the role of militant motherhood was one of the party's positive legacies for the next generation. Many of the Panther women did have babies by Panther men, and a few of these children of the revolution followed in their parents' footsteps, keeping militant attitudes alive in a succeeding generation that would be better known for its apathy than activism.[25]

As revolutionary mothers, Panther women were often sexual partners with Panther men. The ideals of revolutionary manhood and free love that reigned in the late 1960s had both liberating and deleterious effects on sexual relations in the party. In theory, having multiple sexual partners avoided the chauvinistic aspects of "ownership" that traditional monogamy often entailed. However, as the Panthers and other movement groups soon learned, chauvinism was not as easily "smashed" as monogamy. Masai Hewitt remembered that Panther men often took advantage of women recruits, transferring them from office to office to satiate the sexual appetites of party leaders. According to Hewitt, a typical male Panther attitude in the early years was: "'I'm a black king or prince . . . and as a king, I've got a right to as many queens as I want.'" When women first challenged this system, men denounced them, saying, "'Comrade Sister, you're doing the same thing to me that the white man does. You're fucking with my manhood.'"[26]

Far from seeing women as objects of sexual exploitation, Eldridge Cleaver argued that they could and should wield their sexuality as a revolutionary weapon. He shocked audiences by advocating what he referred to as "Pussy Power," exhorting women to leave any man unwilling to join the revolution. "Until he [is] ready to pick up a gun and be a man, don't give him no sugar," Cleaver said. "I don't know how you can stand to have them faggots layin' and suckin' on you. You can always get a real man." As the historian Tracye Matthews observes, Cleaver was treating Panther women's sexuality as a commodity "to be exchanged in service of the revolution." But even if women might have been able to use their sexuality in this way with men outside the party, Hewitt and others suggest that they could rarely assert such "power" with male party leaders.[27]

The rigid gender hierarchy within the party did at times alienate the Panthers from potential allies, but because chauvinism also existed in the predominantly white movement groups, there was initially little resistance to Panther machismo. The antiwar movement, in fact, exhibited similar tendencies in treating women as sexual commodities, urging female war resisters to play their part with the slogan, "Girls Say Yes to Men Who Say No." For a variety of reasons, the antiwar movement proved to be the strongest nexus between the Black Panthers and white movement organizations such as SDS and, later, the Weathermen. The Panthers' masculinist organizing strategy offered militant alternatives for men who were against the war. In antiwar coalitions, the Panthers contributed unique insights into the plight of black GIs and draftees, and they greatly influenced white movement groups that were dealing with similar issues of gender and sexuality.[28]

Many of the Panthers, including cofounder Bobby Seale, were veterans themselves, and they understood why a disproportionately high number of black men were serving and dying in Vietnam. Though Moynihan's recruitment recommendations and programs like Project 100,000 did not help matters, these were not the primary reasons why more black men served in the war. The draft netted more men from impoverished minority backgrounds because these men were less likely to get educational or professional deferments than their wealthy white counterparts. And even if a young black man in this position escaped the draft, he might still be more likely to enlist for the steady pay. During the mid-1960s, when African American unemployment was twice as high as white unemployment, the military offered a quick solution to the economic problems of young, unskilled black men. In conjunction with this economic rationale for enlistment was a psychological motive that the U.S. Army consciously appealed to in its recruiting campaigns. "I passed this recruiting station, and saw in the window a sign that said, 'JOIN THE ARMY AND BE A MAN,'" remembered one black ex-Marine. "For some goddamned reason," he continued, "I believed that the U.S.M.C. made a man out of anybody. And I wanted to be a MAN more than anything in this whole goddamned world." As a veteran, Seale spoke directly to these men in his speeches against the war, challenging the pathway to manhood espoused by Moynihan and the army. "You went into the service for the same reason I [did]," he told them, "'cause it wasn't no jobs. . . . And you feel you'd go into the army and some guy'd sell you some insidious notion about being a man, and all that kind of crap. And you were already a man. . . . [G]oing out trying to prove how many colored peoples you can kill in a foreign land. That's not being a man; that's being a fascist." Because the Panthers used manhood as a recruiting tool in much the same way the armed forces did, they understood the appeal. Seale and other Panthers offered their own ideals of revolutionary masculinity as an alternative to the rite of passage promised by U.S. Army recruiters. In so doing, they forged alliances with white radicals also interested in stopping American involvement in Vietnam, alliances that had an important impact on the direction of the wider movement.[29]

Unlike many militant black nationalist groups founded in the late 1960s such as Ron Karenga's organization "US" that shunned coalitions with white movement groups, the Panthers had been open to interracial alliances almost from the beginning. They first worked with the predominantly white Peace and Freedom Party (PFP), which ran antiwar candidates in the elections of 1968. Eldridge Cleaver became the PFP candidate for president that year. Stokely Carmichael, the former head of SNCC who had briefly joined the Panthers himself, and other black nationalist leaders criticized the Panthers for working so closely with white antiwar activists during an era when Black Power had come to mean black independence for many and separatism for others. The Panthers argued that the alliance was based on pragmatism not dependence, because they believed that coalitions were necessary for a successful movement. The party also formed alliances with Mexican American radicals in the Brown Berets, Puerto Rican militants in the Young Lords, Chinese Americans in the Red Guard, Native Americans in the American Indian Movement, and young working-class white radicals in the Patriots. These alliances deeply impressed a generation of white radical students who were also struggling to form an interracial mass movement based on revolutionary consciousness.[30]

Radical white activists respected the Panthers and supported the Free Huey campaign as a continuation of the civil rights movement's fight against racism. They also struggled to keep up with the radicalization of black movement groups like the Panthers. White movement activists accepted self-defense and violence as viable forms of dissent, in part, to earn the respect of black militants. Todd Gitlin, the former president of SDS, remembers that after one antiwar demonstration that ended in violence, he was overjoyed to hear that some black activists were saying, "OK boys, you've become men. Now, we're ready to talk." Willingness to withstand and, eventually, commit violence in support of the revolution became a badge of "authenticity" among white radicals in much the same way that it became proof of manhood among the Black Panthers. The first time the white movement exhibited such violent militancy en masse occurred in response to police repression during the 1968 Democratic National Convention in Chicago. Though women were involved, Gitlin believed that "men outnumbered women in the Chicago street actions by eight or ten to one." Turning a critical eye on his peers' willingness to use violence, he wrote, "We are living through some profound crisis of masculinity, explained but not wholly justified by the struggle to shake off middle class burdens of bland civility."[31]

While SDS made tentative steps in this direction, its more radical successor, the Weather Underground, jettisoned an allegiance to civility and nonviolence in its attempts to join the Panthers in the revolutionary vanguard. A former member of this group, David Gilbert, reached this point in 1969 when he "turned to armed struggle because the Panthers were being killed, and . . . you could no longer just limit yourself to protest." Acknowledging that a willingness to use violence was a difficult psychological leap for some activists, the Weather Underground used the "gut check" to prepare members for violent action. According to Gilbert, this came out of a "macho culture," which asked, "Are you man enough to stick your head in the lion's den?" Like the Panthers, the Weather Underground welcomed women, but their violent protest thrived on a language and culture of masculinity.[32]

In fact, the white student movement also exhibited the gender and sexual discrimination that plagued the Panthers. Despite its strong adherence to participatory democracy, the white student movement was, from the outset, "highly male-dominated," with many leadership positions and intellectual assignments automatically going to men. Like the Panthers, white movement groups experienced both the liberating and exploitative aspects of free love. For, as David Gilbert explains, "within a structure where there was still male dominance, [free love] meant making women more sexually available for men." The personal politics of sexuality hurt gay men in white student groups as well. Gregory Calvert, who worked with SDS throughout much of the 1960s, was afraid to come out to his peers, and when he finally did, he "got nothing but the most negative kinds of reactions," including gay baiting by other national officers.[33]

Few gay activists raised these issues in white movement organizations until after the Stonewall demonstrations in 1969, but women's liberation became an issue as early as 1965. Movement veterans have recently begun to revise scholarly accounts of the origins of feminist consciousness in the movement. While not denying the chauvinism that existed, these activists argue that scholars have failed to acknowledge the attempts of many movement men to deal with sexism in a more progressive way than men in the wider society. But despite the efforts of both male and female movement feminists, serious discussions and critiques of chauvinism would not be widely addressed until the end of the 1960s. It was then that several of the Panthers began to take a critical look at the masculinist liberation ideology that had guided the group since its inception in 1966.[34]

By 1969 many female Panthers were beginning to chafe at obeisance to revolutionary manhood, though they continued to feel divided racial and gender loyalties. For some, women's liberation had always been a "white girl's thing," not only because their loyalty to the movement kept them focused on the fight against racism, but also because early on, white feminists had difficulty integrating the unique demands of black women into the burgeoning movement. Elaine Brown was one of these women, who, rather than criticizing the Panther's rhetoric of manhood, actively supported it. In the official party anthem, which she wrote and sang, Brown urged young black militants, "We just have to get guns and be men." Others were more critical of the Panthers' masculinist ideology and resulting traditional gender roles. "We would like to be regarded as PANTHERS," June Culberson wrote from southern California in May 1969, "not females (Pantherettes), just Panthers." Culberson and other Panther feminists revised the party's ideal of "revolutionary motherhood" by demanding true equality with Panther men. It was time, these women argued, to crush sexism as well as racism. While they understood that black men were struggling to regain dignity and manhood, they wanted the men to "understand that their manhood is not dependent on keeping their black women subordinate."[35]

Recognizing the problem of sexism and sexual exploitation in the party, male leaders finally began to respond to these internal criticisms in 1969. Eldridge Cleaver asked his comrades to "purge our ranks and our hearts" of chauvinism, though he did not acknowledge that his own ideals of revolutionary manhood had contributed to the problem. Some men in the party had stood against such chauvinism from the beginning. Assata Shakur, a member of the party in New York, wrote lovingly about a fellow Panther named Zayd who "refused to become part of the macho cult that was an official body in the Black Panther Party." Though he was the minister of information for the Bronx chapter, he was often the first person to volunteer to cook dinner, wash dishes, or do other domestic chores. "Zayd had always treated me and all the other sisters with respect," Shakur wrote in her memoir. "I knew this had to be especially hard for him because he was small and his masculinity was always being challenged in some way by the more backward, muscle-headed men in the Party." To support men like Zayd and address gender tensions in the party, the national leadership sent Don Cox and

Masai Hewitt to eradicate "sexual fascism" in local offices across the country by speaking to the men of each chapter about the Panthers' official stance against sexism.[36]

In addition to his efforts in the campaign against sexism, Don Cox also embarked on a fundraising campaign in 1969 that brought the Panthers much needed money but also biting criticism. The writer and journalist Tom Wolfe described one of these fundraising parties in his book *Radical Chic and Mau-Mauing the Flak Catchers*. With his caustic wit, Wolfe caricatured the tough Black Panther emissaries who drummed up support from effete, white socialites while munching on expensive hors d'oeuvres in penthouse apartments high above New York's Park Avenue. In part, Wolfe was critiquing (and the Panthers were skillfully manipulating) white liberal guilt that pried open the wallets and pocketbooks of many would-be philanthropists. Yet Wolfe also addressed the image of militant manhood that the Panthers cultivated to distance themselves from older civil rights leaders and to prove that they were truly radical. "These are no civil rights *Negroes* wearing gray suits three sizes too big," one female guest supposedly gushed at the fundraising event Wolfe observed; "these are *real men*!" According to Wolfe, the Panther machismo and revolutionary rhetoric that won support from these socialites was nothing more than "radical chic," a passing fad. Financial support from such circles dried up quickly in the wake of Wolfe's exposé.[37]

Wolfe also argued that the radical chic of the Panther image served as a model for other young minority men who wanted to "mau-mau" guilty white liberals into giving them funds. The term came from the name of the revolutionary force that overthrew British colonialism in Kenya, but in Wolfe's hands it became a euphemism for "pseudo-revolutionaries" in America, who had found that educated white men had "a deep dark Tarzan mumbo jungle voodoo fear of the black man's masculinity." Wolfe's white male characters looked suspiciously like Cleaver's "omnipotent administrators." These men may have appeared weak, but they were really "flak catchers" for the establishment. "Why do so many bureaucrats, deans, preachers, and college presidents, try to smile when the mau-mauing starts?" Wolfe asked rhetorically. "When some bad dude is challenging your manhood, your smile just proves that he is right and you are chicken shit—unless you are a bad man yourself with so much heart that you can make that smile say, 'Just keep on talking, sucker, because I'm going to count to ten and then *squash* you.'" *Radical Chic* was a response to the masculinist liberation strategies espoused by the Panthers and other groups, a primer on how to deal with angry revolutionaries which implied that all white men in the establishment had to do was call the bluff of militant young men and then reassert their authority once the storm of protest had passed.[38]

White men in positions of power did occasionally respond in this way when confronted by the Panthers. William J. McGill, who was the chancellor of the University of California at San Diego in the late 1960s remembered that withstanding a Panther-inspired student revolt was one of the pivotal moments in his life. As racial tensions at UCSD heated up in 1968, Chancellor McGill passed out in his office due to the stress. Within days of McGill's panic attack, Cleaver spoke on campus, rallying the students to organize a general strike. McGill agreed to address a mass meeting of protesting students even though he was "stricken with anxiety." As he walked through the center of the crowd assembled on the campus commons, he was "immediately embroiled in an argument with black students, with radicals, with kids." The debate lasted for several hours, and when it was over, McGill realized that he had escaped from the protest relatively unscathed. He returned home, took off his figurative flak jacket, and had a drink with his wife. In hindsight, he realized that the demonstrations were merely "a kind of political theater," so "the next morning, I refused to debate them. I said they were violating the rules of the campus." For the Black Panthers and other militant organizations in the late 1960s, this was a danger. Performances of militant masculinity, or what some dubbed "guerilla theater," were often ignored by The Man, because bluster and bravado bounced off even the flimsiest of establishment flak jackets.[39]

Previous critics of Panther machismo have been content to rest with this as their final assessment of the party. Michele Wallace, who focused on the party's "black macho" attitudes, implied that this masculinist rhetoric and posturing hid a lack of substantive programs. But her critique ignores much of the party's grassroots political activism and willingness to address issues of sexism and homophobia within the organization. Even as the Panther leaders preached about revolutionary manhood, they also instituted Survival Programs that served as a new model of activism for thousands of black youths. Newspapers that printed photos of bold Panther men with guns rarely published images of these same Panthers in aprons serving eggs and bacon to hungry kids before school. When the mainstream white press did cover the breakfast programs, reporters often condemned them as indoctrination because the Panthers used the programs to teach children about collective community uplift and socialism. "What you call indoctrination," David Hilliard replied to one such critic, "we call education." Begun in Oakland in 1968, versions of the Panthers' free breakfast program sprang up in urban centers from Seattle, Washington, to Greensboro, North Carolina. By

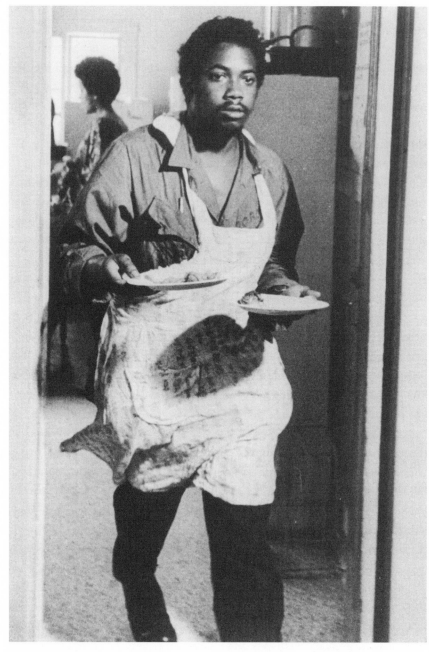

Photographs of Panther men in leather jackets and sunglasses, shouldering shotguns, made good copy for the news media. But mainstream papers rarely published images of these same men in aprons feeding hungry children before school. Here, Charles Bursey works in the Black Panthers' breakfast program at St. Augustine's Episcopal Church in Oakland, California. Courtesy of Pirkle Jones.

late 1969, party officials estimated that local projects provided free breakfast to over 30,000 children a week. In addition to the free breakfast program, party members constructed and staffed free health clinics, sickle cell anemia testing centers, liberation schools, and free busing programs for prisoners' families.[40]

Survival Programs such as the one that provided transportation for families to visit relatives in prison came directly out of the Panthers' own experience with the criminal justice system and understanding of the needs of the black community. In 1970 Huey Newton was only the most famous black prisoner locked behind the bars of an American penal system in which over 50 percent of the inmates were African Americans, the vast majority of whom were young men. After the FBI director, J. Edgar Hoover, dubbed the Panthers the "greatest threat to the internal security of the country" in September 1968, local police and federal law enforcement officials launched concerted attacks on party offices across the country. As FBI files and Panther records show, police harassment of the party was unrelenting. Between March 1968 and January 1970, the police arrested party members more than 650 times on charges ranging from murder to spitting on the sidewalk. For Panther leaders, these arrests led to high profile trials in New York, California, Connecticut, and Illinois, but for the rank and file, arrests often led to prolonged jail time. Ultimately, this concerted attack on the Panthers by federal, state, and local law enforcement agencies would destroy the organization, but in the short run, it linked the party to a population of young black men in prisons who were very receptive to the group's ideology. Like the Black Muslims before them, the Panthers garnered many recruits among inmates with whom their platform to free all political prisoners was widely popular. The Panthers' ideas of revolutionary manhood also spoke to the concerns of black inmates who lived in an entirely masculine world.[41]

By far the most famous inmate recruited by the Panthers was a young man named George Jackson, whose letters and essays written from California prisons became the widely read *Soledad Brother.* Accused and convicted of stealing seventy dollars from a gas station in 1960 at the age of eighteen, Jackson received a one-year-to-life sentence. Jackson's book and his letters to Newton articulate the rage that young black men felt due to the racism that pervaded the criminal justice system. Another dominant theme of the prison letters was anger toward black women for stifling men as a way of protecting them from this racism. One letter that Jackson wrote to his mother in the spring of 1965 — coincidentally, the same time that Daniel Moynihan penned his report on matriarchy in the Negro family — hammers away at her for undermining the masculinity of the men in her family. "You have always had the run of things. You have done father a disservice. You are doing [my brother] Jon a disservice now," Jackson wrote. "This is a man's world. The real world calls for a predatory man's way of thinking. . . . [How could] any of the men of our kind accomplish what we must as men if we think like bourgeoisie women, or let our women think for us?" As Jackson corresponded with Newton and Angela Davis, an ardent advocate of prisoners' rights and a radical political activist, he shifted the target of his angry eloquence. Black women's attempts to protect their husbands and sons, he soon came to realize, were symptomatic of larger problems with racism. Undoubtedly influenced by Davis, Jackson eventually linked the masculinist ideology that had initially attracted him to the Panthers with a broader socialist critique of race, class, and gender in America. By the end of the 1960s, he argued that racism and capitalism together "emasculated" working-class black men. Jackson's letters from this later period reflected a pride in black manhood rather than animosity towards women. Black men, he wrote, "have walked the path of disparity, of regression, of abortion, and yet come out whole. There will be a special page in the book of life for [these] men" that "will tell of utter defeat, ruin, passivity, and subjection in one breath, and in the next, overwhelming victory and fulfillment."[42]

George Jackson never emerged from the prison in which he penned these words because he died in an inmate uprising in 1971, but Newton attended Jackson's memorial service and delivered the eulogy as a free man. He had been released from prison on August 5, 1970, to the cheers of thousands who had helped make the Free Huey campaign a success. That sunny summer day, Newton jumped atop a waiting car to thank the people, his shirt off, his muscles chiseled from years of prison exercise. Newton had honed his mind as well as his body in prison, evolving politically, as had the party during his incarceration. In the first few years of the new decade, Newton and the party would continue to shift their public focus from armed self-defense and the rhetoric of manhood to an emphasis on Survival Programs and political coalition-building that used the language of reform as much as revolution.

In line with this strategy, Newton began to court support from feminist groups and gay liberation organizations in the Bay Area. Ten days after leaving prison, Newton penned a press release entitled "The Women's and Gay Liberation Movements," one of the most progressive statements made by any heterosexual movement leader on issues of gender and sexuality. He first acknowledged Panther prejudices, explaining with frightening frankness that "sometimes our first instinct is to want to hit a homosexual in the mouth, and want a woman to be quiet," because of the fear that homosexuals are a "threat to our manhood" or that feminist women might "castrate us." But he argued that free love included

"THE BADDEST MOTHERFUCKERS"

liberating homosexuality and that gay men and women were in some ways "the most oppressed people in the society." Thus, rather than being somehow weaker than other people in the movement, women and gay activists could be the most militant revolutionaries. Similarly, Newton wrote that if Panthers differed from feminists they should debate them on the issues and "not criticize them [simply] because they are women trying to be free." Newton's statement and attempts by the party to deal with these issues garnered new support for the Panthers and also laid the groundwork for future political coalitions.[43]

Not all Panthers welcomed the shift to reform politics, however. Some, who had been drawn to the party's original mission of armed self-defense, felt stifled by the new emphasis on politics and Survival Programs. One day, several of these Panthers paid a visit to Bobby Seale in the national office. They jacked him up against the wall and said, "We talk this revolutionary shit about 'Off the Pig' and getting arms and having a revolution, and we're [not] doing shit!" Seale tried to explain that they first had to educate the masses through grassroots political programs so that there would be wider support for the revolution, but these men would have none of it. Most of them bolted from the party.[44]

Such divisions eventually produced a larger split between East Coast and West Coast factions in the party that was exacerbated by FBI infiltration and a vicious dispute between Newton and Cleaver. From exile in Algeria, where he had fled to escape charges relating to the ill-fated ambush of April 6, 1968, Cleaver continued to push for armed revolutionary action, and he cultivated support among Panthers in New York who disagreed with the reformist turn of the party leadership in California. When New York Panthers commended the Weathermen for their acceptance of armed struggle in an open letter published in February 1971, they also criticized the national Panther leadership for its "terrible tactics" and "pseudo-machoism." Newton responded by expelling the members of the New York branch, and less than a month later, he locked horns with Cleaver over the same issue of reform versus revolution. In the wake of this battle and Cleaver's subsequent defection from the party, Newton argued that Cleaver's eloquence had amounted to little more than "wild monologues of masculine protest," which had created "an orgy of phallic hysteria." Finally, Newton accused Cleaver of being a closeted homosexual who expressed his "personal problems in political terms." Despite Newton's earlier progressive statements regarding gay liberation, his attacks on Cleaver struck many as homophobic.[45]

The ugly split between Newton and Cleaver, combined with the expulsion or defection of key party organizers on the East Coast and harsh police repression of Panther paramilitary activities, convinced the members of the Oakland leadership that it was time to focus on political activism in the Bay Area. Bobby Seale's and Elaine Brown's 1973 campaigns for city offices in Oakland exemplified this strategy. The broad new political agenda of the Panthers included demands for increasing the availability of public child care and ending job discrimination based on sexual orientation. Behind the scenes, the party wrestled with the implications of this progressive public rhetoric. During staff meetings in 1972, they debated whether to allow an openly gay volunteer to join the Panthers. In the end, they accepted him.[46]

Yet the Panthers' progressive political planks coexisted uneasily with a party underground that became increasingly male-dominated and violent. After Newton's release from prison, he found it difficult to measure up to the unrealistic expectations raised by the Free Huey campaign. The role of martyr proved much easier to play than that of messiah, and though Newton continued to read, speak, and write in support of the revolution, he was enticed by and quickly entangled in the seedier side of the Oakland underworld. One doctor who had worked for the Panthers' Survival Programs later spoke about this transformation. "When I started with the health clinic," he remembered, "I'd come in and there would be some cadre reading [Mao's] Red Book. By the time I left the Party, I'd come in and the same cadre would be reading *The Godfather*." This infatuation with mafia culture reinforced Newton's use of "goon squads" to enforce party discipline, while an addiction to cocaine only exacerbated his volatile temper. Eventually, the Panther leader had to flee the country to escape charges in connection with the murder of an Oakland prostitute and the beating of a local tailor.[47]

Elaine Brown, who became head of the party when Newton fled to Cuba in 1974, explained in her memoir that, by then, Newton's "madness had become as full-blown as his genius. The numerous swaggering 'dicks' who had challenged the hero to prove his manhood had finally taken their toll. Now he had outdone them all, including himself." When Brown stepped up to speak for the first time as the new leader of the party, she looked out over a "sea of predominantly male faces" and wondered whether or not they would take orders from a woman. Brown oversaw the continued emphasis on political activism, including registering voters in the black community and campaigning for the election of Lionel Wilson, the first black mayor of Oakland. Yet Brown was not averse to using physical violence to quell dissent among the Panthers. Though her tenure as party chair was marked by an increasing emphasis on political activism, Brown's continued use of violence to enforce party discipline indicates that the belligerent macho culture of the Panther underground influenced both women and men in the organization. In 1977 Newton's return from exile in Cuba further escalated party violence, and according to Brown, some of this aggression was directed at Panther women in positions of power. Brown's official resignation from the party that same year stated, "Huey's return, then, [has] allowed the Leader and Founder of the Party to re-assume his proper place and relieve me of many duties." Wanting no one to misunderstand her resignation, she wrote that she still believed in the party and agreed with its goals of "total human freedom and dignity and peace." But in a much shorter, private letter to Newton concerning her resignation, she wrote, "Huey—I'm sorry. . . . It seemed too much of a man's world for me. After 10 years of everything—that this could stop me (us). I love you anyway. Elaine."[48]

As Elaine Brown's resignation suggests, a complete understanding of party history must reckon with both the progressive promise of the Panthers' political rhetoric and the problems that their focus on manhood created. The party successfully organized the "brothers on the block" with their ideals of manhood and armed self-defense. With these new recruits, they constructed programs that made civil rights directly relevant to the lives of the urban poor. Through breakfast programs for hungry school children, medical clinics for urban residents too poor to afford health care, and countless other local projects in cities across the country, the Panthers' grassroots activism addressed the real needs of black communities. Their search for gender, racial, and sexual identity exposed prejudices in the movement and the larger society. Critics who belittle the party as nothing more than a "macho" group ignore the Panthers' grassroots activism and efforts to combat sexism and homophobia within their own organization and the larger movement. Without an understanding of these positive aspects of Panther history, Angela Davis asks, how can future activists "position themselves en masse in defense of women's rights and in defense of gay rights if they are not aware of the historical precedents for such positions?"[49]

The Panthers found that the masculinist rhetoric of their early years created an atmosphere in which violence became a means for proving manhood, not for furthering the revolution they had envisioned. White movement groups that turned to violent protest in the late 1960s and early 1970s found themselves entangled in a macho culture as well, and like the Panthers, these groups struggled with internalized norms of gender and sexual oppression. As they grappled with these issues, party leaders tried to shift their focus from assertions of manhood to a broader pursuit of power for all people. This should be the legacy of the Black Panther Party and the goal of future human rights groups, because the quest for manhood may make one the "baddest motherfucker ever to set foot inside of history," but it will not give "Power to the People."

When the White man comes into our society, he goes to war with that society so that he may have free access to the woman. He has conquered us as men, and therefore we cannot be to our women what God commanded us to be until we are made free of the mind and the power of our enemies. —Minister Louis Farrakhan, *The Final Call* (1995)

Conclusion

"The Heartz of Men"

magine that the year is 1971. Night is settling on a small town in the Mississippi Delta not too far away from the birthplace of the Citizens' Councils of America in Indianola and just down the road from the home of state NAACP president Aaron Henry in Clarksdale. The light from a drive-in movie theater slices through the growing darkness as the feature presentation begins. Larger than life images jump from Hollywood's imagination onto a tall white wall, enticing passersby from the highway to park their trucks and large American sedans. As the images come into focus, the audience sees a handsome black man, wearing a stylish black leather coat that hangs snugly from his broad shoulders and swings as he swaggers down the streets of New York City. Confidence radiates from him. As he walks, the syncopated sizzle of a high-hat rhythm picks up the beat of his feet, a funk guitar groove swings to the sway of his hips, and the mellow baritone voice of Isaac Hayes slides into the audience's consciousness. "Who's the man?" he asks. As if there was any doubt, a chorus of female back-up singers shouts, "Shaft!" An orchestral blast of horns and strings punctuates Hayes's reply, "Damn right!"

The protagonist of the movie *Shaft* embodied almost everything that the Citizens' Councils had fought against. A fiercely intelligent and independent black man, John Shaft, played by Richard Roundtree, was beholden to no one. White men feared him. Black men respected him. And women of nearly every color found him irresistible. Undoubtedly, very few Citizens' Councilors saw *Shaft*, but their children might have seen the film alongside the sons and daughters of civil rights activists in a South and a nation that was struggling to come to terms with the legacies of the civil rights movement. Shaft represented a new kind of black manhood made possible by the movement. He was a man who supported and protected his community, but also an individual, free to live his life as he chose, out from under the thumb of "The Man." If his relationships with women on screen seemed untouched by the feminist movement that was challenging such images of dominant masculinity, Shaft did not seem bothered by this. In many ways, Shaft was the cultural embodiment of the hyper-masculine image that the Panthers had initially created for themselves. Echoing the Panthers' earlier claims, Isaac Hayes warns the audience at the beginning of the film, "That man Shaft is a bad mother. . . ." But before he can finish, the female back-up singers stop him with a "Hush yo' mouth!"[1]

The blaxploitation films of the early 1970s represented a commodification and cooptation of militant black masculinity, but the emergence and popular acceptance of characters like Shaft also signified the limited success of a revolution wrought by masculinist organizing strategies and liberation ideologies. These ideas banded men together in an attempt to be men, an attempt to gain power over their lives and in their families. Segregationists marshaled masculinist rhetoric to defend white male supremacy in the South, but a similar rhetoric also inspired black men in America's urban ghettos to confront racism, become heads of their households, and join the Nation of Islam. Masculinist liberation ideologies galvanized sanitation workers into a labor union that challenged white paternalism in Memphis, Tennessee, and spurred the Black Panthers toward a revolutionary vision of American society. The revolution produced by this strategy, however, was not the one that the Panthers had envisioned. Instead of a socialist revolt or a political coup, this was a cultural revolution, an incorporation of black men into the brotherhood of American manhood, and it succeeded, at least temporarily, because it did not directly challenge the many other social, political, and economic facets of racial oppression in America. The more substantive gains of the movement, including desegregation, civil rights legislation, local political involvement, and women's liberation, represented the success of an inclusive, humanistic organizing tradition that empowered both men and women.[2]

Yet in the 1990s, men once again began to rally around masculinist rhetoric, organizing strategies, and liberation theology. This was, as some observers have pointed out, partly a backlash against the feminist movement, but it was also a response to the unfinished business of the civil rights movement. In the 1980s and

1990s, racism, unemployment, drug use, violence, and police brutality continued to plague inner-city black communities. One study conducted in 1990 reported that one in four young black men were entangled in the criminal justice system. By 1995 a follow-up report warned that figure had risen to nearly one-third of the population of young African American men. Clearly, there was a need for action, perhaps another civil rights movement that would call upon the nation's conscience to address issues of racism in the criminal justice system as well as social and economic inequality. Unfortunately, the masculinist movements for racial uplift and reconciliation in the 1990s borrowed from the very strategies of earlier movements that had been least effective in combating prejudice and discrimination. Once again men marched, protested, and spoke up not primarily for social justice or for civil rights, but for recognition and reaffirmation of their manhood. The three most visible manifestations of this were the Million Man March, the Promise Keepers, and the proliferation of gangsta rap in hip-hop culture.[3]

Caravans of automobiles, buses, and trains slowly wound their way into Washington, D.C., for the Million Man March on October 16, 1995. Black men of nearly every class, creed, and shade were present. They had been called by Minister Louis Farrakhan, the leader of the Nation of Islam, a man whose rise to power in the Muslim organization had been boosted by the ousting and assassination of Malcolm X. But Farrakhan had learned something from his old adversary. He had heard the power of Malcolm's preaching, and he understood the appeal of his rhetoric that called for men to take control of their lives and their families. This, in fact, was the impetus for the Million Man March and simultaneous "Day of Absence" called for by Farrakhan. In collaboration with the Reverend Benjamin Chavis Muhammad, Maulana Karenga, and other religious and political leaders, Farrakhan decided that it was time for black men to come together, to atone for their failures as men, and to take charge of the stalled movement for racial equality.[4]

As with the masculinist strategies of the earlier civil rights movement, there were positive and negative ramifications of the Million Man March/Day of Absence. March organizers initially asked black women to show their support by staying home from their jobs and caring for their children. The call for a "Day of Absence" irked many black feminists, both men and women. "This exclusion of women is symptomatic of a general assault on progressive struggle," explained one man who refused to attend the march. He challenged the "patriarchal need to put men in the lead—when the truth of all our movements is that men . . . have been the majority of our leaders." Angela Davis similarly argued, "No march, movement or agenda that defines manhood in the narrowest terms and seeks to make women lesser partners . . . can be considered a positive step."[5]

To their credit, Farrakhan and other march leaders attempted to address the criticisms of feminists by including women speakers on the main platform and changing the strategy for the Day of Absence to include parallel meetings where black women could air their views. Jesse Jackson, who spoke early in the afternoon on the day of the march, addressed criticisms of the demonstration by offering a positive take on its objectives: "America will benefit and ultimately be grateful for this day. When a rising tide for racial justice and gender equality and family stability and inclusion and fairness lifts the boats stuck at the bottom, all boats will benefit." Jackson was one of the few leaders who explicitly called for gender equality at the Million Man March. Instead, many of the speakers emphasized the particular responsibilities of the black men in attendance. In a two-and a-half-hour speech, Farrakhan argued that black men needed to work harder to maintain their families, respect their women, and become politically active so that they could lead the movement against racial oppression in this country. He asked those present to look past the differences that divided them—the variations of skin color, religious affiliation, class, educational status, and so on—and look upon one another as brothers. Answering the oft-asked question of why he called only men to the march, Farrakhan explained, "Because in the beginning, God made man. And if we are at a new beginning, we got to make a man all over again, but make him in the image and likeness of God."[6]

Less than two years after the Million Man March, the Promise Keepers met in Washington with a similar vision of refashioning American manhood with an infusion of spirituality that would allow them to reclaim traditional authority in their families. Begun in 1990 by the head coach of the University of Colorado football team, the Promise Keepers had expanded by the mid-1990s to include hundreds of thousands of followers across the country. Like the men who organized the Million Man March, they too sought to address the unfinished business of the civil rights movement. The Promise Keepers hoped to achieve racial reconciliation by bringing white and black men together with a spiritual bond of interracial brotherhood. The sixth of their seven promises urged men in the movement to "reach beyond any racial and denominational barriers to demonstrate the power of Biblical unity." Given the origin of the movement in the racially integrated and often majority-minority world of college football, it is not surprising that this masculinist religious movement attempted to use gender as the bridge to connect men divided along racial lines. However, the predominantly white constituency of Promise Keeper meetings revealed that interracial unity was not the most successful aspect of their ministry. Instead, the Promise Keepers had the most success when they provided a way for men to address their shaken faith and their fallen status as men. Like the Southern Baptist Convention, which picked up on similar anxieties in the southern evangelical community, the Promise Keepers suggested that men needed to take control not only of their spiritual lives but of their families as well. In opposing women's leadership of the church and the family, these men often cited the New Testament passage Timothy 2:12 in which Paul writes that a woman is not allowed "to teach or to have authority over a man; she must be silent." Though their masculinist theology focused on affirming and supporting manhood, the movements proposed by the Promise Keepers and the organizers of the Million Man March had clear implications for womanhood as well.[7]

The Million Man March and the Promise Keepers reflected some of the same gender anxieties that shaped the rise of another cultural phenomenon of the 1990s, namely gangsta rap. Hip-hop culture, born in the late 1970s, provided a way for inner-city youth not only to relax and party but also to articulate feelings of frustration with racism and oppression. Through break dancing, graffiti, rap music, and fashion, young men and women eloquently expressed themselves in the few forums open to them. In particular, young black men found a voice in rap music. As hip-hop aficionado Nelson George explains, he became "interested in the nature of rapping as art, both as an extension of African-American maleness and as a showcase for the art of verbal dexterity and storytelling." George does not deny that there have been phenomenal female rappers, artists such as Salt-N-Pepa, Queen Latifah, and Lauryn Hill, but he contends that hip-hop has been predominantly a man's game. If this has been true of hip-hop in general, it was even truer of the gangsta rap genre that became popular in the late 1980s and 1990s.[8]

Though he was not an originator of gangsta rap, Tupac Shakur quickly became one of the genre's most widely recognized stars, full of promise and passion, and also a product of the politics and militancy that drove the Black Panthers. Shakur's mother had been a member of the party in New York, but she eventually moved with her son to the Bay Area. Living just miles away from where Huey Newton and Bobby Seale had founded the Black Panther Party less than twenty-five years before, Shakur began to rap about the problems he saw in the Bay Area's black communities. At the beginning of his career, he was a decidedly political rapper, a true child of the revolution that the Black Panthers had begun in the 1960s. "I'm the offspring of the Black Panthers," Shakur proudly told one interviewer in the early 1990s, and his records from that time period reflect his radical upbringing. On *2Pacalypse Now* (1991), *Strictly 4 My N.I.G.G.A.Z.* (1993), and *Me Against the World* (1995), Tupac hit nearly every major problem facing young black men and women growing up in America's inner cities, and he hit them hard. Drugs, teen pregnancy, welfare dependency, single-parent households, political apathy, and police brutality were just a few of the issues that he tackled. Echoing the socialist teachings of his Panther forbearers, Tupac dedicated one of his most explicitly political songs, "Words of Wisdom," to "the masses, the lower classes, the ones you left out." Tupac's political consciousness represented the Panthers' positive legacy in hip-hop culture, a legacy that was similarly reflected in the recordings of hip-hop artists like KRS-One and Public Enemy. Yet Tupac's career also encapsulated many of the controversies and contradictions that had marked the Black Panther Party.[9]

Like the Panthers, Tupac consciously molded an image of confident, militant masculinity that could serve as a model for young black men at the same time it helped to sell his message, but like many other gangsta rappers, Tupac's image, recordings, and actions sent mixed messages about gender relations and violence. "Shakur could sing in respectful praise and defense of women, then turn around and deliver a harangue about 'bitches' and 'ho's,'" one music critic remarked, "or [he] could boast of his gangster prowess one moment, then condemn the same doomed mentality in another track." Tupac's appeal, Michael Eric Dyson observed in a biography, "rested on the divided mind and soul between his revolutionary pedigree and his thug persona." A complex individual and a savvy observer of urban social reality, Tupac both reflected and critiqued the influences of misogyny and violence on poor inner-city communities. It is important to realize that these were not simply products or problems of the inner city. Like urban gangsta rappers, white heavy metal groups from the suburbs laced their lyrics in the 1980s and 1990s with derogatory references to women and gay men in attempts to appear tough or "hard." The white mainstream media, however, focused criticism on rappers like Shakur without highlighting similar problems in the rock world or acknowledging the complexity of the rapper's message. Tupac rapped about and performed this hard-boiled, often misogynistic, masculinity, but he also penned songs like "Brenda's Got a Baby," "Keep Ya Head Up," and the heartfelt "Dear Mama," which voiced deep sympathy and appreciation for black women's strength in overcoming sexism, racism, and poverty to raise their children.[10]

The other side of the "hard" masculinity prominent in gangsta rap of the

1990s was a willingness to use or at least threaten violence in defense of one's manhood. Tupac's song "The Heartz of Men" was just one of many tracks in which he promised retribution for the "pussies" (other rappers) who had dissed him in the press and on their records. Defenders of gangsta rap argue that this was simply a performance and, more to the point, a performance encouraged by white record executives looking to exploit hard gangsta images and lyrics to boost industry sales and profits. Although this was true to a certain extent, Nelson George, Michael Eric Dyson, and other cultural critics suggest that this defense of gangsta rap actually denied the artists' agency and the harsh social reality reflected in their lyrics. This harsh reality came into focus in the rap world during the mid-1990s as the line between performing "hard" masculinity and living it began to blur. Rivalries in hip-hop that had once remained confined to verbal sparring in recordings or stage shows spilled out onto the streets. In 1994 Tupac was shot multiple times when unidentified assailants attempted to rob him in New York—an attack that he later speculated was orchestrated by East Coast rivals jealous of his West Coast sound. He survived the shooting, but this incident and a brief stint in prison fueled Tupac's recordings of the mid-1990s that subsumed much of his earlier political message beneath a torrent of rage directed primarily at rival rappers from the East Coast. Though it has never been proven, many speculate that this East Coast/West Coast rivalry in the 1990s—one that strangely mirrored the split in the Black Panther Party twenty-five years earlier—led to the deaths of Tupac Shakur and Biggie Smalls, two of the most promising artists of their generation.[11]

Gangsta rap, the Promise Keepers, and the masculinist rhetoric that inspired the Million Man March seemed to wane in the late 1990s. Perhaps we can begin to draw some conclusions about how connections between race and manhood influenced American culture and struggles for economic and social equality in the second half of the twentieth century. The men who tried to harness masculinist rhetoric during the civil rights movement and again in the various men's movements of the 1990s came from diverse backgrounds. What these men all shared—black and white, Muslim and Christian, working-class and middle-class—was a sense of powerlessness in their lives. Whether the source of this powerlessness was racism, economic oppression, crumbling patriarchy, or the loss of political hegemony, these men sought to address their own powerlessness by asserting power over other men and women. Often, this masculinist uplift strategy involved replacing one form of discrimination with another. This strategy was a reaction to (or in some cases, a reaffirmation of) the white male supremacy that had long defined American society.

For hundreds of years white men in America positioned themselves as the only "true" men in this country. They attempted to emasculate (both metaphorically and literally) men of color by stripping them of the economic wherewithal and social standing to support and protect their families. When southern white men defended segregation, they were not defending the purity of white womanhood, as many claimed. They were defending their position of authority in a strictly hierarchical society and economy. Black men's military service during the Jim Crow era gave them a new sense of themselves as men and as citizens, but it did not fundamentally alter their position in the social hierarchy of the South or the United States. The civil rights movement sought to bring about those changes. Challenges by civil rights activists and the federal government in the 1950s undermined white supremacy, especially in the South, raising the possibility that white southern men might have to share the power that had been reserved exclusively for them by segregation and disfranchisement. The Citizens' Councils responded by idealizing white manhood and southern honor, while demonizing black manhood. They hoped that this would pressure other white men in the region to band together across class lines to defend white male supremacy. This masculinist strategy led to violent extremism that further undercut southern white men's position of leadership. White brutality against black activists in the American South became embarrassing for the federal government both at home and abroad. SNCC organizers and other civil rights activists used nonviolent direct action to draw attention to violent white supremacy. Resting as much on the threat of federal intervention as on the conscience of America, nonviolence was a savvy political strategy as well as a moral philosophy. The nonviolent movement did not rest on male supremacy, physical power, and aggression, and it was an inclusive one that welcomed women and men, pacifists and military veterans. Because of this, the nonviolent civil rights campaigns of the 1950s and 1960s created new possibilities for black and white men and women to define their own identities, to fashion new definitions of manhood and womanhood.

There were some civil rights activists, however, who were unhappy with nonviolence. These men posited a masculinist uplift strategy that included a willingness to use any means necessary to achieve liberation and attain manhood. To men like Malcolm X, nonviolence and passive resistance seemed unmanly ways to struggle for racial equality, strategies that veered dangerously close to begging the white man for acceptance rather than demanding power. For Malcolm and the generation that picked up the torch after his death, the struggle for racial liberation became inextricably linked to the pursuit of manhood. White liberals in the federal government and radicals in groups such as the Memphis Invaders and the Panthers followed Malcolm's lead in viewing the crux of America's social and economic problems as the failure of downtrodden men to achieve the ideal of American manhood. Masculinist uplift strategies pursued by white and black leaders inspired a sense of dignity and pride in men across the country, but they had the unintended consequences of fostering violence and distracting the nation's attention from some of the deeper problems that the civil rights movement had attempted to address. The story of race and manhood in the movement reveals the contradictions inherent in masculinist uplift strategies. Recognizing these contradictions, future activists may be better equipped to focus their energies, not on the quixotic quest for manhood, but on the more promising and inclusive struggles for social justice and human rights.

Notes

Abbreviations

The following abbreviations are used throughout the notes.

CCCRC	Citizens' Councils/Civil Rights Collection, McCain Library and Archives, University of Southern Mississippi, Hattiesburg, Miss.
CRDP	Civil Rights Documentation Project, Moorland-Spingarn Research Center, Howard University, Washington, D.C.
George Papers	Wesley George Papers, Southern Historical Collection, University of North Carolina, Chapel Hill, N.C.
Johnson Papers	Paul Johnson Family Papers, McCain Library and Archives, University of Southern Mississippi, Hattiesburg, Miss.
LBJ Library	Lyndon Baines Johnson Presidential Library, Austin, Tex.
MLK Papers	Martin Luther King Jr. Papers, King Center for Nonviolent Social Change, Atlanta, Ga.
MOHP	Mississippi Oral History Program, University of Southern Mississippi, Hattiesburg, Miss.
MSDAH	Mississippi State Department of Archives and History, Jackson, Miss.
MSU Collections	Special Collections, Mitchell Memorial Library, Mississippi State University, Starkville, Miss.
MVC	Mississippi Valley Collection, University of Memphis, Memphis, Tenn.
NAACP Papers	National Association for the Advancement of Colored People Papers, Manuscript Division, Library of Congress, Washington, D.C.
Newton Papers	Huey Newton Papers, Special Collections, Stanford University, Palo Alto, Calif.
OHRO	Oral History Research Office, Butler Library, Columbia University, New York, N.Y.
PSOHC	Project South Oral History Collection, Special Collections, Stanford University, Palo Alto, Calif.

RBC	Rare Book Collection, Wilson Library, University of North Carolina, Chapel Hill, N.C.
RJB	Ralph J. Bunche Oral History Program, Moorland-Spingarn Research Center, Howard University, Washington, D.C.
ROHO	Regional Oral History Office, Bancroft Library, University of California, Berkeley, Calif.
SCRBC	Schomburg Center for Research in Black Culture, New York Public Library, New York, N.Y.
SHSW	State Historical Society of Wisconsin, Madison, Wis.
SNCC Papers	Student Nonviolent Coordinating Committee Papers, King Center for Nonviolent Social Change, Atlanta, Ga.
SOHP	Southern Oral History Program Collection, Southern Historical Collection, Wilson Library, University of North Carolina, Chapel Hill, N.C.
WHAF	White House Aides' Files, Lyndon Baines Johnson Presidential Library, Austin, Tex.
WHCF	White House Central Files, Lyndon Baines Johnson Presidential Library, Austin, Tex.
Wirtz Papers	Willard Wirtz Papers, Record Group 174 (Department of Labor), National Archives II, College Park, Md.

Introduction

1. Ellison, *Invisible Man*.

2. For this image, see John Greenleaf Whittier's abolitionist broadside entitled "Our Countrymen in Chains" (New York: Anti-Slavery Office, 1837), Rare Book and Special Collections Division, Library of Congress, Washington, D.C.

3. Brown, *Good Wives*; Wilkins, *Jefferson's Pillow*; Stowe, *Intimacy and Power*; Wyatt-Brown, *Southern Honor*; McCurry, *Masters of Small Worlds*.

4. Douglass, *Narrative*, 298. See also Hine and Jenkins, *Question of Manhood*; and Cullen, "'I's a Man Now.'"

5. Foner, *Short History of Reconstruction*; Edwards, *Gendered Strife and Confusion*; Gilmore, *Gender and Jim Crow*; Kantrowitz, *Ben Tillman*; Bederman, *Manliness and Civilization*; Brown, "Negotiating and Transforming the Public Sphere"; MacLean, *Behind the Mask of Chivalry*; Hall, *Revolt Against Chivalry*; White, *Too Heavy a Load*.

6. Smith, *Killers of the Dream*; Dollard, *Caste and Class*; McMillen, *Dark Journey*. For personal stories of sexual assault during segregation, see the testimony of Endesha Ida Mae Holland in Fields and Mulford, *Freedom on My Mind*. On the other side of this story were the white men and the mixed race offspring of these unions. In 2003 Essie Mae Washington-Williams came forward to claim the recently deceased South Carolina senator and longtime segregationist, Strom Thurmond, as her father. The Thurmond family's African American housekeeper, Carrie Butler, was her mother. Michael Janofsky, "Thurmond Kin Respond to Paternity Claim," *New York Times*, Dec. 16, 2003.

7. Litwack, *Trouble In Mind*, 12, 36; White, *Rope and Faggot*; Dray, *At the Hands of Persons Unknown*. Dray estimates that at least 3,417 African Americans were lynched between 1882 and 1944.

8. Robinson, *Montgomery Bus Boycott*; King, *Stride toward Freedom*, 46–47; E. D. Nixon, interview #139, CRDP; Abernathy, *And the Walls Came Tumbling Down*, 145. King's and Nixon's accounts of the Montgomery movement differ slightly, and the Nixon quotation comes from King's account.

9. For more on manhood in the 1950s, see Cuordileone, "'Politics in an Age of Anxiety'"; Faludi, *Stiffed*; Kimmel, *Manhood in America*; Filene, *Him/Her/Self*; and Ehrenreich, *Hearts of Men*. Each author analyzes different obstacles to the quest for manhood during this period. Few address the mix of economic, social, and political discrimination facing black men.

10. For a definition of feminism, see Kerber and DeHart, *Women's America*, 17–20, 493–521. See Bederman, *Manliness and Civilization*; Gilmore, *Gender and Jim Crow*; Kantrowitz, *Ben Tillman*; Cuordileone, "'Politics in an Age of Anxiety'"; and Wallace, *Black Macho*. No one, as far as I know, has ever claimed to be a "masculinist," but these scholars have begun to analyze the ways that men have used the traditional power associated with manhood—often in conjunction with race—for political, social, or economic ends.

11. Sitkoff, *Struggle for Black Equality*; Branch, *Parting the Waters*; Crawford et al., *Women in the Civil Rights Movement*; Payne, *I've Got the Light of Freedom*; Robnett, *How Long?*; Nasstrom, "Down to Now"; Ling and Monteith, *Gender in the Civil Rights Movement*; and Tyson, *Radio Free Dixie*. Sitkoff and Branch represent the early movement scholarship that paid little attention to gender. Crawford, Payne, Nasstrom, and others called attention to the roles played by women. Ling, Monteith, and Tyson began to analyze masculinity in the movement.

Chapter One

1. Carter interview in Motley, *Invisible Solder*, 106–8.

2. "Torpedo Hit the Arizona First," *New York Times*, Dec. 22, 1941; "Navy Cross for Dorrie Miller," *Pittsburgh Courier*, May 16, 1942; Secretary of the Navy Public Relations Office to Walter White, March 5, 1942, NAACP Papers. As a result of coverage and pressure from black newspapers and civil rights groups, Miller was ultimately awarded the Navy Cross. He returned to duty in the Pacific and perished in 1943.

3. Navy Department Memorandum, Sept. 1940, in Nalty and MacGregor, *Blacks in the Military*, 135. Carter interview in Motley, *Invisible Soldier*, 106–8. As late as 1944, white naval officers were still trying to convince black recruits and draftees to work as messmen.

4. Wynn, *Afro-American and the Second World War*, 21; Dalfiume, *Desegregation of the U.S. Armed Forces*; Kryder, *Divided Arsenal*; Honey, *Creating Rosie the Riveter*; Gluck, *Rosie the Riveter Revisited*.

5. Snyder, *Citizen-Soldiers*; Foner, *Short History of Reconstruction*, 4, 12; Wynn, *Afro-American and the Second World War*, 11–12; Carter interview in Motley, *Invisible Soldier*, 108. Though many of the same issues discussed here are relevant to a history of World War I, the brevity of American combat operations and the conservative (some might say reactionary) mood of the country afterwards limited the social impact of black service during that war.

6. Wynn, *Afro-American and the Second World War*, 40, 55; Motley, *Invisible Soldier*, 26.

7. A. Philip Randolph and Walter White, "Call to Negro to March on Washington for Jobs and Equal Protection" *Black Worker*, May 1941, in Garrow, Kovach, and Polsgrove, *Reporting Civil Rights*, 1:1–4; Arnesen, *Brotherhoods of Color*, 183–92. Rauh interview in Terkel, *"Good*

War," 337–38; Wynn, *Afro-American and the Second World War,* 88. On the executive order against racial discrimination, labor lawyer Joseph Rauh explained to Terkel that he penned a draft of the order and that the president primarily wanted to stop Randolph's march from fear of the political fallout.

8. Dickerson interview in Terkel, *"Good War,"* 340; Wynn, *Afro-American and the Second World War,* 39–55.

9. War College study cited in Sandler, *Segregated Skies,* 8–9; Sitkoff, *New Deal for Blacks,* 298–325; Sitkoff, "Racial Militancy," 664; Sullivan, *Days of Hope;* Lee, *Employment of Negro Troops,* 71–74; memo from Assistant Secretary of War Robert Patterson to Franklin D. Roosevelt, Sept. 1940, in Nalty and MacGregor, *Blacks in the Military,* 107–8. The White House released a nearly verbatim copy of the memo just before the 1940 election. "White House Blesses Jim Crow," *Crisis,* Nov. 1940.

10. Hitler, *Mein Kampf,* 325; Sklaroff, "Constructing G.I. Joe Louis," 958–83; Shirer, *Rise and Fall of the Third Reich,* 1170.

11. Rasmus interview in Terkel, *"Good War,"* 39; Allen, *Port Chicago Mutiny,* 54; Peery, *Black Fire,* 128.

12. D'Emilio, *Lost Prophet,* 72–120; Evanzz, *Messenger,* 143–45; Johnson, *To Stem This Tide,* 94; DeVeaux, *Birth of Bebop,* 246, 253. Johnson's book covers general feelings of African Americans on the home front during the war, showing that conscientious objectors were not alone in their opposition to the war.

13. Nalty, *Right to Fight,* 1, 5–6, 28. According to Nalty, 12,738 of the 19,168 African Americans serving in the marines during World War II went overseas, but the bulk of them were relegated to manual labor as stevedores or stretcher-bearers.

14. McGuire, *Taps for a Jim Crow Army,* 11; Motley, *Invisible Soldier,* 61; Terkel, *"Good War,"* 151.

15. McGuire, *Taps for a Jim Crow Army,* 32, 75. On the issue of promotion, see anonymous letter from a black officer stationed at Fort Huachuca in Arizona to Walter White, Dec. 30, 1943, in "Soldiers' Complaints," NAACP Papers.

16. McGuire, *Taps for a Jim Crow Army,* 11, 14, 32, 42; Sullivan, *Days of Hope,* 136; Service Detachment (Colored), Fort McClellan, Alabama letter to Walter White (n.d.) in "Soldiers' Complaints," NAACP Papers; Nalty and MacGregor, *Blacks in the Military,* 121; Peery, *Black Fire,* 206.

17. Stevens interview in Motley, *Invisible Soldier,* 75–77; Morehouse, "War Stories," 101; Peery, *Black Fire,* 152; Bass interview in Potter, *Liberators,* 189–90. See qualification about *Liberators* in note 41.

18. *Pittsburgh Courier,* Apr. 11, 1942; "For Manhood in National Defense," *Crisis,* Dec. 1940; Finkle, *Forum for Protest,* 66–67, 112, 121, 129–54; *Pittsburgh Courier,* May 16, 1942; *Crisis,* Aug. 1942; Nelson, *Black Press.*

19. Hastie memo to War Department, Sept. 22, 1941, and department response in Nalty and MacGregor, *Blacks in the Military,* 112–15; McGuire, *He, Too, Spoke for Democracy.*

20. Lipsitz, *Rainbow at Midnight,* 55, 73; Taylor, *In Search of the Racial Frontier,* 251–55; Starr, *Embattled Dreams,* viii, 112–13; Johnson, *Second Gold Rush,* 6–8, 52.

21. Eddie Eaton, "In Search of the California Dream: From Houston, Texas to Richmond, California, 1943," 1–32, Lucille Preston, "World War II Journey: From Clarksdale, Mississippi to Richmond, California, 1942," 13–14, and Selena Foster, "Longtime Richmond

Resident from Cherokee County, Texas," 68, oral histories by Judith K. Dunning (1985-1986), ROHO.

22. Richmond City Manager's Office, "An Avalanche Hits Richmond," Office Report, July 1944, 1, Bancroft Library, University of California; Taylor, *In Search of the Racial Frontier*, 255. Eaton interview with Dunning, 38–39; Harry Wheaton Williams and Marguerite Williams, "Reflections of a Longtime Black Family in Richmond," oral history by Dunning (1985), 42, ROHO. These interviews and the City Manager's report reflect a nostalgic longing for the small-town feel that was lost in Richmond during the war.

23. Starr, *Embattled Dreams*, 114; Williams interview with Dunning, 110; Foster interview with Dunning, 78–79; Johnson, *Second Gold Rush*, 47–48, 61. Selena Foster told of how her husband did not want her to work at the shipyards. She snuck in for an interview anyway, but ended up working at Leo's Defense Diner. Marilynn Johnson argues that black women were primarily excluded from skilled positions in the yards, even though women made up more than a quarter of the Kaiser workforce in 1944.

24. Starr, *Embattled Dreams*, 113; and Johnson, *Second Gold Rush*, 41, 65–66.

25. Himes, *Quality of Hurt*, 73–78; see also Himes stories and articles in *Crisis*, Jan., Feb., May, and Nov. 1943 and June 1944.

26. Himes, *If He Hollers Let Him Go*.

27. Johnson, *To Stem This Tide*; Thurgood Marshall, "Sojourner Truth Homes," *Crisis*, Apr. 1942; White, "What Caused the Detroit Riots?," 352; Wynn, *Afro-American and the Second World War*, 68–73; Sitkoff, "Racial Militancy," 670, 673–74.

28. Allen, *Port Chicago Mutiny*, 1–25, 48.

29. Starr, *Embattled Dreams*, 119; Port Chicago "War Diary," July 17, 1944, 4, Bancroft Library, University of California, Berkeley; Small interview with Terkel, *"Good War,"* 392–401.

30. Allen, *Port Chicago Mutiny*, 80–84.

31. *Chicago Defender* quoted in Finkle, *Forum for Protest*, 174; Jefferson Flowers in the Port Chicago Trial Transcript, 174, Charles L. Bridges in Trial Transcript, 163, see also Trial Transcripts, 3–4, 219–20, 300, 366, 444–45, 1433, Bancroft Library, University of California, Berkeley, Calif. (page numbers are from the Berkeley files and do not correspond exactly to the pagination of the original transcript); Allen, *Port Chicago Mutiny*, 80–84. During the trial Small denied saying that he and the other black sailors had the officers "by the balls," but he later admitted to Robert Allen that he probably had said something like this.

32. Port Chicago Trial Transcript, 4, 1505; Small interview with Terkel, *"Good War,"* 399–400; Allen, *Port Chicago Mutiny*, 135–37. In a much less famous confrontation, fifty-four black Wacs, who were trained as technicians, were ordered to clean a hospital while white Wacs were assigned to better duties. The black Wacs refused the assignment and four of them stood trial in 1945. As one of the black women explained, "If it will help my people, I will take a court martial." Cited in Finkle, *Forum for Protest*, 179–81.

33. Smith, *When Jim Crow Met John Bull*, 111, 160; Memos from Franklin D. Roosevelt to Secretary of the Navy Frank Knox, 1942, and "Leadership and the Negro Soldier" in Nalty and MacGregor, *Blacks in the Military*, 128–30, 144–46; Myrdal, *American Dilemma*.

34. Dryden, *A-Train*, 13–14, 22–35, 64–66, 106–8; *Pittsburgh Courier*, May 9, 1942; and Sandler, *Segregated Skies*.

35. Dryden, *A-Train*, 130–35; Motley, *Invisible Soldier*, 233; Smith, *Tuskegee Airman*,

57–63; Sandler, *Segregated Skies*, 45–46. According to Sandler, General Dwight Eisenhower personally congratulated the Tuskegee Airmen after this mission.

36. Sandler, *Segregated Skies*, 47–48; Motley, *Invisible Soldier*, 217, 226.

37. Smith, *When Jim Crow Met John Bull*, 55, 118–19; White, *Rising Wind*, 28; Potter, *Liberators*, 153. See qualification about *Liberators* in note 41.

38. Smith, *When Jim Crow Met John Bull*, 1–4, 185–86.

39. Black interview with Terkel, *"Good War,"* 278–81; Colley, *Road to Victory*, xiv, 182–87.

40. John Long, Eddie Donald, and Horace Evans interviews with Motley, *Invisible Soldier*, 152, 164–65. Members of the 761st Tank Battalion won 11 Silver Stars, 69 Bronze Stars, and 280 Purple Hearts during the course of the war.

41. Stevens's experience related in Potter, *Liberators*, 176–77; Terkel, *"Good War,"* 268. The film *Liberators*, upon which Potter's book is based, was marred by factual errors and was eventually withdrawn from public television. A formal review of the film supported the validity of many of the oral history interviews but found fault with the filmmakers' research and claims about the liberation of the camps at Buchenwald and Dachau. For a complete review of the controversy, see Silverstein, "Examination of *Liberators*."

42. John Long interview with Motley, *Invisible Soldier*, 155; Terkel, *"Good War,"* 280–81; Chamberlin and Feldman, *Liberation*, 23–26; Abzug, *Inside the Vicious Heart*; Silverstein, "An Examination of *Liberators*," 9–10. See note 41 about the liberation controversy. The 71st Infantry Division, which included the Black Panther battalion, was credited as liberating the camp at Gunskirchen Lager (near Lambach, Austria) in May 1945.

43. Peery, *Black Fire*, 271; Hall, *Love, War and the 96th Engineers (Colored)*, 233; letter to the *Chicago Defender* reprinted in McGuire, *Taps for a Jim Crow Army*, 175; and letter to the NAACP from a white North Carolinian in White, *Rising Wind*, 126.

44. Morehouse, "War Stories," 106; Motley, *Invisible Soldier*, 117; Colley, *Blood for Dignity*. In the European theater, black and white troops served together in an all-volunteer integrated unit in the 99th Infantry Division, which proved effective near the end of the war.

45. Dittmer, *Local People*, 2; Dalfiume, *Desegregation*, 123, 134. George McMillan, "Race Justice in Aiken," *Nation*, Nov. 23, 1946, in Garrow, Kovach, and Polsgrove, *Reporting Civil Rights*, 1:82–84; Hampton, Frasier, and Flynn, *Voices of Freedom*, xxiv–xxv; Klarman, "How *Brown* Changed Race Relations"; Patterson, *Brown v. Board of Education*. For more on how military service influenced the growth of the NAACP in the 1940s, see the hundreds of membership applications in the NAACP Papers from 1941–50.

46. Peery, *Black Fire*, 332.

Chapter Two

1. A transcription of this speech can be found in George Papers, box 2, folder 11, series 1.2.

2. Alternate version of this speech appeared as a handbill, introduced by the following: "It is claimed that white people secretly wired the building and recorded the speech as follows." Segregation and Integration Miscellaneous Collection, NAACP folder, 1956–1964, MSU Collections.

3. McMillen, *Citizens' Council*, 36; Carter, *South Strikes Back*, 137–38.

4. Edwards, *Gendered Strife and Confusion*; Gilmore *Gender and Jim Crow*; and Kantrowitz, *Ben Tillman*.

5. Bartley, *Rise of Massive Resistance* and *New South*; McMillen, *Citizens' Council*. Bartley and McMillen deftly depict the political rise of the segregationist movement. They also touch on the gender and sexual dynamics of the struggle, but they do not scrutinize these aspects closely.

6. Martin, *Deep South Says Never*, 1–4; Raines, *My Soul Is Rested*, 297–303; Robert Patterson, *Second Annual Report: August 1956* (Winona: Association of the Citizens' Councils of Mississippi, 1956), Southern Pamphlet Folio 6860, RBC; Klarman, "How *Brown* Changed Race Relations," 81–118.

7. "How the White Citizens' Councils Came to Alabama," *New South*, Dec. 1955, Cox Papers, box I-A, folder 4, MSU Collections; *Birmingham News*, Feb. 19, 1956; and Stowe, "Willie Rainache." Since the anonymous author of the *New South* piece was critical of the councils, he hid the location of the meeting and his own identity for fear of council retaliation. By 1956, the Alabama councils claimed a statewide membership of 40,000 people.

8. Bartley, *Rise of Massive Resistance*, 17–24; Chafe, *Civilities and Civil Rights*.

9. George letter to "Mr. French," Dec. 1954, George Papers, box 2, folder 11; McMillen, *Citizens' Council*, 113–14. George eventually furnished the state of Alabama with a "scientific" treatise on the disastrous consequences of integration entitled "Biology of the Race Problem."

10. Hood letter to George, Feb. 2, 1955, George Papers, box 2, folder 15; Thornton letter to George, Nov. 29, 1954, George Papers, box 2, folder 10.

11. Avant letter to George, Nov. 29, 1954, George Papers, box 2, folder 10; anonymous letter in Daniel, *Lost Revolutions*, 203.

12. *Citizens' Council*, Dec. 1958; Chafe, *Civilities and Civil Rights*, 64–67. Even if the North Carolina organization's integrationist recruitment strategy was merely a rhetorical feint toward interracialism, the irony remains.

13. McIlhenny letter to Brady, Mar. 6, 1957, George Neal McIlhenny Papers, box 2, folder 39, MSU Collections. Brady's pseudo-scientific arguments are representative of a mini-renaissance of scientific racism in the South of the 1950s.

14. Brady, *Black Monday*, 45, 47, 63, 87; Burges, *What Price Integration?*

15. Hampton, Frasier, and Flynn, *Voices of Freedom*, 12–14.

16. "M is for Mississippi and Murder" (New York: NAACP, 1956), CCCRC, box 2, folder 19; McMillen, *Citizens' Council*, 217–18; Whitfield, *Death in the Delta*.

17. McMillen, *Citizens' Council*, 37, 123.

18. *Citizens' Council*, Nov. 1956, Aug. and Nov. 1957; Warren, *Memoirs of Earl Warren*, 291–92.

19. Bartley, *New South*, 188.

20. *Citizens' Council*, Dec. 1958.

21. "Ghost of Robert E. Lee" in the *Citizens' Council*, Feb. 1957; Kilpatrick letter to Simmons, Apr. 19, 1963, State Sovereignty Commission Files, MSDAH. James J. Kilpatrick, the editor of the *Richmond News Leader*, commended Simmons on the councils' work.

22. Blight, *Race and Reunion*; Bonner, "Flag Culture," 293–332.

23. Wyatt-Brown, *Southern Honor*, xv, xvii, 14, 34; Ayers, *Vengeance and Justice*; Nisbett and Cohen, *Culture of Honor*. Here, I am defining honor as the respect and esteem that the

members of a community confer upon an individual, usually a man, who is willing to stand up and often fight for his ideas. Although Wyatt-Brown argues that the southern code of honor began to decline after the Civil War, he suggests that it might be fruitful to study the concept even into the 1950s.

24. Alabama Citizens' Council Constitution, CCCRC, box 1, folder 13. This state council constitution expressly limited membership to "adult white male citizens" in the mid-1950s.

25. McMillen, *Citizens' Councils*, 11.

26. Bartley, *New South*, 201.

27. Forest, Mississippi, Citizens' Council rolls, McIlhenny Papers, box 2, folder 46, MSU Collections.

28. *Citizens' Council*, Nov. 1956.

29. *Citizens' Council*, Feb. 1957. See also a report from the Texas councils in August 1957, which said, "In many of our Councils the men are doing more than the women. We are making a great mistake if we do not enlist the patriotic services of these women."

30. Memo from Robert Patterson, Dec. 30, 1957, "Assoc. of Citizens' Councils of Miss.: Women's Activities" folder, Citizens' Council Collection, MSU Collections; "Women's Aid Sought in Segregation Fight," *Jackson Daily News*, Jan. 3, 1958; McMillen, *Citizens' Council*, 241–42.

31. *Citizens' Council*, Feb. 1957.

32. Herbert Ravenel Sass, *Mixed Schools and Mixed Blood* (Citizens' Councils of America, 1956), Southern Pamphlet #1632, RBC.

33. McMillen, "White Citizens' Council"; Daisy Bates interview with Elizabeth Jacoway, Oct. 11, 1976, SOHP, series G-009.

34. *Citizens' Council*, June 1958.

35. Harry Ashmore interview with John Egerton, June 16, 1990, 10–11, SOHP, series A:3553.

36. Hodding Carter interview with Jack Bass, Apr. 1, 1974, 29, SOHP, series A:100.

37. Martin Luther King Jr., "Letter From Birmingham City Jail" in Carson et al., *Eyes on the Prize Reader*, 156; Belfrage, *Freedom Summer*, 56; Betty Carter interview with John Egerton, Sept. 6, 1990, SOHP, series A:350.

38. Tom Brady, *Review of "Black Monday," an Address to the Indianola Citizens' Councils, Oct. 28, 1954*, 14, Southern Pamphlet #811, RBC.

39. Eskew, *But for Birmingham*, 107–18; McMillen, *Citizens' Councils*, 47–55; Bartley, *Rise of Massive Resistance*, 201–8.

40. Hall, "The Mind That Burns," 61–71.

41. Carter, *South Strikes Back*, 201–2.

42. Mailer, "White Negro," 276–93.

43. Cuordileone, "'Politics in an Age of Anxiety,'" 515–45; Dean, "Masculinity as Ideology," 29–62; "The Challenge to the South and How It Must Be Met," speech to Louisiana Citizens' Councils, July 21, 1960, CCCRC, box 3, folder 12.

44. Cohen, *Masked Men*; Ehrenreich, *Hearts of Men*; Kimmel, *Manhood in America*, 249–58; Meyerowitz, *Not June Cleaver*; Filene, *Him/Her/Self*, 169–76. Filene discusses what he calls the "domestic mystique" for middle-class American men that arose in the 1950s and produced an anxiety about domesticity leading to emasculation.

45. Daniel, *Lost Revolutions*, 121–74; Patterson letter to George, Jan. 25, 1955, George

Papers, box 2, folder 11; Carter, *South Strikes Back*, 160; *Citizens' Council*, Feb. 1957. As Daniel explains, "Rock 'n' roll unlocked women's emotions, but it also threatened white men's control."

46. Reviews and comments concerning the film are located in "Moving Pictures—*Island in the Sun*" folder, Clippings File, SCRBC; *Citizens' Council*, Jan. and Feb. 1957; Daniel, *Lost Revolutions*, 165; and Wilson and Ferris, *Encyclopedia of Southern Culture*, 915–16, 924–27. Klan members picketed a showing of the film in Jacksonville, Florida.

47. *Citizens' Council*, Aug. 1958; Kirby, *Media-Made Dixie*. Caldwell's *Tobacco Road* and many of Williams's plays were turned into feature films in the 1950s and 1960s.

48. Putnam, *Race and Reason*, 27, 44; Schuyler and Schuyler, *Close That Bedroom Door!*, 89–90, 117, 123. Putnam's argument also contains thinly veiled anti-Semitic attacks on anthropologists and sociologists whose work supported integration.

49. Putnam, *Race and Reason*, 22; *Citizens' Council*, Feb. 1959. Eisenhower's intervention in the Little Rock Central High crisis and the Supreme Court's resolution of the Montgomery bus crisis attest to the support of at least gradual southern integration by the federal government. Yet public opinion was divided on the integration question, especially when it came to school desegregation in the North. Carleton Putnam cited a Gallup Poll from 1958 in which 58 percent of northern white parents contacted said they would not send their children to schools with a student body that was more than half black.

50. *Citizens' Council*, Sept. 1959; Barnett speeches, McIlhenny Papers, box 2, folder 38, MSU Collections.

51. Mississippi's House Bill 880 (1956) created the State Sovereignty Commission. See McIlhenny Papers, box 2, folder 60, MSU Collections; Commission director Erle Johnston to William Simmons, Dec. 22, 1960, and Sept. 30, 1963, State Sovereignty Commission Files, MSDAH; Reverend Ed King interview with author (1999).

52. Transcriptions of the phone conversations between the Kennedy brothers and Barnett can be found in Navasky, *Kennedy Justice*, 189–90, 208–11; "Integration of the University of Mississippi" in *Papers of John F. Kennedy*, 4–7; George Leonard, George Harris, and Christopher Wren, "How a Secret Deal Prevented a Massacre at Ole Miss" *Look*, Dec. 31, 1962, 19–36 (italics added).

53. Branch, *Parting the Waters*, 665; "Radio and Television Report to the Nation on the Situation at the University of Mississippi (September 30, 1962)," in *Public Papers: John F. Kennedy*, 726–28; Dean, "Masculinity as Ideology," 29–62. Kennedy was, in fact, a master of masculinist rhetoric in his own right.

54. Aaron Henry interview with Jack Bass, Apr. 2, 1974, 4, 7, SOHP, series A:107.

Chapter Three

1. Charles McLaurin interview with author and Sunflower County Freedom Project (SCFP) students (1999), 11; Council of Federated Organizations (COFO), "Mississippi Handbook for Political Programs" (1964), SNCC Papers, subgroup A, series XV, number 123, A-XV-123.

2. McLaurin speech entitled "To Overcome Fear" (n.d.), SNCC Papers, A-XV-202; McLaurin memo to the SNCC staff relating to the period Aug. 18, 1962–Aug. 31, 1963, SNCC Papers, A-IV-238; Sugarman, *Stranger at the Gates*, 211–13.

3. Moody, *Coming of Age*, Evans, *Personal Politics*; McAdam *Freedom Summer*; McAdam, "Gender as a Mediator," 1211–40; Robnett, *How Long?* I attend to relations between men and women in SNCC throughout this chapter, addressing the infamous, but atypical incidents of chauvinism in the organization.

4. Chafe, *Civilities and Civil Rights*, 83; Branch, *Parting the Waters*, 271–75. Earlier sit-ins had occurred in other southern cities, but none had fired the imagination of young activists the way the Greensboro protest did.

5. Carson, *In Struggle*, 19–30; Payne, "Ella Baker," 885–99; Ella Baker interview with Eugene Walker (1974), 19, 53, SOHP, series G7; Grant, *Ella Baker*, 107–10, 121–30.

6. Carson, *In Struggle*, 46–47; Burner, *And Gently He Shall Lead Them*; "Mississippi: Subversion of the Right to Vote" (1964), 5–7, Segregation and Integration Miscellaneous Collection, SNCC Papers, box 1, folder 24, MSU Collections.

7. Gilmore, *Gender and Jim Crow*, 91–118; Cecelski and Tyson, eds., *Democracy Betrayed*; and Carson, *In Struggle*, 21.

8. Carson, In Struggle, 48; "Mississippi: A Chronicle of Violence and Intimidation in Mississippi since 1961" (1964), 5, Segregation and Integration Miscellaneous Collection, SNCC Papers, box 1, folder 24, MSU Collections.

9. Kapur, *Raising Up a Prophet*, 54–56.

10. For more on self-defense in the Mississippi movement, see Dittmer, *Local People*, 1, 47, 49, 86, 106, 166–67, 188–93, 215, 238, 254, 286, 306–7, 310, 354, 358, 391–98; Payne, *I've Got the Light of Freedom*, 44, 48–51, 54, 59, 61–62, 114, 138–39, 159, 168, 176, 202–6, 209, 279–80, 287, 308, 314; Tyson, *Radio Free Dixie*, 164. The NAACP suspended Robert Williams, and he eventually fled to Cuba to evade U.S. authorities.

11. Payne, *I've Got the Light of Freedom*, 278–80; Rural Organizing and Cultural Center, *Minds Stayed On Freedom*, 152. The story of Turnbow's act of self-defense has taken on a legendary quality in the retelling by local residents of Holmes County and movement activists. It was even immortalized in a folk song sung by volunteers during Freedom Summer.

12. Tyson, "'Black Power,'" 551.

13. Dittmer, *Local People*, 166–67; Jerry DeMuth, "A Guide to Mississippi," unpublished article, DeMuth Papers, SHSW.

14. Reverend Edwin King interview with author (1999).

15. "Mississippi Handbook for Political Programs" (1964), SNCC Papers, A-XV-123; "Mississippi—Is This America?," *Eyes On the Prize*, part 5.

16. "Aaron Henry for Governor Speech," Greenville, Miss., Oct. 24, 1963, 1, SNCC Papers, A-XVI-39; Dittmer, *Local People*, 204–5; Aaron Henry Papers, series 1, box 1, folders 2–4, Special Collections, Tougaloo University; Henry and Curry, *Aaron Henry*. The Henry Papers include an unpublished, incomplete autobiography. Curry's book is a revised version of this autobiography that was completed after Henry's death.

17. Aaron Henry interview with Robert Wright (1968), 9–16, CRDP; Howard "Men Like That," 107–8; Reverend Edwin King interview with the author (1999); Henry and Curry, *Aaron Henry*, 128. Henry did not talk about his own sexuality in interviews, but he did discuss the charges of sexual "misconduct."

18. Chafe, *Never Stop Running*; Bob Moses interview with Anne Romaine, 69–72, Romaine Papers, box 1, folder 11, MLK Papers; diary of Richard "Pete" Andrews (Oct.–Nov. 1963), Miscellaneous Papers, Southern Historical Collection, Wilson Library, University of

North Carolina, Chapel Hill, N.C. Like Henry, Lowenstein was bisexual, but this had little direct impact on his dealings with SNCC. Moses discussed Lowenstein's role in the movement with Romaine.

19. Ivanhoe Donaldson, Field Report (Oct. 30–Nov. 5, 1963), SNCC Papers, A-IV-242.

20. Charlie Cobb interview with John Rachal (1996), vol. 668, MOHP; Hollis Watkins interview with Robert Wright (1968), 36–37, CRDP; SNCC Staff Meeting Minutes (June 9–11, 1964), Robert Clark Papers (uncatalogued), Special Collections, Tougaloo University; "Guideline for Interviewing," Apr. 14, 1964, SNCC Papers, A-VIII-117. COFO also included the Congress of Racial Equality (CORE) and the Southern Christian Leadership Conference (SCLC).

21. McAdam, *Freedom Summer*, 56–60; McAdam, "Gender as a Mediator," 1218–22; Robnett, *How Long?*, 129; Flemming, "Black Women Activists," 72–73; Dave Dennis interview, #442, 6, PSOHC. Robnett's revisions to McAdam suggest that white women who had worked with SNCC for years and black women who desired to volunteer did not face these obstacles to participating in the summer project.

22. McAdam, *Freedom Summer*, 57.

23. Christopher Wren, "Mississippi: The Attack on Bigotry," *Look*, Sept. 8, 1964, 20–28; Belfrage, *Freedom Summer*, 10; Karen Duncanwood interview with Ron Grele (1994), 20, OHRO; Michael Garvel interview with Moore (1981), 184:67, MOHP.

24. Cagin and Dray, *We Are Not Afraid*.

25. *Newsweek*, Feb. 24, 1964; *Student Voice*, May 26 and June 9, 1964; "Genocide in Mississippi" (1964), SNCC Papers, A-VII-117; Sovereignty Commission Operator #79 to Governor Paul Johnson, June 26, 1964, Johnson Papers, box 35, folder 10. In the spring of 1964, Mississippi legislators also attempted to pass a bill that would punish mothers of illegitimate children with sterilization. In the debates surrounding the bill, lawmakers argued that this bill would reduce the welfare rolls and drive poor African Americans out of the state. After SNCC publicly critiqued the bill, the senate passed a version that did not include sterilization.

26. JoAnn Ooiman Robinson interview with author (1999), 6; Duncanwood interview with Grele (1994), 23–24, OHRO; Sutherland, *Letters From Mississippi*, 37–38; JoAnn Robinson diary, June 29, 1964, Robinson Papers, box 2, file 1, SHSW.

27. JoAnn Robinson interview with author (1999), 7.

28. Belfrage, *Freedom Summer*, 42, 45; Fields and Mulford, *Freedom on My Mind*; Robinson interview with author (1999), 13. L. C. Dorsey, a native of Shelby, Mississippi, explained in *Freedom on My Mind* that if you were a black man, "you could be lynched for 'eye rape.'"

29. "Mississippi—Summer of 1964: Troubled State, Troubled Time," *Newsweek*, July 13, 1964; Larry Rubin interview with John Rachal (1995), 624:33–35, MOHP; Willie Peacock comments recorded between 1962 and 1964 on Greenwood documentary tapes, Guy Carawan Collection.

30. Sugarman, *Stranger at the Gates*, 130–32; flyer in Jerry Tecklin Papers, box 1, file 8, SHSW. The meeting flyer included a poem: "Come all who want their freedom / Stand like men in Drew / Cause the police have done wrong / And we have a job to do."

31. McAdam, *Freedom Summer*, 83; "Highlights of One Teacher's Experience," SNCC Papers, A-IV-241; "Freedom School Data," SNCC Papers, A-VIII-122; Freedom School newsletters, SNCC Papers, A-XV-111; JoAnn Robinson interview with author (1999), 9.

32. McAdam, *Freedom Summer*, 108–13; Reverend Edwin King interview with author

(1999), 8. Ed King explained that the originally restricted role for white female volunteers loosened up as the summer progressed.

33. Affidavits of Bessie Turner, Feb. 1962 and May 1964, COFO Collection, box 1, folder 3, Coahoma County, MSDAH (also reprinted in Forman, *Making of Black Revolutionaries*, 242–43); Maggie Gordon memo, June 1965, SNCC Papers, A-VIII-117; affidavit of Paul Klein, reprinted in Belfrage, *Freedom Summer*, 126–27; Sutherland, *Letters From Mississippi*, 146; affidavits of Stuart Rawlings, Lorne Cress, and Martin Mullvain, COFO Collection, box 1, folder 4, Forrest County, MSDAH.

34. Aaron Henry interview with Neil McMillen (1972), 52–53, Aaron Henry Papers; Zoya Zeman interview with John Rachal (1995), vol. 626, MOHP; James A. Campbell affidavit, Ruth Schein (1964) Mississippi Freedom Summer Project Collection, box 1, folder 1, SCRBC; Robert Mandel affidavit, COFO Collection, box 1, folder 3, Coahoma County, MSDAH.

35. Copies of Klan newsletters, SNCC Papers, A-VIII-248 and A-VIII-117; Assistant Attorney General Burke Marshall letter to Dan H. Shell, July 15, 1964, Johnson Papers, box 136, folder 1; Belfrage, *Freedom Summer*, 105–6, 164–65; newsletters in Candy Brown Papers and flyer in Jerry Tecklin Papers, SHSW.

36. Grenville Whitman interview with author (1999), 7; Whitefolks Project Reports, SNCC Papers, A-XV-225.

37. Von Hoffman, *Mississippi Notebook*, 68–72; Harris, *Dreams Die Hard*, 76; Fields and Mulford, *Freedom on My Mind*; Kay Prickett letter to Alice Lake, Aug. 11, 1964, Ellen Lake Papers, SHSW.

38. Sellers, *River of No Return*, 94; McAdam, *Freedom Summer*, 257–82; Charles Cobb interview with John Rachal (1996), 29–30, MOHP; Forman, *Making of Black Revolutionaries*, 374–75; Belfrage, *Freedom Summer*, 182–83.

39. Hill, "Deacons for Defense," 57, 251, 295.

40. Grenville Whitman interview with author (1999), 16; and JoAnn Robinson interview with author (1999), 8.

41. Charles Cobb interview with John Rachal (1996), 17, MOHP; Payne, *I've Got the Light of Freedom*, 265–83; Crawford et al., *Women in the Civil Rights Movement*; Phyl Garland, "Negro Heroines Play a Major Role in Challenging Racist Traditions," *Ebony*, Aug. 1966, 27–37.

42. Sutherland, *Letters From Mississippi*, 60–61; Annie Devine interview, #488, MFDP Card 4, 20–21, and Fannie Lou Hamer interview, #491, MFDP Card 16, 17, PSOHC.

43. Moody, *Coming of Age*, 303–83; JoAnn Robinson interview with author (1999), 9–10; Canton staff lists and incident reports, CORE Papers, box 15, file 2, SHSW; State Sovereignty Commission Files on Chinn, MSDAH; anonymous black man interviewed in Tibbee, Mississippi, #164, MFDP Card 18, 1–2, PSOHC. Both Chinn and his son endured jail and beatings for their participation in the movement.

44. Poussaint, "Stresses of the White Female Worker," 401–7; Belfrage, *Freedom Summer*, 42. As a psychiatrist for movement participants in the South, Alvin Poussaint was the first to analyze gender and sexual tensions.

45. McAdam, *Freedom Summer*, 93–95, 106–9, 137; Evans, *Personal Politics*, 79–81, 88.

46. Forman, *Making of Black Revolutionaries*, xvii; report of Operator #79 (Jackson, Mis-

sissippi), July 3, 1964, Johnson Papers, box 136, folder 1. This spy was more interested in the socialist ideas of these women than their budding feminism.

47. SNCC Position Paper, file "Staff Position Papers," SNCC Papers, A-VI-25 (also reprinted in Evans, *Personal Politics*, 87); Rothschild, *Case of Black and White*; Robnett, *How Long?*, 120; King, *Freedom Song*, 452. Casey Hayden and Mary King both argued that Carmichael's joke was really an expression of his frustration with interracial sex during Freedom Summer.

48. Robnett, *How Long?*, 119; Martha Prescod Norman and Reverend Tommie Jean Lunsford interviews with author (2000); Washington, "We Started from Different Ends," 14–15; Charles Scattergood interview with Robert Wright (1970), 23–24, 54–56, CRDP; Evans, *Personal Politics*, 24–25; Payne, *I've Got the Light of Freedom*, 268. Norman and Lunsford both spoke glowingly to me of the support they got from SNCC men.

49. Lee, *For Freedom's Sake*; Mills, *This Little Light of Mine*.

50. Cagin and Dray, *We Are Not Afraid*.

51. Henry Sias (Chairman of MFDP for Issaquena County) interview with Robert Wright (1968), 19–20, CRDP; Branch, *Pillar of Fire*, 456–76; Chafe, *Unfinished Journey*, 312–13.

52. Hodding Carter interview with Robert Wright (1968), 12, CRDP; Charles McLaurin interview with author and SCFP classes; Amzie Moore interview with Michael Garvey (1981), 184:51–52, MOHP; Aaron Henry interview with Neil McMillen (1972), Aaron Henry Papers, 121–27; Dittmer, *Local People*.

53. Jack Wilmore interview with John Britton (1968), 20–23, CRDP; Davidson and Grofman, *Quiet Revolutions*.

Chapter Four

1. William X Longstreet, "What Islam Has Done For Me," *Muhammad Speaks*, Aug. 30, 1963. See also, Walter 3X (Kemp), "'Islam Made a Man of Me,' Says Muslim from South," *Muhammad Speaks*, Dec. 18, 1964. "What Islam Has Done For Me" was a regular feature in *Muhammad Speaks* throughout the early 1960s.

2. Malcolm X, *Autobiography*, 1–2, 10; DeCaro, *On the Side of My People*, 12–17; Perry, *Malcolm*, 12–13.

3. Malcolm X, *Autobiography*, 11–38; Strickland and Greene, *Malcolm X*, 19.

4. Malcolm X, *Autobiography*, 39–150.

5. Clegg, *Original Man*; Malcolm X, *Autobiography*, 169–210; Elijah Muhammad, *Message to the Blackman*, 110–27. The cosmology and theology of the Nation are complex and convoluted. In brief, Muhammad believed that a mad scientist named Yakub used selective breeding and gene splicing to create a race of "white devils" out of the original black race. Eventually, these white devils came to colonize and rule the Earth, but Muhammad preached that as soon as the "so-called Negroes" united under Islam, they could put an end to the reign of the white devils.

6. Alexander and Lack, *Real Malcolm X*; Charles 37X Kenyatta interview with Robert Wright (1970), CRDP. In an interview for *Real Malcolm X*, historian James Cone estimated that there were only about 400 members of the NOI in 1952.

7. Haley interview in Hampton, Frasier, and Flynn, *Voices of Freedom*, 244–48.

8. Malcolm X, *Autobiography*, 221, 226.

9. Elijah Muhammad, *Message to the Blackman*, 59, 127; Patricia Hill Collins, "Learning to Think for Ourselves," in *Malcolm X*, ed. Joe Wood, 74–81; Farah Jasmine Griffin, "'Ironies of the Saint': Malcolm X, Black Women, and the Price of Protection," in *Sisters in the Struggle*, ed. Bettye Collier-Thomas and V. P. Franklin, 214–29.

10. Charles 37X Kenyatta with Robert Wright (1970), 14, CRDP; Kenneth Clark interviews with Ed Erwin (1976 and 1985), 211, OHRO.

11. Lomax, *When the Word is Given*, 45, 69–71; Malcolm X, *Autobiography*, 227.

12. Betty Shabazz, Susan Taylor, and Audrey Edwards, "Loving and Losing Malcolm," *Essence*, Feb. 1992; Malcolm X, *Autobiography*, 228–32; Perry, *Malcolm*, 171–73, 190.

13. Shabazz, Taylor, and Edwards, "Loving and Losing Malcolm." Betty did decide to leave Malcolm three times, after giving birth to their first three daughters, because of this dispute about her working outside of the home. But "each time I left," she said, "he found me, and I was always happy to see him."

14. A full transcription of *Hate that Hate Produced* can be found in Lomax, *To Kill a Black Man*, 65–76; Haley interview in Hampton, Frasier, and Flynn, *Voices of Freedom*, 244.

15. Carson, *Malcolm X*, 105–6, 108, 160, 226; Malcolm X, *Autobiography*, 106. FBI files report that Malcolm was "found mentally disqualified for military service" on Dec. 4, 1944.

16. Carson, *Malcolm X*, 141; John Buffington interview with Robert Wright (1968), 16–17, CRDP; Branch, *Pillar of Fire*, 260, 318.

17. *Muhammad Speaks*, Oct.–Nov., Dec. 1961; Haley and Fisher, *Playboy Interviews*, 19, 44. The first headline of *Muhammad Speaks* was "Some of this Earth for Our Own or Else."

18. Eldridge Cleaver, "As Crinkly As Yours, Brother" (*Negro History Bulletin*, Mar. 1962), reprinted in *Muhammad Speaks*, June 1962; Wilma Ann, "Should Women Wear Pants or Dresses?," *Muhammad Speaks*, Feb. 1962; "For Men Only," *Muhammad Speaks*, Mar. 1962; Grace (X) Peoples, "Housewife Finds More Rewarding Life in Islam," *Muhammad Speaks*, Nov. 8, 1963; Friedan, *The Feminine Mystique*. Friedan analyzes the relationship between advertising and the cult of domesticity.

19. "Nasser's Advocacy of More Freedom for Egypt Women Opposes Old Time Leaders," *Muhammad Speaks*, Aug. 31, 1962; "Women of Africa, Asia, Latin America Play Vital Role at United Nations," *Muhammad Speaks*, Dec. 15, 1962; Tynetta Deanar, "Women in Islam," *Muhammad Speaks*, Mar. 27, 1964.

20. Deanar, "Women in Islam," *Muhammad Speaks*, July 5, 1963, and (n.d.) 1964; Perry, *Malcolm*, 282; "Sit-Ins Expose Our Women to Horrors," *Muhammad Speaks*, Apr. 1962; Eskew, *But for Birmingham*, 266; Lomax, *To Kill a Black Man*, 99; "The Fire Hoses and the Dogs," *Muhammad Speaks*, May 24, 1963.

21. Perry, *Malcolm X*, 121; Tyson, *Radio Free Dixie*, 145, 205.

22. Malcolm X, *Autobiography*, 278–81, 289; Carson, *Malcolm X*, 245; "Minister Malcolm Exposes 'Farce of D.C. March,'" *Muhammad Speaks*, Oct. 25, 1963; Breitman, *Malcolm X Speaks*, 9; Bayard Rustin interviews with Ed Edwin (1984–86), 218, 243–45, OHRO.

23. Baldwin, *Fire Next Time*, 57; Clegg, *Original Man*, 110–13, 184–94; and Malcolm X, *Autobiography*, 294–300.

24. Lomax, *To Kill a Black Man*, 125–35.

25. Clay, *I Am the Greatest!*; Remnick, *King of the World*, xiii; Bingham and Wallace, *Muhammad Ali's Greatest Fight*; and Sammons, *Beyond the Ring*.

26. Malcolm X, *Autobiography*, 303–8; Ali, *Greatest*.

27. Perry, *Malcolm*, 249; *Muhammad Speaks*, Mar. 13, May 8, and Dec. 4, 1964.

28. "Malcolm X Splits with Muhammad," *New York Times*, Mar. 9, 1964; "The Ominous Malcolm X Exits from the Muslims," *Life*, Mar. 20, 1964; Herman Ferguson interview with Robert Wright (1970), 14, CRDP. Ferguson discussed the ways the NOI restrained Malcolm's intellectual growth and also the formation of the Jamaica Rifle and Pistol Club in Queens, one of the few gun clubs directly inspired by Malcolm's rhetoric.

29. Malcolm X, *Autobiography*, 318–48; Carson, *Malcolm X*, 235–37. This was not Malcolm's first trip to the Middle East, and there is some evidence that the earlier trip had raised questions in his mind regarding Muhammad's teachings. For evidence of Malcolm's earlier acknowledgement of white Muslims, see interview transcript from a Washington, D.C. radio show in 1963 where he says, "The people in the Muslim world don't regard a man according to the color of his skin. When you are a Muslim, you don't look at the color of a man's skin, whether he is black, red, white, or green. . . . [Y]ou judge him according to his conscious behavior." This transcript is included in the FBI files edited by Carson.

30. Goldman, *Death and Life of Malcolm X*, 180; Breitman, *Malcolm X Speaks*, 212.

31. "Malcolm X: Black Revolution is Part of World-Wide Struggle," *Militant*, Apr. 27, 1964, Clippings File, Malcolm X Speeches, SCRBC; Malcolm X, *Autobiography*, 364; John Buffington interview with Robert Wright (1968), 23, CRDP; Malcolm telegram to King in St. Augustine, Florida (n.d.), MLK Papers, box 15, file 16 ("Malcolm X—March 1964–February 1965").

32. Lomax, *To Kill a Black Man*, 131; Davis interview in Hampton, Frasier, and Flynn, *Voices of Freedom*, 260; "Dr. King's Statement on Malcolm X," Mar. 16, 1964, MLK Papers, box 15, file 16; "The Ominous Malcolm X Exits from the Muslims," *Look*, Mar. 20, 1964.

33. "Malcolm Exposed by His Brother," *Muhammad Speaks*, Apr. 10, 1964; "Boston Minister Tells of Malcolm—Muhammad's Biggest Hypocrite," *Muhammad Speaks*, Dec. 4, 1964; "Minister Who Knew Him Best . . . Rips Malcolm's Treachery," *Muhammad Speaks*, May 8, 1964; "A Special Memorandum from the Desk of the Messenger of Allah," *Muhammad Speaks*, Sept. 11, 1964; Perry, *Malcolm X*, 125–26. The final quote in this paragraph reveals the complicated and perhaps contradictory gender ideology underpinning Malcolm's critique of his former mentor. As Patricia Hill Collins noted, "To Malcolm, the immorality of Muhammad's acts hinged not on his immoral treatment of women but on his not acting like a 'man' and owning up to his actions." Collins, "Learning to Think for Ourselves," 78.

34. Goldman, *Death and Life of Malcolm X*, 160–82; DeCaro, *On the Side of My People*, 209–10, 221; Malcolm speech at the Militant Labor Forum, Jan. 7, 1965, reprinted in Breitman, *Malcolm X Speaks*, 197–98.

35. Perry, *Malcolm*, ix, 26, 182; Herman Ferguson interview with Robert Wright (1970), 10–11, CRDP; Sanchez interview in Hampton, Frasier, and Flynn, *Voices of Freedom*, 254–55; Griffin, "Ironies of the Saint," in *Sisters in the Struggle*, ed. Bettye Collier-Thomas and V. P. Franklin, 224. Griffin cites the poet Gwendolyn Brooks, who would later speak in similar terms about Malcolm: "We gasped. We saw the maleness. . . . [Malcolm] opened us—who was a key, who was a man."

36. Perry, *Malcolm*, 319, 336; Amina Rhman (formerly Sharon X) interview in Strickland and Greene, *Malcolm X*, 123; Breitman, *Malcolm X Speaks*, 133–36; Malcolm letter to cousin-in-law, 1965, in Barbara Ransby and Tracy Matthews, "Black Popular Culture and

the Transcendence of Patriarchal Illusions," in *Words of Fire*, ed. Beverly Guy-Sheftall, 530; Perry, *Malcolm X*, 96, 125–26.

37. Carson, *Malcolm X*, 343, 473; Lomax, *To Kill a Black Man*, 252; Peter Bailey interview with Robert Wright (1968), 60, CRDP; excerpts from Davis's eulogy in Malcolm X, *Autobiography*, 454. FBI investigators and many others close to Malcolm believe that police and CIA officials may have known that the militant leader would be assassinated but did nothing to stop it. Strangely, Malcolm himself ordered the guards at his last meeting not to search the crowd for weapons, a custom that he had continued since his days in the NOI.

38. Strickland and Greene, *Malcolm X*, 65.

39. Worth and Perl, *Malcolm X*; Clark, *Dark Ghetto*, 47–48, 70–74. Clark, an African American sociologist, conducted a study of the Harlem Youth Opportunities Unlimited (HARYOU) program, which Daniel Patrick Moynihan cited for support of his report on the black family.

Chapter Five

1. Secretary of Labor Willard Wirtz memo to President Lyndon Johnson, May 4, 1965, Wirtz Papers, box 220, file "1965 — White House-President, May"; Willard Wirtz interview with the author (2000); *The Negro Family: The Case for National Action*, originally released by the Government Printing Office, Washington, D.C., 1965, reprinted in Rainwater and Yancey, *Moynihan Report*, 41–124.

2. Wirtz memo to Johnson, May 4, 1965, Wirtz Papers; Wirtz interview with the author (2000); *Negro Family*.

3. Roemer and Young, *Nothing But a Man*. For published reviews of this film, see the *New York Times Magazine*, Dec. 20, 1964, and *Newsweek*, Jan. 11, 1965.

4. Ehrenreich, *Hearts of Men*; Goldman, *Death and Life of Malcolm X*, 23; Wirtz memo to Lyndon Johnson, May 4, 1965, 4; Clark, *Dark Ghetto*, 32–34.

5. Paul Barton interview with author (2000); Ellen Broderick memo to Frank Erwin, Nov. 4, 1965, Wirtz Papers, box 296, file PI 6-3-6, "1965 Integration, Civil Rights, Voting Rights, and the Negro Family"; Wirtz memo to Bill Moyers, May 23, 1965, Wirtz Papers, box 290, file PE 4–2, "Moynihan, Daniel P." Paul Barton, who was a social science advisor on Moynihan's staff at the DOL in 1964, remembers beginning the research for the *Negro Family* report in December of that year. The only outside reader of the report, according to Ellen Broderick, was Dr. William F. Soskin, a psychologist on the staff of the National Institutes of Health's Office of Planning. Secretary Wirtz sent the report to Moyers with a cover sheet that said, "This is the Moynihan report I called you about. I think it warrants *very serious* consideration. There are *no* other copies in circulation."

6. Schoen, *Pat*, 1.

7. Barton interview with author (2000), 6; Moynihan memo to Wirtz, June 14, 1965, Wirtz Papers, box 290, file PE 4–2, "Moynihan, Daniel P." Although Moynihan originally doubted the influence of the policy planning process, the completion of this report and its initial support from the White House proved to him that his staff had made a real difference in policy.

8. Office of Policy Planning and Research (DOL), *The Negro Family*, 1–14. The numbers cited in this section of the report compare the nonwhite and white populations.

9. Moynihan, *Negro Family*, 15–28. For the analysis of slavery, Moynihan cited his col-

league and co-author Nathan Glazer from Glazer and Moynihan, *Beyond the Melting Pot*, and also the historian Stanley Elkins's *Slavery*. In the late 1960s and early 1970s, historians revised substantially Elkins's original thesis that slavery had emasculated black men, transforming them into "Sambos." See also Frasier, *Negro Family in the United States*. Moynihan and his staff were most worried about the fact that minority male unemployment had actually dropped in the mid-1960s, but family breakdown had continued to worsen.

10. Moynihan, *Negro Family*, 29–40, 44–45; Clark, *Dark Ghetto*; Clark interview with Malaika Lumumba (1970), 31, CRDP. The phrase "tangle of pathology" came from the final report of the Harlem Youth Opportunities Unlimited, Inc. (HARYOU) in 1964, written by the chairman of the board of directors for HARYOU, Kenneth Clark. In the later interview, Clark argued, "Of course, you know that the pathology of the black community can only be understood in terms of the pathology, the sickness, probably the terminal sickness, of the larger society."

11. Moynihan, *Negro Family*, 40–43; Moynihan memo to Wirtz, Jan. 12, 1965, Wirtz Papers, box 290, file PE 4–2, "Moynihan, Daniel P;" Moynihan memo to Harry McPherson, July 16, 1965, WHAF (Harry McPherson), box 21, file "McPherson: Civil Rights." In his January 1965 memo to Wirtz, Moynihan elaborated on his view of using military recruitment "as an instrument of manpower policy."

12. Lemann, *Promised Land*.

13. Billington, "Lyndon B. Johnson and Blacks," 26–42.

14. Moynihan memo to Wirtz, June 1, 1965, Wirtz Papers, box 290, folder PE 4–2, "Moynihan, Daniel P."; Rainwater and Yancey, *Moynihan Report*, 188. The June 1965 memo from Moynihan to Wirtz includes Moynihan's first draft of the speech, which lays out the general themes and ideas echoed in the president's speech. On the impact of slavery, Moynihan wrote, "It is time we faced the fact that American slavery was the most awful the world has ever known. We have had enough of magnolias and banjos. The fact is that American slavery denied the humanity of the slave, destroyed his family, and stripped him of his manhood." According to Moynihan, Wilkins and Young were reportedly "enthusiastic" about the speech. Though some have argued that Martin Luther King Jr. also saw an advance copy of the speech, I have seen no evidence of this.

15. Original of Howard speech, June 4, 1965, Ex SP 3-93, WHCF, box 172 (also reprinted in Rainwater and Yancey, *Moynihan Report*, 125–32).

16. Telegram from King to Johnson, June 7, 1965, MLK Papers, series I, box 13, file 7; letters to Johnson and his response to Wilkins, June-July, 1965, Ex SP 3-93, WHCF, file SP 3-93/Pro-Con/A–Z. Of the many letters the president received, only four (all from white southerners) offered criticisms of the speech.

17. Rainwater and Yancey, *Moynihan Report*, 133–39; Katzmann, *Daniel Patrick Moynihan*.

18. Horne, *Fire This Time*, 3, 12, 39–40, 54–55, 185–243. Horne argues that the Moynihan report created a distorted response to the uprisings, focusing attention not on unemployment, housing, and education, but on gender roles and family structure.

19. Horne, *Fire This Time*, 205, 230; U.S. Commission on Civil Rights, *Time to Listen*, 108; Moynihan, *Miles to Go*, 178–79; Lemann, *Promised Land*, 174–75; Frank Erwin (executive assistant to Wirtz) interview with author (2000); Rainwater and Yancey, *Moynihan Report*, 133–54. As quoted in the notes to *Time to Listen*, the *McCone Commission Report* observed,

"The welfare program that provides for his [Negro male] children is administered so that it injures his position as head of his household, because aid is supplied with less restraint to a family headed by a woman, married or unmarried. Thus, the unemployed male often finds it to his family's advantage to drift away and leave the family to fend for itself. Once he goes, the family unit is broken and seldom restored."

20. Rainwater and Yancey, *Moynihan Report*, 149–51; Ryan, *Blaming the Victim*, 5–11, 63–88.

21. Rainwater and Yancey, *Moynihan Report*, 197; Ryan, *Blaming the Victim*; Bill Moyers's memo to Joe Califano, July 30, 1965, Ex HU2, WHCF, box 3; *Citizen*, Oct. 1965. Ryan also criticized Moynihan's use of illegitimacy data, arguing that the higher access to abortion for white women lowered the number of births to unmarried white couples.

22. Benjamin Payton, "The President, the Social Experts, and the Ghetto: An Analysis of an Emerging Strategy in Civil Rights," Oct. 4, 1965, White House Conference "To Fulfill These Rights," box 67, file "Miscellaneous Papers, Moynihan/Glick," LBJ Library.

23. Mary Dublin Keyserling, "The Negro Woman at Work: Gains and Problems," address to the Conference on the Negro Woman in the U.S.A., Nov. 11, 1965, Washington, D.C., White House Conference "To Fulfill These Rights," master book E, section B, box 72, LBJ Library (Keyserling added the emphasis in the Moynihan quote); Moynihan, "Employment Income, and the Ordeal of the Negro Family," 745–70; Rainwater and Yancey, *Moynihan Report*, 199–203, 395–426; Bayard Rustin interviews with Ed Edwin (1984–1986), 164–65, OHRO.

24. King speeches, "The Dignity of Family Life," Oct. 29, 1965, and "Speech on the Negro Family," Jan. 27, 1966, MLK Papers, "Speeches, Sermons, Etc.," box 9, file "August 1–December 31, 1965," and box 10, file "January–May 1966."

25. Harry McPherson, "Big Six Meeting," Oct. 22, 1965, WHAF, box 21, file "McPherson: Civil Rights—1965"; Herb Gans letter to Richard Goodwin, Aug. 27, 1965, WHAF (Lee White), box 5, file "Equal Rights Conference, 1965"; Payton, "The President, the Social Experts, and the Ghetto," Oct. 14, 1965, White House Conference "To Fulfill These Rights," box 67, file "Miscellaneous Papers—Moynihan/Glick," LBJ Library; Moynihan, *Miles to Go*, 188.

26. Transcript of Planning Session Number 5, "The Family," Nov. 17, 1965, White House Conference "To Fulfill These Rights," box 23, LBJ Library; Rainwater and Yancey, *Moynihan Report*, 252–54; White, *Too Heavy a Load*, 189–211. Despite Height's eloquent testimony here, White criticizes what she sees as Height's general unwillingness to address both race *and* gender issues during the movement era.

27. Hylan Lewis, "The Family Resources for Change," Dec. 1965, White House Conference "To Fulfill These Rights," box 17, file "Family-Preliminary Report," LBJ Library; New York University law professor (unnamed) letter to Joe Califano and attached notes, Dec. 14, 1965, WHAF (Lee White), box 5, file "1966 Spring White House Conference"; Monroe E. Price memo to Willard Wirtz, Dec. 20, 1965, Wirtz Papers, box 240, file "1965—White House Conference on Civil Rights."

28. "Social and Economic Conditions of Negroes in the United States," Oct. 1967, 95, MLK Papers, series I, box 26, file 9; Bureau of Labor Statistics Report Number 332, compiled by the Departments of Labor and the Census, and Wirtz's memo to President Johnson, Dec. 23, 1966, Wirtz Papers, box 322, file "Working Papers, Employment 1966—Unemploy-

ment in the Slums"; Honey, *Black Workers Remember*, 289–90. Poverty levels and unemployment were even worse in southern cities and rural areas. According to Honey, in the 1960s, 57 percent of the black community in Memphis, Tennessee lived below the poverty line (nearly double the figure in Cleveland). In nearby Fayette County, Tennessee (a rural area dominated by agricultural production), almost 70 percent of able-bodied black adults were unemployed.

29. U.S. Commission on Civil Rights, *Time to Listen*, 29–35; "Hearings before the U.S. Commission on Civil Rights" (held in Cleveland, Ohio, Apr. 1–7, 1966), Wirtz Papers, box 341, file "1966—Commission, Civil Rights."

30. *New York Times*, May 24, 1966; "SNCC Statement on White House Conference," May 23, 1966, SNCC Papers, A-VIII-309; conference speeches and "Report of the White House Conference," Wirtz Papers, box 346, file "White House Conference 'To Fulfill These Rights.'"

31. *Washington Post*, May 30, 1966; McPherson memo to cabinet members, June 1966, Wirtz Papers, box 346, file "White House Conference "To Fulfill These Rights'"; Wirtz interview with author (2000). In this interview, Wirtz described the diminishing support for full employment and other labor initiatives as a consequence of the administration's increasing focus on Vietnam.

32. CORE, "Statement of Position on the White House Conference "To Fulfill These Rights,'" June 1966, MLK Papers, series I, box 26, file 23.

33. Moynihan memo to McPherson, July 16, 1965, and "Fact Sheet on 'Negro Participation in the Armed Forces and in Viet Nam,'" Dec. 17, 1965, in WHAF (Harry McPherson), boxes 21 and 22, file "McPherson: Civil Rights"; Barton interview with author (2000); Moynihan speech to Americans for Democratic Action, "The Politics of Stability," Sept. 23, 1967, WHCF, Ex SP/WE, box 55. The total number of U.S. casualties in Vietnam by 1965 was still relatively small. Federal officials explained the high number of African Americans serving in Vietnam by pointing to the higher percentages of black soldiers that reenlisted. In his 1967 speech, Moynihan defended LBJ's actions in Vietnam, even when they impinged on social programs at home.

34. Ruiz and Cummings, "Cultural Identity and the Moynihan Report," 65–72; Grier and Cobbs, *Black Rage*, 22, 31, 60, 83, 87; Hernton, *Sex and Racism* and *White Papers*; Clark, *Dark Ghetto*, 47, 68, 70–74.

35. Staples, "Myth" and *Black Family*; Davis, "Reflections" and *Women, Race, and Class*; Gutman, *Black Family in Slavery and Freedom*; Carol Stack, *All Our Kin*; Zinn, "Family, Race, and Poverty," 856–74; White, *Too Heavy a Load*, 198–203.

36. Jordan, *Technical Difficulties*, 65–80; Sanchez, "Queens of the Universe," 29–34. June Jordan originally published "Memo to Daniel Pretty Moynihan" in the 1970s but reprinted it with an additional discussion of the Moynihan Report in the 1990s.

37. A transcription of Lawrence Spivak, "Meet the Press," NBC Radio and Television, Dec. 12, 1965, can be found in Wirtz Papers, box 290, file PE 4-2, "Moynihan, Daniel P."; Moynihan letter to Harry McPherson, Sept. 22, 1966, WHAF (McPherson), box 22, file "McPherson: Civil Rights"; Moynihan, "President and the Negro," 31–45.

38. "Action for Working Americans," Nov. 1968, U.S. Department of Labor Office of Information, Publications and Reports, Wirtz Papers, box 632, file PI-I, "1968: Summary Plans and Reports"; Moynihan, *Politics of a Guaranteed Income*; Moynihan memo reprinted in

the *New York Times*, Mar. 1, 1970; "A Case of 'Benign Neglect,'" *Newsweek*, Mar. 16, 1970. Moynihan had taken the phrase "benign neglect" from the annals of English history, when officials had suggested that British-Irish relations had gotten so tense that they would benefit from a period of "benign neglect."

39. Barton interview with author (2000), 7; Wirtz interview with author (2000); Rainwater and Yancey, *Moynihan Report*, 22.

40. Moynihan, *Miles to Go*, 171–72; Wilson, *Truly Disadvantaged*; Zinn, "Family, Race, and Poverty"; Collins, "Comparison of Two Works"; Edsall and Edsall, *Chain Reaction*, 53–55, 277–81.

Chapter Six

1. Beifuss, *At the River I Stand*, 244–45.

2. Green, "Battling the Plantation Mentality"; Gary Wills, "Martin Luther King *Is Still on the Case!*," *Esquire*, Aug. 1968, 99; Appleby, Graham, and Ross, *At the River I Stand*; Chafe, *Civilities and Civil Rights*. Chafe's analysis of paternalism or "civility" as stifling the movement is a model for the analysis in this chapter.

3. Faue, "Gender"; Kessler-Harris, "Treating the Male"; Baron, *Work Engendered*; Trotter, "African-American Workers"; Lewis, "Invoking Concepts."

4. Bederman, "'Civilization,'" 13; Goings and Smith, "'Unhidden' Transcripts." Goings and Smith suggest that the lynching campaign in Memphis was an effort to quell working-class political activism in the city.

5. Honey, *Southern Labor*, 20; Honey, "Martin Luther King"; Roediger, *Wages of Whiteness*. Honey shows that segregation undercut wages for unskilled white and black laborers, but white craft union members successfully used exclusion of blacks from their positions to keep wages high by limiting the labor market. Roediger examines racial divisions within the American working class in an earlier period.

6. Honey, *Black Workers Remember*; Korstad and Lichtenstein, "Opportunities Lost." According to Honey, the CIO did successfully unionize black and white workers in the Memphis Firestone, Ford, and Fisher plants during World War II. The Firestone union leaders lent their meeting hall to the sanitation workers during the 1968 strike. Korstad and Lichtenstein look at union drives and civil rights activities during this period.

7. Honey, *Black Workers Remember*, 294; Honey "Martin Luther King, Jr.," 154, 156; Beifuss, *At the River I Stand*, 35.

8. Beifuss, *At the River I Stand*, 19, 30; *Memphis Commercial Appeal*, Feb. 2, 1968.

9. Beifuss, *At the River I Stand*, 32. Dues check-off is a procedure that allows union members' dues to be taken directly out of their paychecks in the same way that state and federal taxes are taken out. This procedure ensures that all union members pay their dues on time.

10. Ezekial Bell interview with Bill Wilson and Jerry Viar (1968), #178, box 20, file 14, 16, MVC; Gwen Awsumb interview with David and Carol Lynn Yellin and Anne Trotter (1968), 8–9, MVC, box 20, file 6; Cornelia Crenshaw interview with James Mosby (1968), interview #243, RJB. Crenshaw remained an outspoken participant in the strike leadership as a member of the strategy committee for the ministers' group, Community on the Move for Equality (COME).

11. Lentz, "Sixty-Five Days in Memphis"; Lentz shows how the two Memphis papers,

which he characterizes as moderate during the desegregation of public facilities in the early 1960s, portray Ciampa as the quintessential northern "outsider," the carpetbagger.

12. Green, "Labor in the South," 170; McKnight, "1968 Memphis Sanitation Strike," 142.

13. Beifuss, *At the River I Stand*, 46; Green, "Labor in the South," 202; James Robinson interview in Honey, *Black Workers Remember*, 307. Green attributes the "I *AM* a Man" slogan to Lucy, but former sanitation worker James Robinson remembers that Reverend Albert Hibbler came up with the slogan.

14. Muddy Waters, *His Best, 1947 to 1955*; Ward, *Just My Soul Responding*, 72–79, 143. For a song with similar themes, see Muddy Waters's "Hoochie Coochie Man."

15. Fred Davis interview with James Mosby (1968), interview #253, RJB; Beifuss, *At the River I Stand*, 75–84; Ezekial Bell interview with Bill Wilson and Jerry Viar (1968), 22, box 21, file 77, MVC. Memphis had just instituted the mayor and city council system of government. The council members were not sure who had the final say in a strike of municipal employees. They decided to pass the political buck on to the mayor.

16. Beifuss, *At the River I Stand*, 86; Ed Gillis interview with David Yellin and Bill Thomas (1968), 36, box 21, file 77, MVC; Jack Wilmore interviewed by John Britton (1968), interview #316, RJB; Appleby, Graham, and Ross, *At the River I Stand*.

17. Green, "Labor in the South," 180–82; Beifuss, *At the River I Stand*, 102–3.

18. Beifuss, *I Am A Man*, 62.

19. Transcript of King's Mason Temple speech, Mar. 18, 1968, 6–7, box 22, file 121, MCV.

20. Peter Ling, "Gender and Generation: Manhood at the Southern Christian Leadership Conference," in *Gender in the Civil Rights Movement*, eds. Ling and Monteith, 111.

21. Fairclough, *To Redeem the Soul of America*, 50; Ling, "Gender and Generation," 101–29. According to Fairclough, King had once said, "The primary obligation of women is motherhood."

22. Juanita Abernathy interview with author (1995); Ling, "Gender and Generation," 101–29. Abernathy noted that the only females who were regularly present at SCLC executive staff meetings, Septima Clark and Dorothy Cotton, were often asked to take notes. Clark and Cotton directed the Citizenship Education Program. This was one of the few avenues to leadership for women in SCLC, because it paralleled a "feminine" occupation in the larger society, the teaching profession.

23. Appleby, Graham, and Ross, *At the River I Stand*; Hosea Williams and R. B. Cotton-reader interviews with author (1995).

24. Calvin Taylor interview with Jerry Viar and Bill Thomas (1968), 18, box 24, file 234, MVC; Beifuss, *At the River I Stand*, 131–32; Charles Ballard and Charles Cabbage interviews with James Mosby (1968), interviews #240 and #255, RJB.

25. Calvin Taylor interview with Jerry Viar and Bill Thomas (1968), 40, box 24, file 234, MVC.

26. Ibid., 34.

27. Beifuss, *At the River I Stand*, 131; Calvin Taylor interview with Jerry Viar and Bill Thomas (1968), 7, box 24, file 234, MVC.

28. Beifuss, *At the River I Stand*, 219; James Lawson interview (1970), 17, box 22, file 141, MVC.

29. King, *Where Do We Go From Here*, 38–47; Ling, "Gender and Generation," 114; Griswold del Castillo and Garcia, *César Chávez*, 87–88. When King came out against the war in Vietnam, he defended his position by explaining, "There is a masculinity and a strength in nonviolence."

30. James Robinson interview in Honey, *Black Workers Remember*, 306; James Lawson interview with Joan Beifuss and Bill Thomas (1969), 44, box 22, file 135, and 4, box 22, file 134, MVC. Lawson argued that people had always questioned the tactics of nonviolence in the movement. "The same question that you get now from among young people about nonviolence, I got them ten years ago from old and young. . . . There has never been an acceptance of the nonviolent approach. And this is why I dismiss those commentators, who say, you know, 'The Negro accepted nonviolence once and now he doesn't.' This is nonsense."

31. Beifuss, *At the River I Stand*, 159, 231; Richard Moon interview with Judy Schultz, Jerry Viar, and Joan Beifuss (1968), 9–10, box 28, file 179, MVC; Maxine Smith interview, 30, box 24, file 217, MVC. Joan Beifuss has a slightly different version of the story that Smith tells in which the police officer called the female NAACP workers "black bitches."

32. Quotes from *Tri-State Defender* in Beifuss, *At the River I Stand*, 248; *Commercial Appeal*, Mar. 31, 1968; Lentz, "Sixty-Five Days in Memphis," 29–30.

33. Calvin Taylor interview with Jerry Viar and Bill Thomas (1968), 41, box 24, file 135, and 50, box 24, file 135, MVC; Beifuss, *At the River I Stand*, 253. Taylor recalled that, when King entered the room, "it seemed like all of a sudden there was a real rush of wind and everything just went out that was bad and peace and calm just settled over everything."

34. King, *I've Been to the Mountaintop*, 12–13.

35. King, *I've Been to the Mountaintop*, 7. SCLC leaders like Jesse Jackson used these same ideas to win a hospital worker's strike in Charleston in 1969 with the slogan "I Am Somebody."

36. Carson, *In Struggle*, 288; Coe interview in Honey, *Black Workers Remember*, 313; Honey, "Martin Luther King," 166. Coe was especially angry when he found out that other black Memphians "weren't going to do nothin'" in terms of an organized, armed insurrection after King was shot. Almost one million dollars of property damage and three deaths resulted from the chaos in Memphis after King's death, but other urban areas witnessed more destruction and even heavier casualties.

37. Stanfield, *In Memphis*, 5; Lewis, "Social Religion," 131.

38. Beifuss, *At the River I Stand*, 150; Appleby, Graham, and Ross, *At the River I Stand*.

39. Beifuss, *At the River I Stand*, 163; Gwen Awsumb interview, 24, box 20, file 8, MVC; Pohlmann and Kirby, *Racial Politics*. Prior to the misquote in the paper, Awsumb had received calls from black women who also disagreed with her position, but she did not note what those callers said. The black community in Memphis was relatively unified during the sanitation strike (especially compared to the white community), but according to Pohlmann and Kirby, class-based divisions within the black community would later limit the power of the city's black voting block for years after the strike.

40. Richard Moon interview with Judy Schultz, Jerry Viar, and Joan Beifuss (1968), 19, box 28, file 179, MVC; James Lawson interview with Joan Beifuss and Bill Thomas (1969), 29, box 22, file 137, MVC; Concerned Women of Memphis, publicity pamphlet and summary, box 7, file 42, item #21, MVC. After the strike, women in Memphis organized to tackle their own issues. Some of the female supporters of the strikers organized as the Concerned Women of

Memphis in 1968. This group pressured Memphis leaders to reach a relatively quick settlement in a hospital strike that followed the sanitation strike.

41. Green, "Battling the Plantation Mentality"; and Giddings, *When and Where I Enter.*

42. Speeches on "Maids" from St. Mary's Episcopal School for Girls, box 23, file 209, MVC; Hunter, *To 'Joy My Freedom.*

43. Hazel McGhee interview with Paul Ortiz (italics in original quote); Green, "Battling the Plantation Mentality," 399; Mr. and Mrs. L. C. Reed interview with Bill Thomas (1968), 18, box 23, file 203, MVC.

44. Maxine Smith interview (1968), 35, box 24, file 217, MVC.

45. Rogers interview in Honey, *Black Workers Remember,* 296–97; Richard Moon interview, 28, box 28, file 178, MVC; Wills, "Martin Luther King," *Esquire,* Aug. 1968, 101.

46. Green, "Labor in the South," 315–16; Appleby, Graham, and Ross, *At the River I Stand*; Hosea Williams interview with author (1995). In this quote, Williams exhibits the disparity between the language of 1968 and 1995—the tension between the "rights of man" and "human rights"—when he says that "a man is someone [that] makes *his or her* own decisions."

47. Honey, "Martin Luther King," 167–68; Henry P. Liefermann, "A Year Later in Memphis," *Nation,* Mar. 31, 1969, 401–3; DRUM song transcript in Van Deburg, *New Day in Babylon,* 97.

Chapter Seven

1. Seale, *Seize the Time,* 102–3.

2. "March of Foolishness and Death," *Black Panther,* May 18, 1968, 2.

3. Eldridge Cleaver interview in Hampton, Frasier, and Flynn, *Voices of Freedom,* 515–16; Eldridge Cleaver affidavit, reprinted in *Black Panther,* June 10, 1968, 18; Cleaver and Linfield, "Education of Kathleen Neal Cleaver," 187. "I think what happened was that the Panthers shot at the police," says Eldridge's former wife Kathleen Cleaver, who did not observe the incident directly. "It could be seen as a decision to strike. If you want to liberate yourself, you've got to get rid of the occupier."

4. Transcript of Eldridge Cleaver speech in Omaha, Neb., Aug. 24, 1968, 11, Black Panther Party—FBI Files, box 1, folder 9, SCRBC; Eldridge Cleaver affidavit, reprinted in *Black Panther,* June 10, 1968, 18.

5. Eldridge Cleaver interview in Hampton, Frasier, and Flynn, *Voices of Freedom,* 514–17; Eldridge Cleaver affidavit, reprinted in *Black Panther,* June 10, 1968, 18; Hilliard and Cole, *This Side of Glory,* 183–88; Pearson, *Shadow of the Panther,* 155–56.

6. "One Year Later," *Black Panther,* Apr. 6, 1969, 4; Cleaver, *Post-Prison Writings,* 40–41.

7. Wallace, *Black Macho,* 34–35, 54–55; Pearson, *Shadow of the Panther*; Matthews, "'No One Ever Asks.'" Journalists, scholars, and many of the Panthers themselves have discussed gender issues in the party. Michele Wallace penned *Black Macho* as a feminist critique of Black Power advocates. Hugh Pearson, a journalist, offers the exposé *Shadow of the Panther,* in which drug abuse, gangsterism, and violent male chauvinism completely eclipsed any positive contributions of the Party. Tracye Matthews's essay in *Black Panther Party (Reconsidered)* revises these accounts by showing that the Panthers wrestled with issues of gender and sexuality.

8. Ten Point Platform, reprinted in every edition of *Black Panther*; Seale, *Seize the Time*, 62–63.

9. Huey Newton, "Fear and Doubt," *Black Panther*, June 10, 1968, 15.

10. Newton, *Revolutionary Suicide*, 24–54; Seale, *Seize the Time*, 12, 34–62. Newton was born in Louisiana, and Seale was born in Texas.

11. Hampton, Frasier, and Flynn, *Voices of Freedom*, 350; Seale, *Seize the Time*, 85–93.

12. *San Francisco Examiner*, Apr. 30, 1967; *New York Times*, May 3, 1967; Executive Mandate #1, reprinted in *Black Panther*, Oct. 26, 1968, 9. A strengthened gun control bill passed in the California legislature in July 1967.

13. Charles E. Jones and Judson L. Jeffries, "'Don't Believe the Hype': Debunking the Panther Mythology," in *Black Panther Party [Reconsidered]*, ed. Charles E. Jones, 41–43; "Eldridge Cleaver: A Candid Conversation with the Revolutionary Leader of the Black Panthers," *Playboy*, Dec. 1968, 108; Hilliard and Cole, *This Side of Glory*, 161; Sanchez interview in Hampton, Frasier, and Flynn, *Voices of Freedom*, 370.

14. Brown, *Taste of Power*, 120, 124–27; "Power! (1967–68)" *Eyes on the Prize II*, part 3; Ray "Masai" Hewitt interview with Ron Grele (1984), 62–67, OHRO.

15. Hilliard and Cole, *This Side of Glory*, 3; Seale's 1991 introduction to *Seize the Time*, ii; Ray "Masai" Hewitt interview with Ron Grele (1984), 116, OHRO; Bobby Seale memo to Panther lawyer Charles Geary, Sept. 16, 1973, Newton Papers, series 2, box 15, folder 8. The Panthers rarely discussed membership numbers during their heyday, but memoirs, interviews, and police estimates have centered on these figures. Seale's memo lists the active chapters in 1973.

16. Eldridge Cleaver speech at Howard University, Sept. 18, 1968, 18–19, Black Panther Party—FBI Files, box 1, folder 9, SCRBC.

17. Cleaver, *Soul on Ice*, 152–53, 165–75.

18. Ibid., 124–25; Cleaver, "Psychology: The Black Bible," in *Post-Prison Writings*, 18, 20; Fanon, *Wretched of the Earth*, 37, 94. Though Fanon does speak of violence as a "cleansing force" that restores self-respect to oppressed colonial peoples, the English translation of his work, at least, speaks little about the role of violence in achieving manhood per se.

19. "Huey Newton Speaks to 'The Movement,'" reprinted by the Tuesday the Ninth Committee and the Berkeley Commune, 7–8, Newton Papers, series 1, box 59, folder 3.

20. Robert Brown interview with Ron Grele (1984), 67–68, OHRO; and "Breaking Capitalism Down," *Black Panther*, Apr. 20, 1969.

21. Cleaver, *Soul on Ice*, 97–106; Cecil Brown, "The Minister of Information Raps: An Interview with Eldridge Cleaver," *Evergreen Review*, Oct. 1968, 46–47; Baraka, "american sexual reference: black male," in *Home*, 216–33; Woodard, *Nation Within a Nation*.

22. D'Emilio, "Homophobia"; Branch, *Parting the Waters*, 172–73, 196–97, 315–16, 861. Aaron Henry, Al Lowenstein, and Bayard Rustin rarely, if ever, discussed their sexuality openly during this period, yet many in the movement knew that they were gay or bisexual.

23. David Major, "poetic pig end," *Black Panther*, Oct. 12, 1968, 13; J. White, "Panther Poem," *Black Panther*, Sept. 7, 1968, 13; *New York Times*, Oct. 3, 1968; Eldridge Cleaver speech at the Berkeley Community Center, reprinted in *Black Panther*, Dec. 21, 1968, 12–13; "An Aside to Ronald Reagan," *Black Panther*, June 21, 1969, 10. At another point, Cleaver threatened to castrate the mayor of San Francisco.

24. Cleaver and Linfield, "Education of Kathleen Neal Cleaver," 186; June Culberson,

"The Role of the Revolutionary Woman," *Black Panther*, May 4, 1969, 9; Madalynn C. Rucker and JoNina M. Abron, "'Comrade Sisters': Two Women of the Black Panther Party," in *Unrelated Kin*, eds. Etter-Lewis and Foster, 163; Black Panther speech in Boston, Black Panther Party—FBI Files, box 1, folder 9, SCRBC. One male Panther told women gathered at a Boston rally to "get your guns for yourselves, because we need some revolutionary women. You all should be able to use those guns too."

25. Brown, *Taste of Power*, 126–36; "Black Survival," *Black Panther*, Oct. 5, 1968, 4; "The Black Revolutionary Woman," *Black Panther*, Sept. 28, 1968, 11.

26. Newton, *Revolutionary Suicide*, 92–93; Gitlin, *Sixties*, 371–72; Masai Hewitt interview with Ron Grele (1984), 2–5, OHRO; "Black Women and the Revolution," *Black Panther*, Mar. 3, 1969, 9; Robert Bowen interview with Ron Grele (1984), 111–12, OHRO; Hilliard and Cole, *This Side of Glory*, 221–25, 234–35. Gitlin looks at the problems of free love becoming exploitative sex in the white movement. Robert Bowen, a member of the party in the Bay Area, remembered a time when female Panthers were told, "If you want to stay in the Black Panther Party, you have to fuck a Panther."

27. Eldridge Cleaver speech at Howard University, Oct. 18, 1968, Black Panther Party—FBI Files, box 1, folder 9, SCRBC; Cleaver speech to the Black Student Union at the University of California at Los Angeles, Aug. 1968, in Robert Igriega, "Eldridge for 'Pussy Power,'" *Open City*, Aug. 9–15, 1968, 1; Matthews, "No One Ever Asks," 281.

28. Gitlin, *Sixties*, 292.

29. "Social and Economic Conditions of Negroes in the United States," published by the Department of Labor's Bureau of Labor Statistics and the Commerce Department's Bureau of the Census, Oct. 1967, 38, 83, MLK Papers, series I, box 26, file 9; Brother Omar, "To My GI Brothers" *Black Panther*, Oct. 4, 1968, 14; Bobby Seale, "Black Soldiers as Revolutionaries to Overthrow the Ruling Class," *Black Panther*, Sept. 20, 1969, 1; "The Negro and the Army," *Washington Post*, May 25, 1966. As early as 1966, black soldiers made up more than twenty percent of some combat units in Vietnam. And they accounted for fifteen percent of the casualties by June 1967.

30. "Editorial: B.P.P. and P.F.P.," *Black Panther Party*, Mar. 16, 1968, 3; "Chicago Panthers Serve the People," *Black Panther*, May 31, 1969, 4. After the idealistic experiment of Freedom Summer, SNCC's black leaders grew more and more wary of white participation in the organization. By 1966, the last remaining white activists were expelled or forced to resign from the group.

31. Gitlin, *Sixties*, 252, 327, 337; Mailer, *Armies of the Night*, 288; Rossinow, *Politics of Authenticity*, 16–17. Norman Mailer observed this same "crisis" of middle class masculinity during an antiwar protest at the Pentagon. Historian Doug Rossinow believes that, though the New Left sought to give voice to all citizens through participatory democracy, like an older generation they "still equated this invigorated citizenship with masculinity, viewing it as a triumph over effeminacy."

32. David Gilbert interview with Ron Grele (1987), 180, 201, 346–47, OHRO. Sentiments also expressed in a letter to the author from David Gilbert. Gilbert qualifies this statement by saying that the members of the Weather Underground accepted that violence was not for everyone and that the movement had room for many different levels of struggle.

33. Evans, *Personal Politics*, 108–19, 152–55, 177–79; Betty Garman Robinson interview with author (2000), 16–17; David Gilbert interview with Ron Grele (1987), 240, Gregory

Calvert interview with Ron Grele (1991), 282–83, 335, OHRO. Betty Garman Robinson, who worked with both SDS and the National Student Association in the early 1960s, described the male chauvinism embedded within these organizations.

34. Marge Percy, "The Movement: For Men Only?" *Guardian*, Jan. 31, Feb. 7 and 14, 1970; Gregory Calvert interview with Ron Grele (1991) 347–50, OHRO; Curry, *Deep in Our Hearts*. In Curry's book, many of the women imply that feminist scholarship on SNCC and other organizations has overemphasized sexism and sexual tensions in the civil rights and student movements.

35. Brown, *Taste of Power*, 191–92; Brown, "The End of Silence," *Seize the Time*; Brown's lyric sheets and liner notes, Newton Papers, series 2, box 41, folder 8; Ward, *Just My Soul Responding*, 370–81, 412–15; June Culberson, "The Role of the Revolutionary Woman," *Black Panther*, May 4, 1969, 9; "Sisters," *Black Panther*, Sept. 13, 1969, 12–13; Cleaver, "Kathleen Cleaver Interview," 54–59; "Agenda for Meeting with Responsible Comrades," May 24, 1972, Newton Papers, series 2, box 4, folder 2. By this 1972 meeting, the Oakland chapter of the party held women's meetings and gender-integrated group discussions of sexism and male-female relationships.

36. Eldridge Cleaver, "Message to Sister Ericka Huggins of the Black Panther Party," *Black Panther*, July 5, 1969, 12–13; Shakur, *Assata*, 223–24; "Interview with D.C.," *Black Panther*, Nov. 1, 1969, 6; Masai Hewitt interview with Ron Grele (1984), 2–3, OHRO.

37. Wolfe, *Radical Chic*, 8, 54 (italics in original).

38. Ibid., 112, 119.

39. William J. McGill interview with Henry Graff (1980), 35–43, OHRO. McGill went on to become chancellor of Columbia University.

40. Baruch and Jones, *Vanguard*; Hilliard on *Face the Nation*, CBS News, Dec. 28, 1968; "Interview with D.C.," *Black Panther*, Nov. 1, 1969, 6; "Chairman Bobby Seale Speaks with Arthur Goldberg of Ramparts Magazine" (1971), Newton Papers, series 2, box 46, folder 10.

41. Hampton, Frasier, and Flynn, *Voices of Freedom*, 512, 543; *Black Panther*, Feb. 21, 1970, 2–26; Churchill and Vander Wall, *Agents of Repression*; O'Reilly, *Racial Matters*.

42. Jackson, *Soledad Brother*, 85–86, 125, 136; Jackson, "Struggle and the Black Man," 248–52; Jackson letters, Newton Papers, series 1, box 3, folder 9 and series 2, box 44, folder 11.

43. Newton, *To Die for the People*, 152–55.

44. Robert Bowen interview with Ron Grele (1984), 73, OHRO.

45. "Open Letter to the Weatherman Underground from Panther 21," *East Village Other*, Jan. 19, 1971, 3; "Newton Expels 12 Panthers," *Guardian*, Feb. 20, 1971, 4; Newton, "Hidden Traitor, Renegade Scab: Eldridge Cleaver," unpublished manuscript, Newton Papers, series 2, box 42, folder 1; Panther memo, Apr. 13, 1973, Newton Papers, series 2, box 4, folder 2. The 1973 memo indicates that other Panthers had difficulty explaining Newton's attacks on Cleaver's sexuality to the press.

46. Community Committee to Elect Bobby Seale and Elaine Brown to City Offices of Oakland, press release, Mar. 5, 1973, and "Why Gay People Should Vote for Bobby Seale and Elaine Brown" (n.d.), Newton Papers, series 2, box 45, folder 19; Central Committee meeting agendas, Aug. 16, Oct. 1 and 2, 1972, Newton Papers, series 2, box 4, folder 2; Brown, *Taste of Power*, 323–27, 400–36. Though the Panther candidates did not win these campaigns, they

did rally large numbers of black voters and liberal Democrats. Seale won 40 percent of the vote in his unsuccessful bid for mayor.

47. Hilliard and Cole, *This Side of Glory*, 339–40; Masai Hewitt interview with Ron Grele (1984), 128–38, OHRO; Brown, *Taste of Power*, 333–52.

48. Brown, *Taste of Power*, 3–7, 441–45; Brown resignation and note, Newton Papers, series 2, box 41, folder 5. Brown's account of her departure from the party highlights the gendered aspects of the violence that accompanied Newton's return. She writes that the beating of one female Panther was "a clear signal that the words 'Panther' and 'comrade' had taken on gender connotations, denoting an inferiority in the female half of us."

49. Davis, "Black Nationalism," 323.

Conclusion

1. Parks, *Shaft*; Bogle, *Toms, Coons, Mulattoes,*; Guerrero, *Framing Blackness*; George, *Black Face.*

2. *Shaft* and *Sweet Sweetback's Baadasss Song* (1971) were the seminal films that inspired the blaxploitation genre. Major Hollywood studios copied the plots, characters, and themes of these movies with only slight alteration in a slew of low-budget action thrillers, riding this genre into the ground by the mid-1970s. The appeal of these films can be seen in their box-office earnings. (In its original release, *Shaft* grossed $7,067,825.) Yet the blaxploitation genre was not universally adored. The NAACP, feminist groups, and others criticized the films for their stereotypical hypermasculinity and sexist overtones.

3. Faludi, *Backlash* and *Stiffed*; Mauer and Huling, *Young Black Americans.* In 1995, Mauer and Huling reported, "Nearly one in three (32.2%) African American males in the age group 20–29 (827,440) is under criminal justice supervision on any given day — in prison or jail, on probation or parole."

4. Booker, *"I Will Wear No Chain!"* 205–7, 220–23.

5. Madhubuti and Karenga, eds., *Million Man March/Day of Absence*, 110; and Booker, *"I Will Wear No Chain!"* 222.

6. Madhubuti and Karenga, *Million Man March*, 13, 20, 32.

7. Abraham, *Who Are the Promise Keepers?*; Brickner, *Promise Keepers.*

8. George, *Hip Hop America*, xiii; Chuck D, *Fight the Power*; Cross, *It's Not About a Salary*; Werner, *Change Is Gonna Come.*

9. Chuck Philips, "2Pac's Gospel Truth," *Rolling Stone*, Oct. 28, 1993, 22.

10. Mikal Gilmore, "Easy Target: Why Tupac Should Be Heard Before He's Buried," *Rolling Stone*, Oct. 31, 1996, 49; Dyson, *Holler If You Here Me*, 14, 181–82. For just a few examples of the misogyny and homophobia in heavy metal lyrics from this period, listen to "Used to Love Her" or "One in a Million" from Guns N' Roses, *Lies.*

11. Shakur, "The Heartz of Men," *All Eyez On Me*; Kevin Powell, "Bury Me Like a G: The Short Life and Violent Death of Tupac Shakur," *Rolling Stone*, Oct. 31, 1996, 38; George, *Hip Hop America*, 47–48; Dyson, *Between God and Gangsta Rap*, 165–86.

Bibliography

Archival Collections

Ralph J. Bunche Oral History Program, Moorland-Spingarn Research Center, Howard University, Washington, D.C.

Guy Carawan Collection, Southern Folklife Collection, University of North Carolina, Chapel Hill, N.C.

Citizens' Councils/Civil Rights Collection, McCain Library and Archives, University of Southern Mississippi, Hattiesburg, Miss.

Civil Rights Documentation Project, Moorland-Spingarn Research Center, Howard University, Washington, D.C.

Wesley George Papers, Southern Historical Collection, University of North Carolina, Chapel Hill, N.C.

Aaron Henry Papers, Special Collections, Tougaloo University, Jackson, Miss.

Paul Johnson Family Papers, McCain Library and Archives, University of Southern Mississippi, Hattiesburg, Miss.

Martin Luther King Jr., Papers, King Center for Nonviolent Social Change, Atlanta, Ga.

Mississippi Oral History Program, University of Southern Mississippi, Hattiesburg, Miss.

Mississippi State Department of Archives and History, Jackson, Miss.

Mississippi Valley Collection, University of Memphis, Memphis, Tenn.

National Association for the Advancement of Colored People Papers, Manuscript Division, Library of Congress, Washington, D.C.

Huey Newton Papers, Special Collections, Stanford University, Palo Alto, Calif.

Oral History Research Office, Butler Library, Columbia University, New York, N.Y.

Project South Oral History Collection, Special Collections, Stanford University, Palo Alto, Calif.

Rare Book and Special Collections Division, Library of Congress, Washington, D.C.

Rare Book Collection, Wilson Library, University of North Carolina, Chapel Hill, N.C.

Regional Oral History Office, Bancroft Library, University of California, Berkeley, Calif.

Schomburg Center for Research in Black Culture, New York Public Library, New York, N.Y.

Southern Oral History Program Collection, Southern Historical Collection, Wilson Library, University of North Carolina, Chapel Hill, N.C.

Special Collections, Mitchell Memorial Library, Mississippi State University, Starkville, Miss.

State Historical Society of Wisconsin, Madison, Wis.

Student Nonviolent Coordinating Committee Papers, King Center for Nonviolent Social Change, Atlanta, Ga.

White House Central Files, White House Aides' Files, and White House Conference Files, Lyndon B. Johnson Presidential Library, Austin, Tex.

Willard Wirtz Papers, Record Group 174 (Department of Labor), National Archives II, College Park, Md.

Oral History Interviews

Juanita Abernathy (January 1995)
Paul Barton (March 2000)
R. B. Cottonreader (January 1995)
Frank Erwin (May 2000)
June Johnson (February 2001)
Margaret Kibbee (July 2000)
Ed King (June 1999)
Tommie Jean Lunsford (July 2000)
Charles McLaurin (June 1999, July 2000)
Martha Norman Prescod (May 2000)
Bernice Johnson Reagon (March 1997)
Betty Garman Robinson (April 2000)
JoAnn Ooiman Robinson (May 1999)
Cleveland Sellers (April 2002)
Grenville Whitman (April 1999)
Hosea Williams (January 1995)
Willard Wirtz (March 2000)

Newspapers and Periodicals

Black Panther
Citizens' Council
Crisis
Ebony
Esquire
Essence
Look
Memphis Commercial-Appeal
Muhammad Speaks
Nation
Newsweek

New York Times
Pittsburgh Courier
Playboy
Rolling Stone
San Francisco Examiner
Student Voice
Washington Post

Books

Abernathy, Ralph David. *And the Walls Came Tumbling Down*. New York: Harper and Row, 1989.

Abraham, Ken. *Who Are the Promise Keepers?: Understanding the Christian Men's Movement*. New York: Doubleday, 1997.

Abzug, Robert H. *Inside the Vicious Heart: Americans and the Liberation of Nazi Concentration Camps*. Oxford: Oxford University Press, 1985.

Ali, Muhammad, *The Greatest, My Own Story*. With Richard Durham. New York: Random House, 1975.

Allen, Robert. *The Port Chicago Mutiny*. New York: Warner Books, 1989.

Arnesen, Eric. *Brotherhoods of Color: Black Railroad Workers and the Struggle for Equality*. Boston: Harvard University Press, 2001.

Ayers, Edward L. *Vengeance and Justice: Crime and Punishment in the 19th Century American South*. New York: Oxford University Press, 1984.

Baldwin, James. *The Fire Next Time*. New York: Dial Press, 1963.

———. *Nobody Knows My Name*. New York: Dial Press, 1961.

Baraka, Amiri. *Home*. New York: William Morrow, 1966.

Baron, Ava. *Work Engendered: Toward a New History of American Labor*. Ithaca, N.Y.: Cornell University Press, 1991.

Bartley, Numan. *The New South, 1945–1980*. Baton Rouge: Louisiana State University Press, 1995.

———. *The Rise of Massive Resistance: Race and Politics in the South during the 1950's*. Baton Rouge: Louisiana State University Press, 1969.

Baruch, Ruth Marion, and Pirkle Jones. *The Vanguard: A Photographic Essay on the Black Panthers*. Boston: Beacon Press, 1970.

Bederman, Gail. *Manliness and Civilization: A Cultural History of Gender and Race in the United States, 1880–1917*. Chicago: University of Chicago Press, 1995.

Beifuss, Joan Turner. *At the River I Stand: Memphis, the 1968 Strike, and Martin Luther King*. Memphis: B&W Books, 1985.

———. *I Am A Man: Photographs of the 1968 Memphis Sanitation Strike and Dr. Martin Luther King, Jr*. Memphis, Tenn.: Memphis, 1993.

Belfrage, Sally. *Freedom Summer*. Charlottesville: University Press of Virginia, 1965.

Biggs, Bradley. *The Triple Nickels: America's First All-Black Paratroop Unit*. Hamden, Conn.: Archon Books, 1986.

Bingham, Howard, and Max Wallace. *Muhammad Ali's Greatest Fight: Cassius Clay vs. the United States of America*. New York: M. Evans and Company, 2000.

Blight, David W. *Race and Reunion: The Civil War in American Memory*. Cambridge: Harvard University Press, 2001.

Bogle, Donald. *Toms, Coons, Mulattoes, Mammies, and Bucks*. New York: Bantam Books, 1973.

Booker, Christopher B. *"I Will Wear No Chain!": A Social History of African American Males*. Westport, Conn.: Praeger, 2000.

Brady, Tom P. *Black Monday*. Winona, Miss.: Association of Citizens' Councils, 1955.

Branch, Taylor. *Parting the Waters: America in the King Years, 1954–1963*. New York: Simon and Schuster, 1988.

———. *Pillar of Fire: America in the King Years, 1963–1965*. Simon and Schuster, 1998.

Breitman, George. *The Assassination of Malcolm X*. New York: Pathfinder Press, 1988.

———. *The Last Year of Malcolm X: The Evolution of a Revolutionary*. New York: Merit, 1967.

Breitman, George, ed. *Malcolm X Speaks*. New York: Grove Press, 1965.

Brickner, Bryan W. *The Promise Keepers: Politics and Promises*. Lanham, Md.: Lexington Books, 1999.

Brown, Elaine. *A Taste of Power: A Black Woman's Story*. New York: Pantheon Books, 1992.

Brown, Kathleen M. *Good Wives, Nasty Wenches, and Anxious Patriarchs: Gender, Race, and Power in Colonial Virginia*. Chapel Hill: University of North Carolina Press, 1996.

Burges, Austin Earl. *What Price Integration?* Dallas: American Guild Press, 1956.

Burner, Eric. *And Gently He Shall Lead Them: Robert Parris Moses and Civil Rights in Mississippi*. New York: New York University Press, 1994.

Cagin, Seth, and Philip Dray. *We Are Not Afraid: The Story of Goodman, Schwerner, and Chaney and the Civil Rights Campaign for Mississippi*. New York: Macmillan, 1988.

Carson, Clayborne. *Malcolm X: The FBI File*. New York: Carroll and Graf, 1991.

———. *In Struggle: SNCC and the Black Awakening of the 1960s*. Cambridge: Harvard University Press, 1981.

Carson, Clayborne, et al., eds., *The Eyes on the Prize Civil Rights Reader*. New York: Penguin Books, 1991.

Carter, Hodding. *The South Strikes Back*. Garden City, N.Y.: Doubleday, 1959.

Cecelski, David, and Tim Tyson, eds., *Democracy Betrayed: The Wilmington Race Riot of 1898 and Its Legacy*. Chapel Hill: University of North Carolina Press, 1998.

Chafe, William. *Civilities and Civil Rights: Greensboro, North Carolina, and the Black Struggle for Freedom*. Oxford: Oxford University Press, 1980.

———. *Never Stop Running: Allard Lowenstein and the Struggle to Save American Liberalism*. New York: Basic Books, 1993.

———. *The Unfinished Journey: America since World War II*. New York: Oxford University Press, 1995.

Chamberlin, Brewster, and Marcia Feldman, eds. *The Liberation of the Nazi Concentration Camps 1945: Eyewitness Accounts of the Liberators*. Washington, D.C.: United States Holocaust Memorial Council, 1987.

Churchill, Ward and Jim Vander Wall. *Agents of Repression: The FBI's Secret Wars against the Black Panther Party and the American Indian Movement*. Boston: South End Press, 1988.

Clark, Kenneth. *Dark Ghetto: The Dilemmas of Social Power*. New York: Harper and Row, 1965.

Clark, Steve. *Malcolm X: The Final Speeches*. New York: Pathfinder, 1992.

Cleaver, Eldridge. *Post-Prison Writings and Speeches*. New York: Random House, 1969.

———. *Soul on Ice*. New York: Dell, 1968.

Clegg, Claude Andrew. *An Original Man: The Life and Times of Elijah Muhammad*. New York: St. Martin's Press, 1997.

Clinton, Catherine, and Nina Silber, eds., *Divided Houses: Gender and the Civil War*. Oxford: Oxford University Press, 1992.

Cohen, Steven. *Masked Men: Masculinity and the Movies in the Fifties*. Bloomington: Indiana University Press, 1997.

Colley, David. *Blood for Dignity: The Story of the First Integrated Combat Unit in the U.S. Army*. New York: St. Martin's Press, 2003.

———. *The Road to Victory: The Untold Story of World War II's Red Ball Express*. Washington: Brassey's, 2000.

Collier-Thomas, Bettye, and V. P. Franklin, eds., *Sisters in the Struggle: African American Women in the Civil Rights-Black Power Movement*. New York: New York University Press, 2001.

Crawford, Vicki L., Jacqueline Anne Rouse, and Barbara Woods, eds. *Women in the Civil Rights Movement: Trailblazers and Torchbearers, 1941–1965*. Brooklyn: Carlson, 1990.

Cross, Brian. *It's Not About a Salary: Rap, Race and Resistance in Los Angeles*. London: Verso, 1993.

Curry, Constance, et al., eds. *Deep in Our Hearts: Nine White Women in the Freedom Movement*. Athens: University of Georgia Press, 2000.

D., Chuck. *Fight the Power: Rap, Race, and Reality*. With Yusuf Jah. New York: Delacourte Press, 1997.

Dalfiume, Richard M. *Desegregation of the U.S. Armed Forces: Fighting on Two Fronts, 1939–1953*. Columbia: University of Missouri Press, 1969.

Daniel, Pete. *Lost Revolutions: The South in the 1950s*. Chapel Hill: University of North Carolina Press, 2000.

Davidson, Chandler, and Bernard Grofman, eds., *Quiet Revolutions in the South: The Impact of the Voting Rights Act, 1965–1990*. Princeton: Princeton University Press, 1994.

Davis, Angela Y. *Women, Race, and Class*. New York: Random House, 1981.

DeCaro, Louis A. *On the Side of My People: A Religious Life of Malcolm X*. New York: New York University Press, 1995.

D'Emilio, John. *Lost Prophet: The Life and Times of Bayard Rustin*. New York: Free Press, 2003.

DeVeaux, Scott. *The Birth of Bebop: A Social and Musical History*. Berkeley: University of California Press, 1997.

Dittmer, John. *Local People: The Struggle for Civil Rights in Mississippi*. Chicago: University of Illinois Press, 1995.

Dollard, John. *Caste and Class in a Southern Town*. New York: Harper, 1949.

Douglass, Frederick. *Narrative of the Life of Frederick Douglass*. In *The Classic Slave Narratives*, edited by Henry Louis Gates Jr. New York: Penguin Books, 1987.

Dray, Philip. *At the Hands of Persons Unknown: The Lynching of Black America*. New York: Random House, 2002.

Dryden, Charles W. *A-Train: Memoirs of a Tuskegee Airman*. Tuscaloosa: University of Alabama Press, 1997.

Dyson, Michael Eric. *Between God and Gangsta Rap: Bearing Witness to Black Culture*. New York: Oxford University Press, 1996.

———. *Holler If You Here Me: Searching for Tupac Shakur*. New York: Basic Civitas Books, 2001.

———. *Making Malcolm: The Myth and Meaning of Malcolm X*. New York: Oxford University Press, 1995.

Edsall, Thomas Byrne, and Mary D. Edsall, *Chain Reaction: The Impact of Race, Rights, and Taxes on American Politics*. New York: W. W. Norton, 1992.

Edwards, Laura. *Gendered Strife and Confusion: The Politics and Culture of Reconstruction*. Urbana: University of Illinois Press, 1997.

Ehrenreich, Barbara. *The Hearts of Men: American Dreams and the Flight from Commitment*. Garden City, N.Y.: Anchor Books, 1983.

Elijah Muhammad. *Message to the Blackman in American*. Chicago: Muhammad Mosque of Islam No. 2, 1965.

Elkins, Stanley. *Slavery: A Problem in American Institutional and Intellectual Life*. Chicago: University of Chicago Press, 1959.

Ellison, Ralph. *Invisible Man*. New York: Random House, 1952.

Epps, Archie, ed. *The Speeches of Malcolm X at Harvard*. New York: W. Morrow, 1968.

Eskew, Glenn T. *But for Birmingham: The Local and National Movements in the Civil Rights Struggle*. Chapel Hill: University of North Carolina Press, 1997.

Etter-Lewis, Gwendolyn, and Michéle Foster, eds. *Unrelated Kin: Race and Gender in Women's Personal Narratives*. New York: Routledge, 1996.

Evans, Sara. *Personal Politics: The Roots of Women's Liberation in the Civil Rights Movement and the New Left*. New York: Vintage Books, 1979.

Evanzz, Karl. *The Messenger: The Rise and Fall of Elijah Muhammad*. New York: Pantheon Books, 1999.

Fairclough, Adam. *To Redeem the Soul of America: The Southern Christian Leadership Conference and Martin Luther King, Jr.* Athens: University of Georgia Press, 1987.

Faludi, Susan. *Backlash: The Undeclared War against American Women*. New York: Crown Books, 1992.

———. *Stiffed: The Betrayal of the American Man*. William Morrow, 1999.

Fanon, Frantz. *Black Skin, White Masks*. New York: Grove Press, 1967.

———. *The Wretched of the Earth*. New York: Grove Press, 1963.

Filene, Peter. *Him/Her/Self: Sex Roles in Modern America*. Baltimore: Johns Hopkins University Press, 1986.

Finkle, Leo. *Forum for Protest: The Black Press during World War II*. Cranbury, N.J.: Associated University Press, 1975.

Foner, Eric. *A Short History of Reconstruction, 1863–1877*. New York: Harper and Row, 1990.

Foner, Philip S. *The Black Panthers Speak*. New York: Da Capo Press, 1995.

Forman, James. *The Making of Black Revolutionaries: A Personal Account*. Washington, D.C.: Open Hand, 1985.

Frasier, E. Franklin. *The Negro Family in the United States*. Chicago: University of Chicago Press, 1939.

Friedan, Betty. *The Feminine Mystique*. New York: W. W. Norton, 1963.

Gallen, David. *Malcolm X: As They Knew Him*. New York: Carol and Graf, 1992.

Garrow, David J., Bill Kovach, and Carol Polsgrove, eds. *Reporting Civil Rights*. Part 1, *American Journalism, 1941–1963*. New York: Library of America, 2003.

George, Nelson. *Blackface: Reflections on African Americans and the Movies*. New York: HarperCollins, 1994.

———. *Hip Hop America*. New York: Penguin Books, 1998.

Giddings, Paula. *When and Where I Enter: The Impact of Black Women on Race and Sex in America*. New York: Morrow, 1984.

Gilmore, Glenda. *Gender and Jim Crow: Women and the Politics of White Supremacy in North Carolina, 1896–1920*. Chapel Hill: University of North Carolina Press, 1996.

Ginsberg, Carl. *Race and Media: The Enduring Life of the Moynihan Report*. New York: New York Institute for Media Analysis, 1989.

Gitlin, Todd. *The Sixties: Years of Hope, Days of Rage*. New York: Bantam Books, 1987.

Glazer, Nathan, and Daniel Patrick Moynihan, *Beyond the Melting Pot*. Cambridge: M.I.T. Press and Harvard University Press, 1963.

Gluck, Sherna Berger. *Rosie the Riveter Revisited: Women, the War, and Social Change*. Boston: Twayne, 1987.

Goldman, Peter Louis. *The Death and Life of Malcolm X*. New York: Harper and Row, 1973.

Grant, Joanne. *Ella Baker: Freedom Bound*. New York: John Wiley and Sons, 1998.

Grier, William H., and Price M. Cobbs, *Black Rage*. New York: Basic Books, 1968.

Griswold del Castillo, Richard, and Richard A. Garcia, *César Chávez: A Triumph of Spirit*. Norman: University of Oklahoma Press, 1995.

Guerrero, Ed. *Framing Blackness: The African American Image in Film*. Philadelphia: Temple University Press, 1993.

Gutman, Herbert G. *The Black Family in Slavery and Freedom, 1750–1925*. New York: Pantheon Books, 1976.

Guy-Sheftall, Beverly, ed. *Words of Fire: An Anthology of African American Feminist Thought*. New York: New Press, 1995.

Haley, Alex, and Murray Fisher, eds. *The Playboy Interviews*. New York: Ballantine Books, 1993.

Hall, Gwendolyn Midlo, ed. *Love, War, and the 96th Engineers (Colored): The World War II New Guinea Diaries of Captain Hyman Samuelson*. Urbana: University of Illinois Press, 1995.

Hall, Jacquelyn Dowd. *Revolt against Chivalry: Jessie Daniel Ames and the Women's Campaign against Lynching*. New York: Columbia University Press, 1979.

Hampton, Henry, Steve Frasier, and Sarah Flynn, eds. *Voices of Freedom: An Oral History of the Civil Rights Movement, from the 1950s through the 1980s*. New York: Bantam Books, 1990.

Harris, David. *Dreams Die Hard*. New York: St. Martin's Press, 1982.

Henry, Aaron. *Aaron Henry: The Fire Ever Burning*. With Constance Curry. Jackson: University of Mississippi Press, 2000.

Hernton, Calvin C. *Sex and Racism in America*. New York: Grove Press, 1965.

————. *White Papers for White Americans*. Westport, Conn.: Greenwood Press, 1966.

Hilliard, David, and Lewis Cole. *This Side of Glory: The Autobiography of David Hilliard and the Story of the Black Panther Party*. Boston: Little and Brown, 1993.

Himes, Chester. *If He Hollers Let Him Go*. New York: Thunder's Mouth Press, 1945.

————. *The Quality of Hurt: The Autobiography of Chester Himes*. New York: Doubleday, 1972.

Hine, Darlene Clark, and Earnestine Jenkins, eds. *A Question of Manhood: A Reader in U.S. Black Men's History and Masculinity*. Bloomington: Indiana University Press, 1999.

Hitler, Adolph. *Mein Kampf*. Translated by Ralph Manheim. Boston: Houghton Mifflin, 1943.

Honey, Maureen. *Creating Rosie the Riveter: Class, Gender, and Propaganda during World War II*. Amherst: University of Massachusetts Press, 1984.

Honey, Michael. *Black Workers Remember: An Oral History of Segregation, Unionism, and the Freedom Struggle*. Berkeley: University of California Press, 1999.

————. *Southern Labor and Civil Rights: Organizing Memphis Workers*. Urbana and Chicago: University of Illinois Press, 1993.

Horne, Gerald. *Fire This Time: The Watts Uprising and the 1960s*. Charlottesville: University Press of Virginia, 1995.

Hunter, Tera W. *To 'Joy My Freedom: Southern Black Women's Lives and Labor after the Civil War*. Cambridge: Harvard University Press, 1998.

Jackson, George. *Soledad Brother*. New York: Coward-McCann, 1970.

Johnson, Charles S. *To Stem This Tide: A Survey of Racial Tensions in the United States*. Boston: Pilgrim Press, 1943.

Johnson, Marilynn S. *The Second Gold Rush: Oakland and the East Bay in World War II*. Berkeley: University of California Press, 1993.

Jones, Charles E., ed. *The Black Panther Party (Reconsidered)*. Baltimore, Md.: Black Classic Press, 1998.

Jordan, June. *Technical Difficulties: African-American Notes on the State of the Union*. New York: Pantheon Books, 1992.

Kantrowitz, Stephen David. *Ben Tillman and the Reconstruction of White Supremacy*. Chapel Hill: University of North Carolina Press, 2000.

Kapur, Sudarshan. *Raising Up a Prophet: The African-American Encounter with Gandhi*. Boston: Beacon Press, 1992.

Katzmann, Robert A., ed. *Daniel Patrick Moynihan: The Intellectual in Public Life*. Washington, D.C.: Woodrow Wilson Center Press, 1998.

Kerber, Linda, and Jane Sherron DeHart, *Women's America: Refocusing the Past*. Oxford: Oxford University Press, 1991.

Kimmel, Michael. *Manhood in America: A Cultural History*. New York: Free Press, 1996.

King, Martin Luther, Jr. *I've Been to the Mountaintop*. San Francisco: HarperSanFrancisco, 1994.

————. *Stride toward Freedom: The Montgomery Story*. New York: Ballantine Books, 1958.

————. *Where Do We Go from Here: Chaos or Community?* New York: Harper and Row, 1967.

King, Mary. *Freedom Song: A Personal Story of the 1960s Civil Rights Movement.* New York: Morrow, 1987.

Kirby, Jack Temple. *Media-Made Dixie: The South in the American Imagination.* Athens: University of Georgia Press, 1986.

Kryder, Daniel. *Divided Arsenal: Race and the American State During World War II.* Cambridge: Cambridge University Press, 2000.

Lee, Chana Kai. *For Freedom's Sake: The Life of Fannie Lou Hamer.* Urbana: University of Illinois Press, 1999.

Lee, Ulysses. *The Employment of Negro Troops.* Washington, D.C.: Department of Defense, 1966.

Lemann, Nicholas. *The Promised Land: The Great Black Migration and How It Changed America.* New York: Alfred Knopf, 1991.

Ling, Peter, and Sharon Monteith, eds. *Gender in the Civil Rights Movement.* New York: Garland, 1999.

Lipsitz, George. *Rainbow at Midnight: Labor and Culture in the 1940s.* Urbana: University of Illinois Press, 1994.

Litwack, Leon. *Trouble In Mind: Black Southerners in the Age of Jim Crow.* New York: Alfred Knopf, 1998.

Lomax, Louis. *To Kill a Black Man.* Los Angeles: Holloway, 1987.

———. *When the Word Is Given.* Westport, Conn.: Greenwood Press, 1963.

MacLean, Nancy. *Behind the Mask of Chivalry: The Making of the Second Ku Klux Klan.* New York: Oxford University Press, 1994.

Madhubuti, Haki R., and Maulana Karenga. *Million Man March/Day of Absence: A Commemorative Anthology.* Chicago: Third World Press, 1996.

Mailer, Norman. *The Armies of the Night: History as Novel, The Novel as History.* New York: Penguin Books, 1968.

Martin, John Barlow. *The Deep South Says Never.* New York, Ballantine Books, 1957.

Martínez, Elizabeth Sutherland, ed. *Letters from Mississippi.* New York: McGraw-Hill, 1965.

Mauer, Marc, and Tracy Huling, *Young Black Americans in the Criminal Justice System: Five Years Later.* Washington, D.C.: Sentencing Project, 1995)

McAdam, Doug. *Freedom Summer.* New York: Oxford University Press, 1988.

McCurry, Stephanie. *Masters of Small Worlds: Yeomen Households, Gender Relations, and the Political Culture of the Antebellum South Carolina Low Country.* New York: Oxford University Press, 1995.

McGuire, Phillip. *He, Too, Spoke for Democracy: Judge Hastie, World War II, and the Black Soldier.* New York: Greenwood Press, 1988.

McGuire, Phillip, ed. *Taps for a Jim Crow Army: Letters from Black Soldiers in World War II.* Lexington: University Press of Kentucky, 1983.

McMillen, Neil R. *The Citizens' Council: Organized Resistance to the Second Reconstruction, 1954–1964.* Urbana: University of Illinois Press, 1994.

———. *Dark Journey: Black Mississippians in the Age of Jim Crow.* Urbana: University of Illinois Press, 1989.

Meyerowitz, Joanne, ed. *Not June Cleaver: Women and Gender in Postwar America, 1945–1960.* Philadelphia: Temple University Press, 1994.

Mills, Kay. *This Little Light of Mine: The Life of Fannie Lou Hamer.* New York: Dutton, 1993.

Moody, Anne, *Coming of Age in Mississippi.* New York: Dell, 1968.

Motley, Mary Penick, ed. *The Invisible Soldier: The Experience of the Black Soldier, World War II.* Detroit: Wayne State University Press, 1975.

Moynihan, Daniel Patrick. *Family and Nation.* San Diego: Harcourt Brace Jovanovich, 1986.

———. *Maximum Feasible Misunderstanding: Community Action in the War on Poverty.* New York: Free Press, 1969.

———. *Miles to Go: A Personal History of Social Policy.* Cambridge: Harvard University Press, 1996.

———. *The Negro Family: A Case for National Action.* Washington, D.C.: United States Department of Labor, Office of Policy Planning and Research, 1965.

———. *The Politics of a Guaranteed Income: The Nixon Administration and the Family Assistance Plan .* New York: Random House, 1973.

Myrdal, Gunnar. *An American Dilemma: The Negro Problem and Modern Democracy.* New York: Harper and Brothers, 1944.

Nalty, Bernard. *The Right to Fight: African American Marines in World War II.* Washington, D.C.: Marine Corps Historical Center, 1995.

Nalty, Bernard, and Morris J. MacGregor. *Blacks in the Military: Essential Documents.* Wilmington, Del.: Scholarly Resources, 1981.

Navasky, Victor S. *Kennedy Justice.* New York: Atheneum, 1971.

Newton, Huey. *Revolutionary Suicide.* New York: Harcourt Brace Jovanovich, 1973.

———. *To Die for the People: The Writings of Huey P. Newton.* New York: Vintage Books, 1972.

Nisbett, Richard E., and Dov Cohen. *Culture of Honor: The Psychology of Violence in the South.* Boulder, Colo.: Westview Press, 1996.

O'Reilly, Kenneth. *Racial Matters: The FBI's Secret File on Black America, 1960–1972.* New York: Free Press, 1989.

Papers of John F. Kennedy, Presidential Papers, President's Office Files: Presidential Recordings, Transcripts. Boston: John F. Kennedy Library, 1984.

Patterson, James. *Brown v. Board of Education.* New York: Oxford University Press, 2001.

Payne, Charles. *I've Got the Light of Freedom: The Organizing Tradition and the Mississippi Freedom Struggle.* Berkeley: University of California Press, 1995.

Pearson, Hugh. *The Shadow of the Panther: Huey Newton and the Price of Black Power in America.* Reading, Mass.: Addison-Wesley, 1994.

Peery, Nelson. *Black Fire: The Making of an American Revolutionary.* New York: New Press, 1994.

Perry, Bruce. *Malcolm: The Life of a Man Who Changed Black America .* Barrytown, N.Y.: Station Hill, 1991.

Perry, Bruce, ed. *Malcolm X: The Last Speeches.* New York: Pathfinder, 1989.

Pohlmann, Marcus D., and Michael P. Kirby. *Racial Politics at the Crossroads: Memphis Elects Dr. W. W. Herenton.* Knoxville: University of Tennessee Press, 1996.

Potter, Lou. *Liberators: Fighting on Two Fronts in World War II.* New York: Harcourt Brace Jovanovich, 1992.

Public Papers of the Presidents of the United States: John F. Kennedy, 1962. Washington, D.C.: U.S. Government Printing Office, 1963.

Putnam, Carleton. *Race and Reason: A Yankee View.* Washington, D.C.: Public Affairs Press, 1961.

Raines, Howell. *My Soul Is Rested: Movement Days in the Deep South Remembered.* New York: Penguin Books, 1983.

Rainwater, Lee, and William L. Yancey. *The Moynihan Report and the Politics of Controversy.* Cambridge: M. I. T. Press, 1967.

Remnick, David. *King of the World: Muhammad Ali and the Rise of an American Hero.* New York: Random House, 1998.

Robinson, JoAnn Gibson. *The Montgomery Bus Boycott and the Women Who Started It.* Knoxville: University of Tennessee Press, 1987.

Robnett, Belinda. *How Long? How Long?: African-American Women in the Struggle for Civil Rights.* New York: Oxford University Press, 1997.

Roediger, David R. *The Wages of Whiteness: Race and the Making of the American Working Class.* London: Verso, 1991.

Rossinow, Doug. *The Politics of Authenticity: Liberalism, Christianity, and the New Left in America.* New York: Columbia University Press, 1998.

Rothschild, Mary Aiken. *A Case of Black and White: Northern Volunteers and the Southern Freedom Summers, 1964–1965.* Westport, Conn.: Greenwood Press, 1982.

Rural Organizing and Cultural Center. *Minds Stayed On Freedom: The Civil Rights Struggle in the Rural South: An Oral History.* Boulder, Colo.: Westview Press, 1991.

Ryan, William F. *Blaming the Victim.* New York: Vintage Books, 1971.

Sammons, Jeffrey T. *Beyond the Ring: The Role of Boxing in American Society.* Urbana: University of Illinois Press, 1988.

Sandler, Stanley. *Segregated Skies: All-Black Combat Squadrons of World War II.* Washington, D.C.: Smithsonian Institution Press, 1992.

Schoen, Douglas E. *Pat: A Biography of Daniel Patrick Moynihan.* New York: Harper and Row, 1979.

Schuyler, Lambert, and Nora Patricia Schuyler. *Close That Bedroom Door!* Seattle, Wash.: Heron House, 1957.

Seale, Bobby. *A Lonely Rage: The Autobiography of Bobby Seale.* New York: Times Books, 1977.

———. *Seize the Time: The Story of the Black Panther Party and Huey Newton.* New York: Random House, 1970.

Sellers, Cleveland. *The River of No Return: The Autobiography of a Black Militant and the Life and Death of SNCC.* New York: Morrow, 1973.

Shakur, Assata. *Assata: An Autobiography.* Chicago: Lawrence Hill Books, 1987.

Shirer, William L. *The Rise and Fall of the Third Reich: A History of Nazi Germany.* New York: Simon and Schuster, 1960.

Sitkoff, Harvard. *A New Deal for Blacks: The Emergence of Civil Rights as a National Issue.* New York: Oxford University Press, 1978.

———. *The Struggle for Black Equality, 1954–1992.* New York: Hill and Wang, 1992.

Smith, Charlene E. McGee. *Tuskegee Airman: The Biography of Charles E. McGee, Air Force Fighter Combat Record Holder.* Boston: Brandon, 1999.

Smith, Graham A. *When Jim Crow Met John Bull: Black American Soldiers in World War II Britain*. New York: St. Martin's Press, 1987.

Smith, Lillian. *Killers of the Dream*. New York: W. W. Norton, 1949.

Snyder, R. Claire. *Citizen-Soldiers and Manly Warriors: Military Service and Gender in the Civic Republic Tradition*. Lanham, Md.: Rowan and Littlefield, 1999.

Stack, Carol. *All Our Kin: Strategies for Survival in the Black Community*. New York: Harper and Row, 1974.

Stanfield, J. Edwin. *In Memphis: Mirror to America?* Atlanta: Southern Regional Council, 1968.

Staples, Robert. *The Black Family: Essays and Studies*. Belmont, Calif.: Wadsworth, 1971.

Starr, Kevin. *Embattled Dreams: California in War and Peace, 1940–1950*. New York: Oxford University Press, 2002.

Stowe, Steven. *Intimacy and Power in the Old South: Ritual in the Lives of the Planters*. Baltimore, Md.: Johns Hopkins University Press, 1987.

Strickland, William, and Cheryll Y. Greene, eds. *Malcolm X: Make It Plain*. New York: Viking, 1994.

Sugarman, Tracy. *Stranger at the Gates: A Summer in Mississippi*. New York: Hill and Wang, 1966.

Sullivan, Patricia. *Days of Hope: Race and Democracy in the New Deal Era*. Chapel Hill: University of North Carolina Press, 1996.

Sutherland, Elizabeth. *Letters From Mississippi*. New York: McGraw-Hill, 1965.

Taylor, Quintard. *In Search of the Racial Frontier: African Americans in the American West, 1528–1990*. New York: W. W. Norton, 1998.

Terkel, Studs. *"The Good War": An Oral History of World War II*. New York: Pantheon Books, 1984.

Tyson, Tim. *Radio Free Dixie: Robert F. Williams and the Roots of Black Power*. Chapel Hill: University of North Carolina Press, 1999.

U.S. Commission on Civil Rights. *A Time to Listen . . . A Time to Act: Voices from the Ghettos of the Nation's Cities*. Washington, D.C.: Government Printing Office, 1967.

Van Deburg, William L. *New Day in Babylon: The Black Power Movement and American Culture*. Chicago: University of Chicago Press, 1992.

Von Hoffman, Nicholas. *Mississippi Notebook*. New York: David White, 1964.

Wallace, Michele. *Black Macho and the Myth of the Superwoman*. New York: Dial Press, 1978.

Ward, Brian. *Just My Soul Responding: Rhythm and Blues, Black Consciousness, and Race Relations*. Berkeley: University of California Press, 1998.

Warren, Earl. *The Memoirs of Earl Warren*. New York: Doubleday, 1977.

Werner, Craig. *A Change Is Gonna Come: Music, Race and the Soul of America*. New York: Penguin Books, 1999.

White, Deborah Gray. *Too Heavy a Load: Black Women in Defense of Themselves, 1894–1994*. New York: W. W. Norton, 1999.

White, Walter. *A Rising Wind*. New York: Doubleday, Doran, 1945.

———. *Rope and Faggot: A Biography of Judge Lynch*. New York: Alfred Knopf, 1929.

Whitfield, Stephen J. *A Death in the Delta: The Story of Emmett Till*. New York: Free Press, 1988.

Wilkins, Roger. *Jefferson's Pillow: The Founding Fathers and the Dilemma of Black Patriotism*. New York: Beacon Press, 2002)

Wilson, Charles Reagan, and William Ferris, eds. *Encyclopedia of Southern Culture*. Chapel Hill: University of North Carolina Press, 1989.

Wilson, William J. *The Truly Disadvantaged: The Inner City, the Underclass, and Public Policy*. Chicago: University of Chicago Press, 1987.

Wolfe, Tom. *Radical Chic and Mau Mauing the Flak Catchers*. New York: Farrar, Straus, and Giroux, 1970.

Wood, Joe, ed. *Malcolm X: In Our Own Image*. New York: St. Martin's Press, 1992.

Woodard, Komozi. *A Nation within a Nation: Amiri Baraka (Leroi Jones) and Black Power Politics*. Chapel Hill: University of North Carolina Press, 1999.

Wyatt-Brown, Bertram. *Southern Honor: Ethics and Behavior in the Old South*. Oxford: Oxford University Press, 1982.

Wynn, Neil A. *The Afro-American and the Second World War*. New York: Holmes and Meier, 1993.

X, Malcolm. *The Autobiography of Malcolm X*. With Alex Haley. New York: Ballantine Books, 1965.

Articles and Essays

Bederman, Gail. "'Civilization': The Decline of Middle-Class Manliness, and Ida B. Wells' Antilynching Campaign, 1892–1894." *Radical History Review* 52 (November 1992): 5–30.

Billington, Monroe. "Lyndon B. Johnson and Blacks: The Early Years." *Journal of Negro History* 62 (January 1977): 26–42.

"*Black Scholar* Interviews Kathleen Cleaver." *Black Scholar* 3 (December 1971): 54–59.

Bonner, Robert E. "Flag Culture and the Consolidation of Confederate Nationalism." *Journal of Southern History* 68 (May 2002): 293–332.

Brown, Elsa Barkley. "Negotiating and Transforming the Public Sphere: African American Political Life in the Transition from Slavery to Freedom." *Public Culture* 7 (Fall 1994): 107–46.

Brownell, Herbert. "Eisenhower's Civil Rights Program: A Personal Assessment." *Presidential Studies Quarterly* 21 (June 1991): 235–42.

Cleaver, Kathleen Neal, and Susie Linfield. "The Education of Kathleen Neal Cleaver." *Transition* 0 (1998): 172–95.

———. "Kathleen Cleaver Interview." *Black Scholar* 3 (December 1971): 54–59.

Collins, Patricia Hill. "A Comparison of Two Works on Black Family Life." *Signs* 14 (Summer 1989): 875–84.

Cullen, Jim. "'I's a Man Now': Gender and African American Men." In *Divided Houses: Gender and the Civil War*, edited by Catherine Clinton and Nina Silber, 76–91. New York: Oxford University Press, 1992.

Cuordileone, K. A. "'Politics in an Age of Anxiety': Cold War Political Culture and the Crisis in American Masculinity, 1949–1960." *Journal of American History* 87 (September 2000): 515–45.

Davis, Angela Y. "Black Nationalism: The Sixties and the Nineties." In *Black Popular Culture*, edited by Gina Dent and Michele Wallace, 317–24. Seattle, Wash.: Bay Press, 1992.

———. "Reflections on the Black Woman's Role in the Community of Slaves." *Black Scholar* 3 (December 1971): 2–15.

Dean, Robert D. "Masculinity as Ideology: John F. Kennedy and the Domestic Politics of Foreign Policy." *Diplomatic History* 22 (Winter 1998): 29–62.

D'Emilio, John. "Homophobia and the Trajectory of Postwar American Radicalism: The Career of Bayard Rustin." *Radical History Review* 62 (Spring 1995): 80–103.

Faue, Elizabeth. "Gender and the Reconstruction of Labor History." *Labor History* 34 (Spring-Summer 1993): 169–77.

Fleming, Cynthia Griggs. "Black Women Activists and the Student Nonviolent Coordinating Committee: The Case of Ruby Doris Smith Robinson." *Journal of Women's History* 4 (Winter 1993): 64–82.

Goings, Kenneth W., and Gerald L. Smith. "'Unhidden' Transcripts: Memphis and African American Agency, 1862–1920." *Journal of Urban History* 21 (March 1995): 372–94.

Graham, Hugh Davis. "Race, History, and Policy: African Americans and Civil Rights Since 1964." *Journal of Policy History* 6 (Winter 1994): 12–39.

———. "The Storm Over Black Power." *Virginia Quarterly Review* 43 (August 1967): 545–65.

Hall, Jacquelyn Dowd. "The Mind That Burns in Each Body: Women, Rape, and Racial Violence." *Southern Exposure* 12 (November/December 1984): 61–71.

Harper, Frederick D. "The Influence of Malcolm X on Black Militancy." *Journal of Black Studies* 1 (June 1971): 387–402.

Harrington, Michael. "The Welfare State and Its Neoconservative Critics." *Dissent* 20, no. 4 (1973): 435–54.

Honey, Michael. "Martin Luther King, Jr., the Crisis of the Black Working Class, and the Memphis Sanitation Strike." In *Southern Labor in Transition, 1940–1995*, edited by Robert H. Zieger, 147–75. Knoxville: University of Tennessee Press, 1997.

Horne, Gerald. "Myth and the Making of Malcolm X." *American Historical Review* 98 (April 1993): 440–50.

Jackson, George. "Struggle and the Black Man." *Black Scholar* 2 (June 1971): 248–52.

Jones, Charles E. "The Political Repression of the Black Panther Party 1966–1971: The Case of the Oakland Bay Area." *Journal of Black Studies* 18 (June 1988): 415–34.

Kessler-Harris, Alice. "Treating the Male as 'Other': Redefining the Parameters of Labor History." *Labor History* 34 (Spring-Summer 1993): 190–204.

Kissack, Terence. "Freaking Fag Revolutionaries: New York's Gay Liberation Front, 1969–1971." *Radical History Review* 62 (Spring 1995): 104–34.

Klarman, Michael. "How *Brown* Changed Race Relations: The Backlash Thesis." *Journal of American History* 81 (June 1994): 81–118.

Korstad, Robert, and Nelson Lichtenstein. "Opportunities Lost: Labor, Radicals, and the Early Civil Rights Movement." *Journal of American History* 75 (December 1988): 786–811.

Lentz, Richard. "Sixty-Five Days in Memphis: A Study of Culture, Symbols, and the Press." *Journalism Monographs* 98 (1986): 1–40.

Lewis, Earl. "Invoking Concepts, Problematizing Identities: The Life of Charles N. Hunter and the Implications for the Study of Gender and Labor." *Labor History* 34 (Spring-Summer 1993): 292–308.

BIBLIOGRAPHY

Mailer, Norman. "The White Negro." *Dissent* 4 (Summer 1957): 276–93.

Matthews, Tracye. "'No One Ever Asks, What a Man's Place in the Revolution Is': Gender and the Politics of the Black Panther Party, 1966–1971." In *The Black Panther Party [Reconsidered]*, edited by Charles E. Jones, 267–304. Baltimore, Md.: Black Classic Press, 1998.

McAdam, Doug. "Gender as a Mediator of the Activist Experience: The Case of Freedom Summer." *American Journal of Sociology* 97 (March 1992): 1211–40.

———. "Specifying the Relationship Between Social Ties and Activism." *American Journal of Sociology* 99 (November 1993): 640–67.

McKnight, Gerald. "The 1968 Memphis Sanitation Strike and the FBI: A Case Study in Urban Surveillance." *South Atlantic Quarterly* 83 (Spring 1984): 138–56.

McMillen, Neil R. "White Citizens' Council and Resistance to School Desegregation in Arkansas." *Arkansas Historical Quarterly* 30 (Summer 1971): 95–122.

Moynihan, Daniel P. "Employment, Income, and the Ordeal of the Negro Family." *Daedelus* 94 (Fall 1965): 745–70.

———. "The President and the Negro: The Moment Lost." *Commentary* 43 (February 1967): 31–45.

Nasstrom, Kathryn. "Down to Now: Memory, Narrative, and Women's Leadership in the Civil Rights Movement in Atlanta, Georgia." *Gender and History* 11 (April 1999): 113–44.

Payne, Charles. "Ella Baker and Models of Social Change." *Signs* 14 (Summer 1989): 885–99.

Perry, Bruce. "Malcolm X and the Politics of Masculinity." *Psychohistory Review* 13 (Winter 1985): 18–25.

Poussaint, Alvin. "The Stresses of the White Female Worker in the Civil Rights Movement in the South." *American Journal of Psychiatry* 123 (October 1966): 401–7.

Ruiz, Dorothy Smith, and Robert G. Cummings. "Cultural Identity and the Moynihan Report." *Western Journal of Black Studies* 17 (Summer 1993): 31–45.

Sanchez, Sonia. "Queens of the Universe." *Black Scholar* 1 (Fall/Winter 1970): 29–34.

Scott, Daryl Michael. "The Politics of Pathology: The Ideological Origins of the Moynihan Controversy." *Journal of Policy History* 8 (Winter 1996): 81–105.

Silverstein, Morton. "An Examination of *Liberators: Fighting on Two Fronts in World War II.*" WNET Office Report. New York: Thirteen/WNET, 1993.

Sitkoff, Harvard. "Racial Militancy and Interracial Violence in the Second World War." *Journal of American History* 58 (December 1971): 661–81.

Sklaroff, Lauren Rebecca. "Constructing G.I. Joe Louis: Cultural Solutions to the 'Negro Problem' during World War II." *Journal of American History* 89 (December 2002): 958–83.

Staples, Robert. "The Myth of the Impotent Black Male." *Black Scholar* 2 (June 1971): 2–9.

Trotter, Joe William, Jr. "African-American Workers: New Directions in U.S. Labor Historiography." *Labor History* 35 (Fall 1994): 495–523.

Tyson, Tim. "'Black Power,' and the Roots of the African American Freedom Struggle." *Journal of American History* 85 (September 1998): 540–70.

Washington, Cynthia. "We Started from Different Ends of the Spectrum." *Southern Exposure* 4 (Winter 1977): 14–15.

White, Walter. "What Caused the Detroit Riots?" Reprinted in Thomas R. Frazier, *Afro-American History*, 341–54. New York: Harcourt, Brace, 1970.

Zinn, Maxine Baca. "Family, Race, and Poverty in the Eighties." *Signs* 14 (1989): 856–74.

Dissertations and Theses

Green, Earl, Jr. "Labor in the South: A Case Study of Memphis: The 1968 Sanitation Strike and Its Effect on an Urban Community." Ph.D. diss., New York University, 1980.

Green, Laurie Beth. "Battling the Plantation Mentality: Consciousness, Culture, and the Politics of Race, Class and Gender in Memphis, 1940–1968." Ph.D. diss., University of Chicago, 1999.

Hill, Lance E. "The Deacons for Defense and Justice: Armed Self-Defense and the Civil Rights Movement." Ph.D. diss., Tulane University, 1997.

Holder, Kit Kim. "The History of the Black Panther Party." Ph.D. diss., University of Massachusetts, 1990.

Howard, John. "Men Like That: Male Homosexuals in Mississippi, 1945–1985." Ph.D. diss., Emory University, 1997.

Lewis, Selma Seligman. "Social Religion and the Memphis Sanitation Strike." Ph.D. diss., Memphis State University, 1976.

Morehouse, Maggi M. "War Stories: Personal Battles of Black Soldiers in the 93rd Infantry Division during World War II." Master's thesis, San Francisco State University, 1997.

Newton, Huey P. "War Against the Panthers: A Study of Repression in America." Ph.D. diss., University of California-Santa Cruz, 1980.

Romano, Renee Christine. "Crossing the Line: Black-White Interracial Marriage in the United States, 1945–1990." Ph.D. diss., Stanford University, 1996.

Sales, William W., Jr. "Malcolm X and the Organization of Afro-American Unity: A Case Study in Afro-American Nationalism." Ph.D. diss., Columbia University, 1991.

Schultz, Debra L. "'We Didn't Think in Those Terms Then': Narratives of Jewish Women in the Southern Civil Rights Movement, 1960–1966." Ph.D. diss., Union Institute, 1995.

Stowe, William McFerrin, Jr. "Willie Rainache and the Defense of Segregation in Louisiana." Ph.D. diss., Texas Christian University, 1989.

Films and Sound Recordings

Alexander, Brett, and Andrew Lack. *The Real Malcolm X: An Intimate Portrait of the Man.* Beverly Hills, Calif.: CBS News: Fox Video, 1992.

Appleby, David, Allison Graham, and Steven John Ross. *At the River I Stand.* San Francisco: California Newsreel, 1993.

Brown, Elaine. *Seize the Time.* Vault Records, 1969.

Clay, Cassius. *I Am the Greatest!* Sony Entertainment, 1963.

Fields, Connie, and Marilyn Mulford. *Freedom on My Mind.* Berkeley, Calif.: Clarity Educational Productions, 1994.

Eyes On the Prize: America's Civil Rights Years, 1954–1965. Produced by Blackside and the Corporation for Public Broadcasting. Alexandria, Va.: PBS Video, 1987.

Eyes on the Prize II: America at the Racial Crossroads, 1965–1985. Produced by Blackside and the Corporation for Public Broadcasting. Alexandria, Va.: PBS Video, 1989.

Guns N' Roses. *Lies.* Geffen Records, 1988.

Malcolm X: Make It Plain. Produced by Blackside and Roja Productions. Boston: PBS Video, 1994.

Muddy Waters. *His Best, 1947 to 1955: The Chess 50th Anniversary Collection.* Chess/MCA, 1997.

Nelson, Stanley. *The Black Press: Soldiers Without Swords.* Berkeley, Calif.: California Newsreel, 1999.

Parks, Gordon, Sr. *Shaft.* Metro-Goldwyn-Mayer, 1971.

Roemer, Michael, and Robert Young. *Nothing But a Man.* Nothing But a Man Co.-Du Art Film Label, 1964.

Shakur, Tupac. *All Eyez On Me.* Death Row Records, 1996.

———. *Me Against the World.* Interscope Records, 1995.

———. *Strictly 4 My N.I.G.G.A.Z.* Interscope Records, 1993.

———. *2Pacalypse Now.* Interscope Records, 1991.

Worth, Marvin, and Arnold Perl. *Malcolm X.* Warner Brothers Communications, 1972.

Van Peebles, Melvin. *Sweet Sweetback's Baadasss Song.* Xenon Pictures, 1971.

X, Malcolm. *Malcolm X Speaks Out.* Kansas City: Andrews and McMeel, 1992.

Index

Jackson, George, 173–74

Jackson, Jesse, 182

Jim Crow, 6, 17, 20, 23, 33, 36, 48, 186. *See also* Segregation

Johnson, Lyndon, 85, 107, 113–16, 120, 123, 127, 140

Johnson, Paul, 69, 71

Jordan, June, 126–27

Karenga, Ron (Maulana Karenga), 167, 181

Kennedy, John F., 57, 58–59, 77, 98, 114

Kennedy, Robert, 57–58, 77

Keyserling, Mary Dublin, 118–19

King, Coretta Scott, 103

King, Ed, 68–69, 78, 84–85, 200 (n. 32)

King, Martin Luther, Jr., 6, 7, 50, 63–64, 107, 108, 162; on nonviolence, 65–66, 143; compared to Malcolm X, 88, 97–98, 99 (ill.), 103, 104; on family, 115, 119–20; in Memphis, 129, 131–32, 138–40, 142–43, 145–46; assassination of, 145–46, 147, 150, 153–54, 210 (n. 36)

King, Martin Luther, Sr., 138–39

King, Mary, 82–83, 201 (n. 47)

Ku Klux Klan, 5, 50–52, 66, 77, 84, 86, 97, 103

Lawson, James, 64, 65–66, 138, 140, 142–43, 144, 210 (n. 30)

Loeb, Henry, 131–32, 135–36, 138, 143, 146, 147, 149–50

Longstreet, William X, 87–88

Louisiana, 21, 24, 35, 53, 64, 78–79

Lowenstein, Allard, 69, 76, 162

Lucy, Bill, 136, 150

Lynching, 2, 5–6, 20–21, 44–45, 50, 59, 80, 190 (n. 7)

Mailer, Norman, 52, 213 (n. 31)

Malcolm X (El-Hajj Malik El-Shabazz): in Nation of Islam, 88, 90–101; upbringing of, 88–90; marriage of, 92–93; on nonviolence, 96–99, 103, 104, 203 (n. 29); and Martin Luther King Jr., 97–98,

99 (ill.), 103; hajj to Mecca, 101–2, 203 (n. 29); assassination of, 105–6, 107, 204 (n. 37); legacy of, 108, 109, 119, 123, 128, 140, 141, 144, 157–58, 161, 181, 186–87

Marshall, Thurgood, 28–29, 36

Masculinism: definition of, 7–8, 190 (n. 10); in Citizens' Councils, 51, 52–53, 56, 59; in SNCC, 62, 70; in Nation of Islam, 88, 89, 101, 102, 105, 109; in Black Panther Party, 151, 155, 159–77 passim. *See also* Feminism

McAdam, Doug, 70, 75, 81

McCorkle, Sara, 48

McLaurin, Charles, 61–62, 66, 71, 73, 74, 83, 84, 85

Memphis, Tennessee, 86, 129, 131–51, 180, 186

Meredith, James, 57–59

Michigan, 89, 90, 151

Miller, Dorie, 12, 15 (ill.), 18

Million Man March, 8, 181–83, 185

Mississippi, 6, 87, 89, 113, 122, 133, 136, 162, 179; and World War II, 21, 36, 37; Citizens' Councils in, 39–40, 41, 43–45, 47, 50, 56–59; civil rights movement in, 61–62, 64, 65, 66–85, 103

Mississippi State Sovereignty Commission, 56–57, 71–72, 82

Montgomery, Alabama, 6–7, 55, 63, 65

Moore, Amzie, 36, 64, 71, 85

Moses, Bob, 64–65, 68, 69, 70–71

Moyers, Bill, 110, 117

Moynihan, Daniel Patrick: in Department of Labor, 107–8, 110–13, 116; and Martin Luther King Jr., 108, 119–20, 139, 140; upbringing of, 110; and Lyndon Johnson, 113, 115, 127; on military recruitment, 113, 124–25, 166; in Nixon administration, 114 (ill.), 127–28; critics of, 118–19, 120–21, 122, 124 (ill.), 125–27. See also *The Negro Family*

Muhammad, Elijah: opposition to World War II, 18–19, 90; relationship with Malcolm X, 91, 93, 94, 96, 97–99, 100–101, 104, 106; theology of, 201 (n. 5)